COUNTING ON
THE CENSUS?

COUNTING ON THE CENSUS?

*Race, Group Identity,
and the Evasion of Politics*

P ETER S KERRY

BROOKINGS INSTITUTION PRESS
Washington, D.C.

150226

Copyright © 2000
THE BROOKINGS INSTITUTION
1775 Massachusetts Avenue, N.W.
Washington, D.C. 20036
www.brookings.edu

Library of Congress Cataloging-in-Publication data

Skerry, Peter.
  Counting on the census? : Race, group identity, and the evasion of
politics / Peter Skerry.
    p.   cm.
Includes bibliographical references and index.
  ISBN 0-8157-7964-X (hc : acid-free)
  1. Race. 2. Group identity—United States. 3. Census.
  4. Apportionment (Election law)—United States. 5. United States—Census.
I. Title.
  HT1521 .S535 2000   00-008352
  304.6'07'23--dc21   CIP

9 8 7 6 5 4 3 2 1

The paper used in this publication meets minimum requirements of the
American National Standard for Information Sciences—Permanence of Paper
for Printed Library Materials: ANSI Z39.48-1984.

Typeset in Sabon

Composition by Oakland Street Publishing
Arlington, Virginia

Printed by R. R. Donnelley and Sons

To Gil Steiner

Foreword

From the very beginning, when the U.S. Constitution instructed that slaves be counted as three-fifths of a person, the census has been caught up in the nation's racial dilemmas. Today the bicentennial count is torn by controversies over affirmative action, shifting racial identities, and the persistent problem of minority group undercounts.

In this timely and provocative volume, Peter Skerry, a nonresident senior fellow of the Brookings Governmental Studies program, confronts each of these issues. To those who object to census questions about race and ethnicity, Skerry argues that they are appropriate and necessary public policy instruments. To those who define the census as a scientific enterprise that is above politics, Skerry contends that it is inherently and properly a political undertaking.

Moreover, to those who call for statistical adjustment to remedy the census undercount, Skerry demonstrates that the stakes, both for political parties and for minority groups, have been misunderstood and exaggerated. Acknowledging that the census is critical to the administration of policies affecting racial and ethnic minorities, he calls for greater realism about the limits of census data in a society where identities are more mutable and fluid than ever, and for greater tolerance of the untidy politics necessarily involved in gathering such data.

Finally, Skerry points out that statistical adjustment of the census is an arcane procedure that threatens to frustrate the legitimate aspirations of disadvantaged minorities and to undermine public confidence in what has been one of the most respected functions of the federal government. And, most important, he concludes that in the context of an administrative state with a largely demobilized electorate, the battle over census adjustment is a distraction from the more fundamental challenges of empowering the disadvantaged.

Skerry acknowledges the aid of numerous professionals, in and out of government, who shared with him their expertise and insights about the census and the federal statistical system generally. He is particularly grateful for the guidance of David McMillen and the late W. Allen Wallis. For the opportunity to present his research findings to colleagues at various academic institutions, Skerry is indebted to Bruce Cain and Jack Citrin (University of California, Berkeley), David Heer (University of Southern California), Glenn Loury (Boston University), Jack Peltason and Mark Petracca (University of California, Irvine), and Roger Waldinger (University of California, Los Angeles). He also thanks those who read and commented on all or part of the manuscript: Nathan Glazer, R. Shep Melnick, Peter Morrison, Steven Teles, Stephan Thernstrom, James Q. Wilson, Maggie Wittenburg, Don Ylvisaker, and one anonymous reviewer. In particular, Skerry acknowledges the unstinting support and wise counsel of Thomas Mann.

For its generous and patient support of his work on this project, Skerry thanks the William H. Donner Foundation, in particular, James V. Capua and William T. Alpert.

Skerry further wishes to thank his wife, Martha Bayles, for her keen and frequently called upon editorial advice.

Research assistance was ably provided by Michael Hartman, Anil Kakani, Won Kim, and Stephen Rockwell. Skerry is immeasurably grateful to Jon Shields for assistance far beyond any call of duty. At the Brookings Institution Press, he thanks for their skillful and swift assistance Larry Converse, Nancy Davidson, and Janet Walker; Vicky Macintyre copyedited the manuscript, Carlotta Ribar proofread the pages, and Mary Mortensen indexed them. Susan Stewart of the Brookings Governmental Studies program cheerfully dealt with the inevitable administrative issues.

This project was nearing completion as Paul Light assumed his new duties as director of the Brookings Governmental Studies program. He graciously facilitated those final, critical steps.

The views expressed here are solely those of the author and should not be ascribed to any persons or institutions acknowledged above or to the trustees, officers, or other staff members of the Brookings Institution.

MICHAEL H. ARMACOST
President

March 2000
Washington, D.C.

Contents

Appendixes

CHAPTER ONE

Introduction

This book has its origins around the time of the 1990 census, when minority leaders were expressing dismay that
once again hundreds of thousands of individuals would not be enumerated
in the decennial count. To compensate for the undercount, some were advocating statistical adjustment of census results. Today, after a decade of litigation and controversy, the issue is hardly resolved. While the Supreme Court
has virtually assured that apportionment of the Congress will not rely on
adjusted data from the 2000 census, the Bureau of the Census will nevertheless produce a set of adjusted numbers that may well be used for redistricting, allocation of funds, and other purposes. Meanwhile, concern about
the minority undercount continues unabated, as does the pressure for census adjustment.

In part, this book is a brief against census adjustment. It begins by arguing that the inherent unreliability of racial and ethnic data requires a more
realistic standard of accuracy than has typically been adopted by adjustment advocates. It also maintains that the implications of the undercount
for both minorities and nonminorities—including the partisan interests of
Democrats and Republicans—are grossly exaggerated and misunderstood.
A novel intervention into a highly complex system, adjustment would produce all sorts of unpredictable results. In some cases minorities could end
up with relatively lower population totals with adjustment than without it.

Moreover, adjusted census data would get fed into complicated fiscal formulas and redistricting calculations whose outcomes would be similarly counterintuitive. Thus I argue that adjustment would not benefit minorities as much as advocates believe and might well disadvantage them.

At the same time, the risks of adjustment have been underestimated. Adjustment could further undermine already weak incentives to cooperate with the census and thereby exacerbate the problem it was intended to remedy. Advocates have depicted the process as little more than an exercise in the science of statistical sampling. But adjustment would be much more: a huge logistical undertaking of which sampling would be merely one part. Not only would this process be difficult to explain and interpret to the American people, but its very complexities would create new opportunities for error. In my view, the possibility that adjustment could undermine public confidence in one of government's most basic functions greatly outweighs whatever benefits might be realized.

But for me, and I hope for the reader, the case against adjustment is not the whole story. The controversy over census adjustment opens an invaluable window onto American politics at the end of the twentieth century. In the context of the modern administrative state, political elites have become acclimated to an increasingly demobilized electorate; rather than confront the genuine social and political problems of the disadvantaged, political elites prefer to argue about how best to tweak data for marginal gains. Indeed, the debate over census adjustment seems less about the empowerment of disadvantaged minorities than about the impoverishment of contemporary politics.

Yet here a question arises: why do the participants in this debate—Republican party leaders, Census Bureau officials, minority advocates, big city officials and politicians, editorial page writers, elected officials—take the positions they do? As in many controversies, interest calculations here are complicated and not necessarily obvious. Republicans, for example, have argued so forcefully against adjustment because of their traumatic experiences with redistricting at the hands of Democrats in 1990 and especially in 1980. City officials have sued for adjustment in part because this is one issue where local boosterism and minority concerns coincide. As for minorities, their concern about the undercount has not always translated into unhesitating support for adjustment. Actually, minorities are quite distrustful of the bureau's efforts to "modernize" the census.[1]

Just as striking is the way affirmative action figures into this debate. Much of the energy directed against adjustment derives from hostility to affirmative action. Critics routinely express hostility to the census because they regard it as a vital cog in the machinery by which the federal government "counts by race." Yet at the individual level, there is no direct connection between affirmative action and the census: unlike someone filling out a college application, an individual identifying himself on a census form as belonging to a protected minority group does not stand to benefit directly. If members of minority groups did benefit from so identifying themselves on the census, then the undercount would be greatly diminished.

Also looming in this debate are the ongoing controversies over diversity and multiculturalism. The debate itself—and certainly the efforts by racial and ethnic groups to maximize their census counts—is routinely taken as one more indication that American society is balkanizing into contending racial and ethnic groups.[2] Yet an important finding of this study is that much of this controversy over the census arises not because Americans are breaking up into hard-edged groups, but because we are intermixing as individuals to the point where group barriers are breaking down, making it increasingly difficult for the census to count racial and ethnic identities meaningfully. This intermixing is one reason why racial and ethnic data lack reliability. Of course, this may lend credence to the view that the census should stop asking Americans about their racial and ethnic backgrounds. But this is *not* my argument. My view is that racial and ethnic data—however much lacking reliability—are too important to be discontinued. At the same time, we need to be more realistic about the limitations of these data and their potential uses.

Such issues underline that the census is inextricably bound up with race, and so I believed when I first embarked on this project. Fairly soon, however, I conceived doubts about focusing unduly on such controversial flashpoints as the minority undercount and adjustment. Encouraging these doubts were some of my colleagues and several of the individuals I was interviewing. They tried, usually subtly and rarely explicitly, to divert my focus. I was specifically steered away from racial issues by senior officials at the Census Bureau, some of whom directed my attention, for example, to privacy issues. It is probably no accident that during this same period the bureau in its public pronouncements was doing its best to discount the importance of race—for example, by justifying statistical adjustment in terms not of racial equity but of reducing costs.

Not everyone adopted this stance. Eugene Ericksen, a sociologist who has served as an adviser to the secretary of commerce on census adjustment, observed in 1991 congressional testimony about adjustment: "Were it not for the civil rights aspects of this issue, it would not be something we would be focusing on so much."[3] In 2000 any avoidance of race seems increasingly implausible, and it has accordingly been less evident. Nevertheless, as I will argue here, there is a persistent and pervasive tendency at the Census Bureau and at the Office of Management and Budget to downplay racial matters and even to deny their importance.

There is scant historical justification for such efforts. Starting with Article I of the Constitution—which stipulates how the enumeration is to be conducted, explicitly in the case of Indians and implicitly in the case of Negro slaves—the census has always been entwined with race. Certainly the debate over the undercount and the proposed remedies for it are all about race. This seemingly obvious point needs to be emphasized up front, before I explore the complex and somewhat technical matters that any serious discussion of the census necessarily involves.

Why has the Census Bureau sought to downplay race? One reason is that the agency has long been dominated by demographers, statisticians, and other highly trained professionals who pride themselves on their technical expertise. Emphasizing their politically neutral role as "factfinders for the nation," census professionals do not typically see themselves as political actors or policymakers.[4] They certainly do not gravitate readily to a controversial subject such as race—unless, as we shall see, it is possible to do so in a way that transcends (or appears to transcend) politics.

A related factor is the tension between the extremely technical character of the census and the emotional, highly symbolic nature of race politics. A particular problem is the degree of misinformation and confusion that envelops public discussions of the census, whether of adjustment procedures or simply of the methods used to collect racial data. Such confusion is evident among elites and ordinary Americans alike.

Indeed, elites are not very interested in or focused on the census. Newspapers, for instance, are prone to decry the "racial injustice" of the census undercount.[5] But editors are also leery of devoting much space to such a technical and (as far as their readers are concerned) tedious topic. The unhappy result is episodic coverage that is often ill-informed or downright misleading, punctuated by high-minded editorial posturing. Similarly, most politicians, including most members of Congress, would place the census at the very bottom of any list of compelling topics. These same politicians, however, are more than prepared to express moral outrage about the negative impact of the census undercount on disadvantaged minorities.

Elites behave this way for good reasons, of course. Although they may find the census tedious, they realize that it packs an emotional wallop for minorities, especially black Americans. Yet the technical nature of census discussions remains jarring to minorities and their allies, who tend to feel that basic human needs are getting lost in a welter of statistical minutiae. In a curious way this problem is exacerbated by the Census Bureau's openness in providing an abundance of data and a wealth of technical analyses about its operations and products. In this regard the census is an activist's nightmare and a policy wonk's dream.

This is precisely the problem: in the sea of information about this massive undertaking, it is easy to lose sight not only of the more fundamental issues at stake—for example, what this most basic of governmental functions tells us about the nature of citizenship in late-twentieth-century America—but also of the larger symbolic issues. A mantra repeated in this debate is that the census is "a national ceremony." It is taken from the statistician William Kruskal:

> The census is one of our relatively few national, secular ceremonies. It provides a sense of social cohesion, and a kind of non-religious communion: we enter the census apparatus as individual identities with a handful of characteristics; then later we receive from the census a group snapshot of ourselves at the ceremony date.[6]

No one wants to be left out of a group snapshot—even if, as we shall see, the absence of many individuals is due at least as much to their own choices as to shortcomings of the Census Bureau. This desire not to be left out is all the stronger among black Americans in particular, given the Constitution's original provision that slaves would be counted as three-fifths of a person. It is impossible to overemphasize the importance of that single historical datum in this controversy.

These symbolic aspects of census politics are crucial, and I have tried to be attentive to them. But I have also resisted becoming overly preoccupied with them, out of a strong conviction that racial politics in the United States has too frequently been allowed to be overwhelmed by symbols.

But if the U.S. census has always been bound up with race, our notion of race has also been undergoing enormous change. Most obviously, race in the United States has become more diverse and more complex. The racial spectrum no longer consists merely of whites, blacks, and American Indians. In addition to Asians, that spectrum now includes Hispanics, a group whose racial status is quite ambiguous but increasingly important.

Of even greater significance is the transformation in our very conceptualization of race, and of ethnicity. Until quite recently social scientists regarded these as social constructs that reflected one's ties to other individuals and institutions. In the context of the census, these constructs were reported on by enumerators. Today, race and ethnicity are seen more as matters of individual psychology, of an individual's subjective feelings of attachment to a group, or groups. Moreover, this identification is now reported to the census not through an enumerator, but directly by each individual.[7] Indeed, "self-identification" of a respondent's racial and ethnic background is now a principle to which the Census Bureau proudly adheres.

This conceptual shift helps to explain what I have already emphasized: the ambiguity of racial and ethnic data. Moreover, while race and ethnicity have become increasingly subjective categories, they have grown more critical to public policy. This then points to a conflict between the vagaries of personal identity and the requirements of bureaucratic rationality, a conflict most evident when the Census Bureau, seeking to impose order on what would otherwise be chaos, violates its commitment to racial and ethnic self-identification and forces the myriad of self-identified responses into established categories. This exercise of governmental authority in such a personal and controversial realm is a delicate balancing act: understandably, the bureau is not eager to acknowledge its inevitable role in the rationalization of racial and ethnic identity.

This balancing act is hardly an isolated example. On the contrary, it is typical of how authority in general is wielded in the contemporary administrative state. As various students of what has come to be called "the new American political system" point out, in recent decades substantive policy goals have come to be pursued less and less through conventional political and legislative means and increasingly through arcane legal and administrative channels that leave many ordinary Americans feeling bewildered and excluded.[8]

In a regime that emphasizes administration over politics, it is perhaps not surprising that the numbers necessary to administer outcomes get an enormous amount of attention. The most revealing aspect of the census controversy is the tendency for all of the disputants to equate census numbers with political power. Adjustment advocates are particularly prone to this equation, deemphasizing the importance of actual voting or other forms of political effort. Some of these advocates go so far as to charge that to be uncounted in the census is to be "disenfranchised." While such perspectives reflect the administrative realities of the new American political system, this is a curious line of argument in an era when the quality of citizenship and of civic engagement is being criticized from all sides as thin.

Nor in such a regime should it be surprising that there would be an effort to cleanse the census of politics. This is no mean feat, since the census was originally designed by the Framers to deal with the fundamental political tasks of taxation and representation. Nevertheless, adjustment advocates argue that the census does—or ought to—transcend politics. Specifically, they insist that the census is a scientific undertaking into which politicians have no business intruding; alternatively, they maintain that there is a right to be counted that is denied by the census undercount. Science and rights are both characteristically American ways of seeking the advantages of political power without having to acknowledge the pursuit of politics or of power. These now enjoy renewed currency in our new American political system. And in this new regime, it is increasingly important—and difficult—to discern that the census is not only a critical tool in the administration of governmental benefits, but also an instrument of state power and authority.

Readers primarily concerned with the policy debate over the undercount and adjustment might want to turn directly to chapter 5, "The Politics of Census Adjustment." There the various points sketched above are developed in detail. Chapter 6, "The Census in the New American Political System," broadens the argument by relating the census to the sweeping changes in American politics over the past thirty years. While those changes have often been criticized for contributing to the shift from the representation of individuals to that of groups, equally important has been the shift from a focus on the political participation of the disadvantaged to a formalistic notion of their representation. Chapter 6 also explores how the dynamics of public interest organizations have been fueling this controversy and how, in the context of this new regime, adjustment would benefit various elites more than the disadvantaged minorities who are its presumed beneficiaries.

But the reader is encouraged to take the scenic route by beginning at the beginning. Chapter 2 examines the politics of the census process and the bureaucratic politics of the Census Bureau. Relying on Aristotle as well as the Framers, I argue that the census is inherently—and properly—political in nature. But contrary to popular perception, politics does not typically impinge on the census through the gross manipulation of data. Where politics does play an essential role is the creation of the racial and ethnic categories that appear on the census questionnaire. At the same time, the Census Bureau, like any government agency, strives to control its environment and to protect its prerogatives and mission. It does this by presenting itself as a neutral fact finder and by maintaining a rigorous if delimited notion of professionalism. What the bureau has not done (at least until recently) is define its mission as primarily scientific in nature—a stance that, as we shall see, distinguishes it from many advocates of adjustment.

Chapter 3 scrutinizes the bureau's racial and ethnic categories, clearly the most politicized and contentious aspect of the census, and explores the necessarily limited precision of these data, which may be a bigger problem than the actual undercount of minorities. Further, chapter 3 examines the implications of the tension between our societal commitment to self-identification and our equally strong need to generate authoritative racial and ethnic data on which public policy can be based.

Chapter 4 confirms that the undercount is persistent and indeed has grown worse over the past fifty years. But after a review of the extensive body of ethnographic research sponsored by the Census Bureau into the causes of the undercount, two things become clear. First, responsibility for the undercount cannot be wholly laid at the door of the bureau. Second, noncooperation with the census occurs for a fascinating and surprising variety of reasons, many of them all too understandable from the viewpoint of those who do not cooperate. Finally, chapter 4 looks closely at the specific sampling and adjustment programs that have been proposed to remedy the undercount.

The book concludes with some admittedly imperfect crystal ball gazing in chapter 7 about possible (and impossible) alternatives to census adjustment. For a variety of reasons, the controversy is not likely to be resolved in the near future. This suggests that we may simply have to learn to live with the ambiguity that suffuses racial and ethnic data, and with the politics that inescapably pervades the census. As we begin the new millennium, one of the main challenges we face may well be learning to tolerate the untidiness that accompanies the diversity we have come to value.

CHAPTER TWO

Census Politics: Boundaries and Bureaucracies

Nᴇw *York Times* journalist Steven Holmes has observed that the Census Bureau is "one of the most apolitical of all federal agencies" and indeed has been "traditionally apolitical."[1] This chapter will explore why such a characterization of the bureau is mistaken.

Even a casual reading of history suggests that the bureau has been anything but apolitical. It is true that at certain periods the results of the census were not crucial to important political interests. But that is not the same as being apolitical, if apolitical means having essentially nothing to do with politics. The Census Bureau has never been apolitical in that sense. Focusing perhaps on the twentieth century, Holmes may have in mind something closer to "nonpartisan." Yet as will soon be evident, partisanship hardly exhausts the possible dimensions of the political.

In Aristotelian terms, the census is an aspect of the statesman's role of ordering the parts that make up the polis. Those parts are not to be taken as given: they are themselves shaped by political competition and conflict. This suggests that the census is not simply about counting in the abstract, but about counting certain group characteristics whose salience is determined through politics. The census is therefore concerned with establishing the boundaries that define the parts, or groups, that constitute the political community. This is inescapably a political undertaking.

In ancient Rome the censors had enormous power over citizens, and the census was clearly understood to be an instrument of state authority. Similarly, the Framers conceived of the census as a mechanism to levy taxes as well as to apportion representation. This critical aspect of the census is now obscured by the politics of the modern welfare state, in which the state is seen as satisfying needs more than wielding power.

Today, the governmental structure set in motion by the Framers enmeshes the Census Bureau in bureaucratic politics, an exploration of which gives flesh and blood to the argument that census-taking is fundamentally political in nature. To be sure, the bureau seeks, as does any bureaucracy, to stabilize its environment and in particular to minimize external political interference with its operations. Toward this end the Census Bureau presents itself either as a technocratic fact finder or as a collegium of professionals.

Either stance has strengths and weaknesses. But what the bureau has not typically done is to present itself as engaged in scientific research that should not be interfered with by politicians. To that degree it has acknowledged that the census is an instrument of state authority. In the controversy over the census undercount and what to do about it, by contrast, advocates of adjustment have invoked science in precisely these apolitical terms. As this chapter demonstrates, the stance of these advocates is contradicted by the evidence. But even more to the point, their mistake reminds us of how the suspicion of state authority in American political culture has often resulted in the frustrating and wrongheaded pursuit of political goals through seemingly nonpolitical means.

The first thing to note about the census is that it is much more than a nose count. As demographer Nathan Keyfitz writes:

> The purpose of the census is not to establish the total population of the United States—that can be equally well obtained from births, immigration, and other sources—but to find the populations and characteristics of some 39,000 states, cities, and smaller jurisdictions, an even larger number of census tracts, and other geographical detail.[2]

In contemporary America the census attempts to situate individuals in specific social categories and political jurisdictions. After all, these are the data needed to satisfy the one remaining constitutional purpose of the census: congressional apportionment. The point is expressed by Herman Habermann, director of statistical programs for the United Nations:

A census is a picture of a nation. In that snapshot in time the census lets us understand the boundaries of our nation, where its strengths are, what weaknesses need to be corrected and the relationship of its parts. A census lets each of us as individuals think about his or her place in the country.[3]

The key word here is "boundaries." The essential, defining characteristic of any census is the drawing of boundaries.

Understood as boundary drawing, the census is *an inherently political exercise*, in the Aristotelian sense of the proper ordering and maintenance of the diverse parts that make up the whole. While Plato sought to unify the polis by eliminating the categories and distinctions that he saw pulling it apart (such as between men and women, family and polis, young and old, private and public), Aristotle took such competing and partial claims of justice as inevitable and regarded the statesman's role as responding to and balancing those claims. In that task, the creation of categories and the drawing of boundaries were fundamental.

Yet Aristotle also understood that these activities of the statesman are fraught with difficulty and strife. Precisely because nature provides no definitive guides for such boundaries and categories, those created are invariably subject to challenge. Political theorist Arlene Saxonhouse explains: "Because we ourselves, as a composite of a multiplicity of characteristics, vary along so many dimensions, the political regime is forced to establish boundaries and select criteria to define the order of its polity, but always those boundaries are subject to dispute and to counterclaims."[4] Put differently, Aristotle would not be surprised to see the modern census engulfed by political contention.

An Instrument of State Authority

The census is hardly a modern invention. Census-taking has been one of those fundamental tasks of political authorities since the beginning of history.[5] The earliest recorded census was undertaken around 3800 B.C. by the ancient Babylonians.[6] Several censuses are recounted in the Bible. In the Book of *Numbers* the Lord twice commands Moses to number the people of Israel. Yet when King David undertakes a census, he incurs the wrath of God, stigmatizing census-taking for some believers down to the time of America's first enumeration.[7] Note, too, that Christ was born in Bethlehem as Joseph and Mary were complying with the Roman emperor's decree that "all the world should be enrolled."[8] The word "census" comes to us from the Latin *censere*, to assess. The goal of this assessment was, typically, to levy taxes. This was certainly the purpose of the census of England undertaken by William the Conqueror from 1085 to 1086. The data thus gathered were brought together in the Domesday Book.

"Domesday" is a variant of "doomsday," which of course means "day of judgment."[9] In the contemporary era, when government has come to be regarded primarily as a source of benefits, this authoritative facet of the census has been obscured. But in ancient Rome, the *census* was the official list of the Roman people for purposes of military service and taxation. It was maintained by the *censors*, two magistrates who wielded enormous authority: if for any reason both censors indicated their official disapproval of a man's conduct, the censured individual could be removed from his tribe and consequently lose his right to vote. This specific authority is clearly cognate with our term "censorship," though the connection is almost never made today.

Taking a census is therefore a critical stage in the process of nation-building. The U.S. census is the world's longest-lived such effort, first undertaken in 1790 and every decade thereafter, as prescribed under Article I, Section 2, of the Constitution: "The actual Enumeration shall be made within three Years after the first Meeting of the Congress of the United States, and within every subsequent Term of ten Years." It was only after the United States successfully completed its first census that the modern nations of Europe undertook their own.[10] And it is no accident that one of the first projects of the new black-majority government of South Africa was a census.

Yet here, too, it is crucial to highlight the fact that the Framers envisioned the census as a means not only of apportioning representation among the states but also of assessing taxes. As they wrote in Article I, Section 2, of the Constitution: "Representatives and direct Taxes shall be apportioned among the several States which may be included within this Union, according to their respective Numbers." To be sure, such direct taxes were seldom levied on the states and were eventually obviated by income taxes levied on individuals.

Today the census is inextricably bound up with the administrative needs of the welfare state. In that environment the needs of claimants distract our attention from the power the state must exercise in order to meet those needs. Nevertheless, the heavy hand of governmental authority and the coercive power of the state continue to inhere in the census.

Boundaries in Three Dimensions

The boundary drawing of the modern census has a revealing precedent in sixth-century Athens, where in 508 B.C. the statesman Cleisthenes implemented sweeping reforms in how Athenians were to be classified and governed. Boldly, Cleisthenes abolished the centuries-old, kinship-based system of rule and replaced it with a regime based on residence in newly created geographically defined jurisdictions, called *demes*. These hundred or more demes became the basic unit for voting and military conscription, and with their distinct boundaries, they were equivalent to what today we would call townships. To further his goal of undermining the old tribal ties and, in Aristotle's terms, "mixing up the citizens" to create a unified whole, Cleisthenes assigned several noncontiguous demes to each of ten new "tribes."[11] The social theorist Robert Nisbet concludes: "Instead of the traditional, kinship-based pluralism of Athenian authority, there is now a monolithic unity that arises from a governmental system reaching directly down to the individual citizen."[12] Nisbet adds that Cleisthenes' reforms set the stage for the important military victories of the Athenians over the Persians early in the fifth century B.C. and for the extraordinary cultural and intellectual achievements that followed.[13]

In the same vein, our census today is not just about arithmetic or abstract numbers. Rather it is about numbers in three dimensions: geographical space, temporal space, and social space.

In the first instance, a census must draw a boundary around the nation. For example, the Census Bureau must decide whether Americans living abroad, whether diplomats or military personnel, are to be included in the census, and if so, where they are to be situated geographically.[14] Alternatively, the bureau must deal with the thorny issue of whether illegal aliens residing in the United States are to be included in the decennial count. In this instance, the decision has been made by the federal courts, which have ruled that illegal aliens are to be included.[15]

The next geographical boundaries to be drawn are internal. The Census Bureau has never had the authority to draw county or state lines, but it has had to decide where individuals living astride jurisdictional boundaries are deemed to live for purposes of counting. The bureau has also been involved in the definition and drawing of new geographical entities. Most obvious and least controversial have been census tracts and blocks, the areas into which the bureau subdivides the nation in order to go about its work.[16]

And the bureau has worked with the Office of Management and Budget (OMB) on the definition and creation of various types of metropolitan statistical areas (MSAs). How an MSA gets defined is of critical importance to local political and business leaders, and both OMB and the Census Bureau feel that heat.

The second type of boundary, temporal, is less obvious but equally important. As Habermann points out, a census is "a snapshot *in time*" (emphasis added). The Census Bureau has often had to decide at what point in time its snapshot is best taken. Over the last two centuries the census has been taken in August, then June, then April, then January. Since 1930 the date of the census has been April 1. Each of these dates has had strengths and weaknesses. Around the turn of the century, for example, a June enumeration missed city dwellers who had already left on vacation, while farmers did not recall enough about the previous year's crops for the agricultural census.[17] Today, those pressing for more accurate counts of migrant farmworkers argue for a census date later in the growing season.[18] Others concerned about the undercounting of renters argue for a day other than the first of the month.

Finally, there are the social boundaries that the census must draw. Many of these—for example, between men and women or among age categories—are taken for granted and barely noted. Much more visible and controversial have been the boundaries between ethnic and especially racial groups. The Constitution, it will be recalled, drew the first such boundaries. As stipulated in Article I, Section 2, state census totals were to be obtained by "adding to the whole Number of free Persons, including those bound to Service for a Term of Years, and excluding Indians not taxed, three fifths of all other Persons." In other words, at the founding of our republic, census boundaries were drawn around Indians not under U.S. jurisdiction and slaves.

Over the decades these boundaries have changed. In 1868 the Fourteenth Amendment ensured that thenceforward all persons (again, excluding Indians not taxed) would be counted as whole persons, although the boundary between the races was maintained and blacks tabulated separately. Then in 1890, the census began to count all Indians.[19] At the same time, other boundaries—between mulattoes, quadroons, and octoroons, for instance, or between presumed Mexican and non-Mexican racial groups—have appeared and disappeared.[20]

As should be evident, there are no obviously correct or incorrect ways to draw any of these various boundaries. Affecting various groups and interests differently, these are fundamentally political questions. The point is that none of the three dimensions—geographical, temporal, or social—comes in any natural units. Each is calibrated according to conventions that have been arrived at through a process of societal decisionmaking that is inevitably political.

Naiveté, Cynicism, and Realism

This understanding of the census as inextricably bound up with politics collides with several of the perspectives revealed in the contemporary debate. One widely voiced perspective naively maintains that the census can and ought to be above politics. Accusing the census of having been "corrupted by politics," this perspective implicitly downplays the fact that the census imposes obligations on Americans, and more generally that it is an instrument of political rule. Widely voiced by statisticians, demographers, and both supporters and opponents of adjustment, this naive perspective tends to emphasize the role of rights and science in the census.

A second, cynical perspective regards politics as inevitably playing a role but nevertheless condemns the census process in recent years as having been "overrun by politics." This perspective has been most forcefully articulated by demographer William Petersen, who is critical of the ethnic and racial advisory panels that the bureau established in the mid-1970s.[21] Emphasizing that historically such advisory panels were composed of demographers, statisticians, and other such experts, Petersen stresses that the ethnic and racial panels are made up of minority leaders and activists who, in his view, simply lobby the bureau in behalf of their groups.[22] His point is that this degree of politics surpasses what prudence and especially science would dictate.

A third, realistic perspective has been articulated by Vincent Barabba, twice director of the Census Bureau (under Richard Nixon and Jimmy Carter):

> The census is one of the most political things we do. They [the Census Bureau] don't like to use that word, but it is a political event. . . . [T]o somehow say, "We are going to get rid of all that," is naive. You have to find a way to deal with it in the political arena.[23]

Barabba's disagreement with the naive perspective is self-evident. At the same time, it was Barabba who established the racial and ethnic advisory panels that have so antagonized "cynics" like Petersen.

A deeper source of the realistic perspective is found in the Framers themselves. They conceived of the census as an inherently political undertaking, which did not mean that they simply abandoned the process to sheer power politics. Rather, as was their wont, they embedded the census process in a political architecture that, taking as a given the self-interested political motives of all actors, sought to balance one set of political motives or interests against others. As already mentioned, it was the Framers' original conception that census numbers would be used to levy direct taxes on the states as well as to apportion congressional representatives among them. The former would of course encourage states to minimize their population counts, while the latter would work in the other direction. This balancing act is explained in *Federalist* No. 54:

> The establishment of a common measure for representation and taxation will have a very salutary effect. As the accuracy of the census to be obtained by the Congress will necessarily depend . . . on the disposition, if not on the cooperation, of the States, it is of great importance that the States should feel as little bias as possible, to swell or to reduce the amount of their numbers. Were their share of representation alone to be governed by this rule, they would have an interest in exaggerating their inhabitants. Were the rule to decide their share of taxation alone, a contrary temptation would prevail. By extending the rule to both objects, the States will have opposite interests, which will control and balance each other, and produce the requisite impartiality.[24]

It is important to note here that as conceived of by the Framers the census does not somehow keep politics at bay or within certain bounds. Rather the census relies on politics as the very mechanism by which an impartial result will be achieved.

Moreover, *Federalist* No. 54 uses the term "impartiality"—not, for example, "accuracy." While it would be foolish to argue that the Framers and their contemporaries were not concerned with accuracy, they clearly did not make a fetish of it or elevate it to an absolute standard. This was in part because when used to levy taxes the census was understood to be an approximate indicator of wealth.[25] Thus the Framers strove for accuracy within the bounds of political pragmatism.

But the Framers' stance toward the census also reflects a deeper philosophical thrust. As the intellectual historian John Diggins writes: "Skeptical of man's intellectual capacities, the theorists of the Constitution doubted that Americans could know their true and ultimate interests, and thus the Federalists settled for moderation, tolerance, compromise, and pluralism."[26] This philosophical disposition also led the Framers away from any notion of the census as an absolute measure of population.

Varieties of Census Politics

Admittedly, it only gets us so far to argue in such broad historical and philosophical terms that the census is inherently and properly a political undertaking. Different observers attach different meanings to the term "politics," and one naturally wants to know how politics in the contemporary sense manifests itself in the census.

My surmise is that most Americans would subscribe to the common-sense notion that politics in the census is found in the gross manipulation of numbers—the statistical equivalent of stuffing ballot boxes. Reflecting this common-sense view of census politics is Winston Churchill's pithy observation: "When I call for statistics about the rate of infant mortality, what I want is proof that fewer babies died when I was prime minister than when anyone else was prime minister."[27]

Yet as noted by James Bonnen, former director of President Carter's Reorganization Project for the Federal Statistical System, "Politicizing statistics only rarely involves 'cooking the numbers.'"[28] Declares Morris Hansen, whose career at the Census Bureau spanned almost half a century:

> I do not think I have seen much evidence where there was any effort to influence the data, as such, from the outside. I have seen some things that bothered me, but it did not amount to much—where someone got a release [of data] speeded up or had the release held back. . . . Not much of that, but I have seen some isolated instances. They are rare exceptions.[29]

Echoing Hansen's judgment is C. Louis Kincannon, deputy director of the bureau from 1982 to 1992:

> In these years as deputy director, there have never been any efforts by higher authorities to influence the numbers this way or that. Nothing that crude. There have been arguments about definition, but they seemed to me to have been legitimate. Where we thought political authorities wanted to investigate a definition at the wrong time— merely for the way it might affect an outcome—we have said it was not something we would do.[30]

Both Hansen and Kincannon suggest that politics manifests itself not through cooking the numbers but through precisely those boundaries—especially social and temporal—that I have highlighted.

To be sure, American history has seen many incidents of chicanery and disputed census results. In the early days of the republic, such problems appear to have arisen from the practice of paying enumerators by the number of individuals registered on the census.[31] Since this method of payment persisted through 1940, these problems extended well into the modern era.[32] When the policy finally changed and enumerators began to be paid by the hour (as they are today), census results became susceptible to manipulation by falsifying answers or simply by throwing forms away—a practice known as "curbstoning."

Politics has also permeated the census to the extent that the Framers intended it to be a creature of Congress.[33] Throughout the nineteenth century Congress not only got directly involved in the writing of census questions but also relied on the census as a source of patronage. Until the creation of the Government Printing Office in the mid–nineteenth century, census patronage included contracts to private printing firms.[34] Also important was the hiring of thousands of enumerators for the house-to-house canvass that was the primary means of gathering census data until 1960, when the census began to rely on self-enumeration.[35] Under what the Census Bureau delicately refers to as "the referral system," field supervisors and enumerators for the decennial census have long been hired on recommendation by U.S. senators and congressmen.[36] And while the referral system is relied upon less today than in the past, Senator Charles Schumer (Democrat of New York) recalls that for the 1980 census the Carter administration hired enumerators in New York City on the basis of referrals from local Democratic political clubs.[37] During the 1990 census the bureau had a political appointee dealing with referrals from members of Congress.[38]

As it happened, the Carter administration attempted to wrest control of census hiring away from Congress, an effort that prompted Senator Ernest Hollings of South Carolina to rebuke Census Director Vincent Barabba: "You explain to the President that I will determine who will conduct the census in South Carolina. . . . This is the way it has been done, and this is the way it will be done."[39] Such politically influenced hiring has undoubtedly compromised the professionalism and quality of the census down through the decades. Yet there is a case to be made in favor of the referral system as a means of gaining for the census the enthusiastic support and local knowledge of elected officials. Certainly, there have been arguments for and against the referral system among professionals within the Census Bureau itself.[40]

On Not Cooking the Numbers

With the diminished role of the referral system, the locus of political influence on the census has shifted back to the fundamental issues of boundary drawing. Often the boundaries at issue are temporal, involving the timing of the collection—or especially (as Morris Hansen has indicated) of the publication—of census data. In the extreme, political considerations have led to a decision not to release data at all.

For example, under the Bush administration a political appointee at the Census Bureau sought (unsuccessfully) to bury a report by a bureau economist that demonstrated a sharp increase in the percentage of low-paying jobs.[41] At the time, this episode was noted as being unusual. During the Nixon administration, however, it would not have been. Nixon launched what must be seen as the most aggressive effort of this century to exert political control over the Census Bureau and other statistical agencies.

At the Bureau of Labor Statistics (BLS), the Nixon administration sought to counteract the steady stream of unfavorable unemployment and inflation data by discontinuing the monthly technical briefings that BLS professionals had been conducting for the press since 1953.[42] At the Census Bureau, Nixon placed several political operatives, including a former employee of the Republican National Committee, to work with high-level professionals. Recalls Conrad Taeuber, then associate director of the census for demographic fields: "There was a serious effort from the Department [of Commerce], and I suppose from the White House, [to place] the more politically sensitive people in positions where they could influence the flow of data."[43]

Facing the first redistricting since the federal courts' one-person/one-vote rulings, the Nixonites were particularly concerned with expediting the release of small-area data from the 1970 census to certain users. They were also concerned about the steady stream of data highlighting poverty that was coming out of the bureau's Population Division. As a result, a public relations officer was assigned to the division to monitor its output. According to Taeuber, "Nothing was suppressed. It was more a matter of emphasis—why go into the unpleasant aspects of life in the U.S.?"[44]

One consequence of these efforts to extend political control over the bureau was the departure of several high-level professionals, including members of the "Class of '40," the cohort that had come to the Census Bureau during the Great Depression, worked on the census of 1940, and contributed mightily to the agency's enhanced reputation.[45] Under Nixon, morale hit what was probably an all-time low, and many saw this as the beginning of the end of the glory days.[46]

Yet without minimizing the import of the Nixon administration's efforts, it is worth noting that not only were they unsuccessful, they also did not focus on "cooking the numbers." Rather they focused on the boundaries: on the categories of data (such as poverty versus nonpoverty) and on matters of timing. In the words of Vincent Barabba:

> I would imagine at that time there had been discussions within the Nixon administration about trying to get hold of sensitive statistical information. Now, I was not involved in those, but it has never been clear to me whether they were saying, "We have to handle this information more sensitively than it's been handled before," or "We've got to make it look good." I don't think it was the latter. I think it was more sensitive about what was collected and how it was distributed, because as pragmatic as those people were, they were not dumb. I think they would have a sense that you couldn't hide that kind of stuff. So I would think the whole purpose of that was, in essence, to put sort of a "communication" clamp on the whole statistical system to make sure that you didn't have people running around trying to embarrass the Administration.[47]

One of the remarkable things about such episodes is that there have not been more of them. A possible explanation is suggested by Raymond Vernon. Examining the politics of economic statistics in developing nations, Vernon readily acknowledges official manipulation of such data but makes the further point that politicians in these nations typically have less control over the numbers than may at first appear. This is due to the often complex and contradictory outcomes of statistical manipulations. Vernon cites the example of officials tempted to orchestrate lower official price indexes having to ponder whether their actions would also depress GNP estimates.[48] With substantially less latitude to manipulate government statistics than their counterparts in the developing world, American officials face similar uncertainties. This point will take on added significance when I turn to the politics of the census undercount and the controversy over adjustment.

Another reason why there has been little gross manipulation of census data is the relative autonomy the Census Bureau has enjoyed for much of its history. I emphasize *relative* because Congress has clearly played an active role in the census. Yet as historian Margo Anderson has noted, the emergence of the census as a permanent bureaucratic agency late in the nineteenth century coincided with the decreasing political salience of census results, because until 1920 Congress minimized zero-sum conflicts over apportionment by expanding the size of the House each decade. Moreover, during this same period, the other constitutional purpose of the census—levying direct taxes on the states—fell into complete disuse as the inauguration of the federal income tax obviated any such rationale for the enumeration. As Anderson writes: "Ironically, but perhaps predictably, the successful campaign for a permanent census office got going in earnest at a point when the constitutional purposes of the census seemed so innocuous and routine that the statisticians could be called on to do new and different things."[49] In essence, by the beginning of World War I bureaucrats and statisticians had their agency, Congress its patronage, and the Constitution its decennial apportionment.

This equilibrium lasted through the mid-1960's, when both Congress and the Department of Commerce still afforded the bureau considerable latitude and discretion. This is confirmed by Richard Scammon, bureau director from 1961 to 1965. Scammon cites routine dealings with members of Congress over patronage and redistricting issues.[50] But in general he emphasizes what a quiet and uneventful period it was:

> I don't really recall we had any particular squabbles with Congress. . . . We never had any questions that I can recall from the general oversight function exercised in Congress. I think that the reason for that is that we never were really that important. . . . The members of Congress would pay attention to it really only when it affected them or their districts.[51]

Scammon cites the same benign neglect from the Department of Commerce, enhanced by the physical separation of the bureau in suburban Maryland from department headquarters in downtown Washington.[52]

Scammon's watch ended just before the explosion in federal grant programs whose formulas would rely on census data, before the impact of the 1960s one-person/one-vote court rulings on the 1970 redistricting, and before the Nixon administration began the storm of political interference mentioned above. Even so, by today's standards, the bureau continued to enjoy a remarkable degree of autonomy well into the 1970s and 1980s. In 1971 President Nixon's Commission on Federal Statistics (the Wallis Commission) reported that "Congress reviews the Bureau of the Census less as an adjunct of the Department of Commerce than as an independent agency."[53] This finding, arguably suspect for presenting the Nixon administration in a favorable light, was nevertheless echoed in 1975 by statistical policy analyst Judith Innes:

> Agencies like the Census Bureau and BLS have been directed by professionals rather than politicians and allowed some autonomy. They have direct relationships, not filtered through the Secretary, with Congress, the users, and the public through the press and their own publications. The situation has encouraged them to serve that public rather than simply the political leadership of the moment.[54]

This autonomous status was still very much in evidence during the 1980 census. For example, the critical decision not to adjust that census was made exclusively by the bureau.[55] The secretary of commerce seldom focused on the activities of the Census Bureau,[56] and at OMB the sentiment was, according to one official, "When you are up to your armpits in alligators, you don't worry much about statistics."[57] All this was to change very quickly in the next few years.

A Bureaucratic "Takeover"?

At this juncture it is helpful to situate the Census Bureau within the larger federal bureaucracy. Perhaps most salient is the fact that the bureau has remarkably few political appointees, which is all the more striking since its parent agency, the Department of Commerce, is renowned for being overloaded with them.[58] During the 1980s, for example, the department had so many political appointees beholden to Vice President George Bush that administration insiders dubbed it "Bush Gardens."[59]

By contrast, there are still only three political appointees among the more than 10,000 individuals employed by the Census Bureau.[60] This low number of such officials contributes to a lack of political savvy and to an overall vulnerability to political forces external to the agency. Consider the terms of tenure of the director: appointed by the president with the consent of the Senate and serving at the pleasure of the president, the census director routinely resigns with the election of a new chief executive. Further, the census director now reports to two other presidential appointees, the secretary of commerce and the deputy secretary of commerce through the under secretary for economic affairs.[61]

This rather anomalous chain of command reflects the bureau's more general subordination to the Department of Commerce. In recent years there has been what former census director Barbara Bryant calls a "takeover" of the bureau by the Commerce Department.[62] This takeover is nowhere more evident than in the decision to adjust the results of the decennial census. As indicated above, for the 1980 census the decision was explicitly left up to the director. But by 1987 the under secretary of commerce was intervening in bureau deliberations and ruling that there would be no adjustment of the 1990 census. After much controversy, litigation, and study, this same decision against adjustment was made in 1991 by Secretary of Commerce Robert Mosbacher, who explicitly overruled the recommendation of Census Director Bryant.

The increasing involvement of the Commerce Department in the planning and implementation of the decennial census has not gone unnoted by bureau professionals. Edwin Goldfield, a former high-level Census Bureau administrator of many years, commented in a 1991 interview:

> Certainly, some of us who observe the Bureau have seen what seems to be an increasing degree of micromanagement. It is almost embarrassing to the Census Bureau that when congressional committees or subcommittees hold a hearing on the decennial census . . . that the spokesman is the Under Secretary of Commerce or the Deputy Under Secretary, with maybe the Director of the Census Bureau sitting off to one side. It used to be that the Director would be the chief witness.[63]

This vulnerability to outside political forces is highlighted when compared with the Bureau of Labor Statistics (BLS), the second pillar of the federal statistical system. Like the census director, the commissioner of labor statistics is appointed by the president with the consent of the Senate. But unlike the census director, the BLS commissioner does not serve at the pleasure of the president and has a four-year term of office. Moreover, reappointment to more than one term has become a BLS tradition. Since its creation in 1884, the BLS has had only eleven commissioners (fewer than any other statistical agency, including the Census Bureau).[64] The immediate past commissioner, Janet Norwood, served more than twelve years. During her tenure at the BLS, the Census Bureau went through seven leadership changes: four directors plus three interim acting directors. The BLS commissioner does not have to negotiate the same complicated chain of command as the census director: she reports directly to her departmental superior, the secretary of labor. Moreover, the highly sensitive data on unemployment and inflation that the BLS releases each month do not have to be cleared by the Department of Labor.[65] Unquestionably, the BLS enjoys more visibility and independence within the Department of Labor than the Census Bureau enjoys within the Department of Commerce.

The Political Weakness of the Bureau

What accounts for the Census Bureau's weakness? To some degree its ambiguous relationship to the Department of Commerce is responsible. Intensive oversight by an under secretary whose staff and budget pertain largely to the census has clearly exacerbated the natural tensions between any agency head and his departmental superiors.[66] As former deputy census director Kincannon has observed, "Those relationships [between census directors and under secretaries] have ranged from merely tense, where there was strong but careful working together, to really almost a complete breakdown."[67] One way these tensions have played out is by the department asserting its political will over the bureau in the name of insulating it from politics. The result, whether intended or not, has been to politically weaken and marginalize the bureau. Until fairly recently, for example, the Census Bureau would routinely assign a senior staffer to the House subcommittee overseeing the census. Yet this practice, which was intended to afford Congress expertise in federal statistical policy but which also helped the bureau to develop insight into the ways of Congress, was eventually discontinued by the Commerce Department.[68] In the same vein, former under secretary of commerce Everett Ehrlich is reported to have directed congressional staffers to take their problems directly to him, not to the census director, whom he did not want involved in politics.

Such efforts have arguably contributed to the bureau's underdeveloped political skills. The bureau gets exceptionally low marks from congressional staffers, who grumble about census professionals who are technically proficient but politically inept. Such complaints run the gamut from the mundane to the substantive. House committee staffers complain that census personnel fail to keep them informed of critical meetings at the bureau. One staffer noted that Director Martha Riche was so poorly briefed when she first made the rounds on Capitol Hill, she was unaware that the name of her oversight committee had been changed. Another complaint was that the bureau's 1991 adjusted numbers originally presented to members were aggregated not at the state level, which is naturally of most concern to members of Congress, but at the regional level.

The political ineptitude of the bureau also comes through in its management of the ethnic and racial advisory committees. It is evident from their meetings that the bureau has missed the opportunity to use these committees to inform minority advocates about political realities. On the contrary, briefings seem to work the other way. During one memorable session, an earnest congressional staffer tried to alert both bureau professionals and committee members to the difficulties of getting members of Congress focused on the census. In response, he was greeted with condescending lectures about the need for aides to "educate" their bosses about the importance of the census.[69]

Not all such complaints of political ineptitude come from outside the bureau. Former deputy director Louis Kincannon diplomatically observes: "I think one of the worst shortcomings of my time at the Census Bureau has been our failure to develop and adhere consistently to an effective strategy with Congress."[70] While stressing that the bureau has very little pork to hand out to Congress, Kincannon says that even when bureau officials do have a bit of bacon, they do not make use of it. Specifically, when the bureau decides to build large processing facilities—something that any member of Congress would welcome into his or her district—it simply does not take political relationships into account. Kincannon points to a regional computing center that was eventually built in Charlotte, North Carolina, and notes: "We just put it where it worked best, without any cognizance of whether that did us any good or not. As a consequence, we have it where it works very well, and I don't know that we have reaped any benefit other than the efficient operation of it."[71] While not advocating that such decisions should be made on purely political grounds, Kincannon argues that the bureau consistently fails to keep political relationships and benefits in mind.

Part of the problem may be the paucity of political appointees, who (in spite of the problems they might create) would lend the bureau more savvy. More broadly, though, the bureau has never been the kind of place that attracts those adept at bureaucratic infighting or political maneuvering. Quite the opposite: for several decades beginning in the 1930s, the Census Bureau has resembled a graduate school as much as a government agency. Former director Bryant is not too far off the mark when she observes: "While there's no ivy on the walls of its headquarters in Suitland, Maryland, the Census Bureau's full-time professional staff of analysts, survey designers, computer scientists, mathematical statisticians, and demographers are like the social sciences faculty at an elite research university."[72]

By the end of the depression the bureau had become a haven for leading figures in the emerging fields of statistics and survey sampling.[73] Prominent academic demographers such as Philip Hauser of the University of Chicago came and brought their graduate students with them. The bureau had a reputation as a center of innovation in its field: quality control guru Edward Demming worked there, and the bureau provided the impetus for computer technology. The latter dates back to the turn of the century, when a bureau employee developed the first modern computing machine that eventually led to the birth of IBM. At the close of World War II, the bureau played a key role in developing nonmilitary uses for the modern computer and was one of the first customers for the early postwar mainframes.[74]

The bureau's critical mass of talented professionals and social scientists has not only lacked political savvy but created other political problems. Along with other federal statistical agencies, the bureau developed a reputation for sometimes sacrificing timeliness to other professional criteria.[75] More generally, Congress has often expressed annoyance at spending taxpayer money on research that did not have some obvious and immediate benefit.[76]

Over time, events have removed much of the burnish from the bureau's sterling professional reputation. By the late 1960s the prestigious "Class of '40" was beginning to retire or move on to other positions, a process of natural attrition that was undoubtedly accelerated by the aforementioned political pressures applied by the Nixon administration.[77] Yet it would not be accurate to trace the decline in the bureau's prestige simply to political events. In many respects the Census Bureau has been a victim of its own successes. Having pioneered the gathering and processing of survey data, it could not long monopolize the field. Having helped to create the American computer industry, the bureau, like any government agency, could not keep up with the dizzying pace of innovation that now characterizes that sector.[78] At the same time, with statistics having become an acknowledged profession and with major universities churning out highly trained specialists, the Census Bureau must now compete for talent not only with other professionalized statistical agencies at the federal, state, and local levels but also with private industry and universities.[79]

Moreover, the social scientific and technical orientation of most Census Bureau professionals makes it difficult for them to explain their concepts and programs to Congress and the public. Technique and process tend to override organizational and political imperatives. At one meeting at the bureau in the mid-1990s, when plans for the 2000 census were first being announced, the big news was that statistical sampling and adjustment were

going to be built into a "one-number census." Accordingly, the agenda for
the meeting included a discussion of the complicated mechanics of sampling. But the schedule for the two-day conference left this discussion for
the late afternoon of the last day, a Friday, just when many participants
would be departing. Upon realizing their mistake, bureau officials resched-
uled the sampling discussion for Friday morning, explaining that they had
originally planned to hold it at the end of the conference because sampling
and adjustment come at the end of the decennial census process![80]

Ironically, in recent years the bureau's decline in professional standing
may have reduced its ability to recruit top political executives. The increased
constraints placed on the Census Bureau by the Department of Commerce
have not made the job of director any more appealing. There have been
unfortunate stretches when the director's post has gone unfilled, and the
tenure of President Bill Clinton's first census director, Martha Riche, was
stormy and unusually brief. It may be that the political pressures on the
bureau have become untenable for any director. Nevertheless, it is hard to
avoid the conclusion that recent high-level officials there have lacked some
of the political skills of former director Richard Scammon. As he recounts:

> If you are Director, and if any Member calls, you talk to him. You
> don't let anybody else talk to him because you want the Member to
> feel that you are concerned. You know enough in advance; you can
> bone up a little on the particular districts. Just being able to talk in
> some way, not as an expert, with these people is helpful. I don't know
> if Barbara [Bryant] or the people who have been [in the Director's
> position] between me and Barbara do that now.[81]

Boredom on the Hill

If Census Bureau specialists have a hard time explaining to politicians and
the public what their agency does, this is due not only to their own limitations but also to the low tolerance many nonspecialists have for the technical nature of the bureau's work. As Senator Warren Rudman commented
to Census Director Bryant, "I don't know how you get excited about these
numbers. They tend to put me to sleep."[82] Because the fates of senators do
not hang on the apportionment or redistricting implications of the decennial results, Rudman's reaction should not surprise us. But his sentiment is
shared by the vast majority of House members, whose political fates *do*
depend more directly on census results.

Throughout the 1990s staffers working on census issues complained of the difficulty of getting their bosses focused on the census—and these were the members whose committee assignments pertained directly to the census. Undoubtedly, this lack of interest has something to do with the fact that seats on the census subcommittee were not highly sought after.[83] In the same vein, a staffer at the General Accounting Office (GAO) complained that his division had not received a single request for information about the census from any members from 1993 to 1997—years when the bureau was making important and controversial decisions about the 2000 census.

Members can afford to be indifferent to the Census Bureau in part because there are so few organized constituencies pushing them to show interest. Many government agencies enforce laws that depend on the census for specific kinds of data; the Voting Rights Act and its need for block-level data on race and ethnicity come to mind. But these agencies are not the kind of constituents—organizations capable of mobilizing broad public support or narrowly focused constituencies with substantial resources at their disposal—that capture the attention of Congress.

Specific interests are always lobbying for items to be placed on the decennial questionnaire. A classic example is the swimming pool industry, which pushes for a question about pool ownership; or pet food producers, who routinely seek a question on household pets. But such interests are really just trying to free-ride on what is already there: they seldom organize on behalf of the census when it comes time to appropriate budgets.

As various commentators have noted, the census is essentially a public good with no well-organized or highly visible constituencies prepared to support it. Senator Daniel Patrick Moynihan observed some time ago:

> To declare that the Census is without friends would be absurd. But partisans? When Census appropriations are cut, who bleeds on Capitol Hill or in the Executive Office of the President? The answer is almost everyone in general, and therefore no one in particular. But the result, too often, is the neglect, even the abuse, of an indispensable public institution, which often of late has served better than it has been served.[84]

In some respects, the bureau has found it convenient to have no specific constituencies beyond "the public"; in this way it manages to avoid relationships with specific interests that might lead to controversy and thus to maintain an "objective" stance.[85] Unfortunately, the price of this arrangement is the absence of supporters in times of need.

Here again, it is useful to compare the Census Bureau with the Bureau of Labor Statistics, which suffers far less from this public-good effect. Because the BLS produces figures each month that are highly visible and have a direct impact on very specific organized interests, it has a number of constituencies invested in its operations. The Census Bureau, by contrast, focuses on a once-in-a-decade event whose implications, while enormous, are so diffuse that they inspire only the weakest kind of organized interests.

This analysis suggests that the Census Bureau has always been politically weak and vulnerable to outside forces. Yet only recently, especially since the 1960s, has it become clear that the benign neglect enjoyed by the bureau for much of its history reflected neither the bureau's strength nor the respect it commanded; rather it reflected the bureau's political marginality. Now that the political stakes in the census have been heightened, neglect has turned to preoccupation.

The Politics of "Depoliticization"

A further irony of recent census history is that the Commerce Department's takeover of the Census Bureau has been facilitated by those who, while criticizing the undercount of minorities and arguing for census adjustment, assert that the census is a scientific enterprise that must not be sullied by politics. Former director Bryant explains:

> The cities, in suing the secretary of commerce, the Department of Commerce, and the Census Bureau in 1980 and 1990, precipitated the department's 'takeover' of the Census Bureau. Once the secretary of commerce was sued, the General Counsel's Office at the department had to take on the secretary's defense. The Census Bureau was no longer a quiet statistical agency out in Maryland, but a problem for the department and its secretary. The lawsuits have diminished the bureau's autonomy, moving adjustment decisions away from the purely statistical arena.[86]

To illustrate the point, Bryant describes a typical process in which it took six weeks and sixteen steps to produce a response to a friendly inquiry from Senator Paul Sarbanes (Democrat of Maryland) that was acceptable to everyone.[87]

In one important sense, the Census Bureau would benefit from more politics, not less. Strictly speaking, the concentration of political control at the Department of Commerce has "depoliticized" the bureau. As we have seen, the effect has been to render the bureau weaker politically and more susceptible to external political influences. Thus the bureau could benefit from a few well-organized constituencies to counterbalance such influences. This counterbalancing of competing political interests is clearly what the Framers had in mind for our political system generally. But it is also how they saw the census functioning: by means of competing interests organized around the uses of the census for representation on the one hand and taxation on the other.

To glance again at the BLS, there is no doubt that it is a more independent agency than the Census Bureau, more able to defend its mission and prerogatives as a highly professional statistical agency. But this is not because the BLS is "apolitical," but because it has many specific *political* allies and adversaries who both support and criticize it. Because the BLS is less of a public good than the Census Bureau, it is more able to withstand intrusions from outside its ranks. Again, what is called for is not an effort to make the bureau apolitical but ways to make it a stronger political actor.[88]

"Conservative and Cautious"?

Further misunderstanding arises when analysts assert that the Census Bureau, like statistical agencies everywhere, is reluctant to change its methods in any way that would threaten continuity in data sets. As sociologist Stanley Lieberson observes about census operations generally:

> Census-taking organizations are cautious and not readily inclined towards making changes in either the questions or their coded responses. The organization in each country is likely to be conservative; there will be a preference, when in doubt, to use the existing question. When there is unavoidable doubt or pressure about the existing procedure, then the tendency will be to modify (if at all possible) an existing question. If this is impossible and no recourse is available, a new question is introduced.[89]

Christopher Jencks, commenting specifically on the United States, presses the point: "We have created a political system in which federal statistical agencies often find it safer to go on doing something wrong year after year than to make improvements."[90] Sociologist Paul Starr puts it succinctly: "Statistical systems are conservative in an institutional rather than political sense."[91] This perspective reflects a sort of modern folk wisdom about government bureaucracies, along with the oft-heard maxim that bureaucrats always seek to maximize their budgets. The point about budgets has been demonstrated to be incorrect, and that about institutional conservatism—at least concerning the Census Bureau—merits the same treatment.[92]

The confusion surrounding this issue is evident in a recent monograph on racial and ethnic statistics by the National Academy of Sciences (NAS). At one point editor Barry Edmonston and his colleagues echo the conventional wisdom: "Statistical categories are often adapting to change that has already occurred, rather than to change that is anticipated. One reason is that statistical administration is usually conservative and cautious."[93] A very different interpretation is offered when the NAS Edmonston report highlights the Census Bureau's leading role in popularizing the term "Hispanic": "The designation 'Hispanic' was not in common usage prior to its adoption by the Bureau of the Census in the early 1970s, yet its government-wide use as a referent for heterogeneous populations has bolstered the growth of Hispanic or Latino/a identity."[94] Confirming this interpretation are the frequent complaints of Latino activists and scholars who reject "Hispanic" as foisted on them by federal bureaucrats in Washington.[95]

The point is also illustrated by the bureau's decision to undertake a count of the homeless for the 1990 decennial census. Its highly publicized effort on the night of March 20, 1990—so-called S Night, for "shelters and streets"—was not only innovative and unprecedented, it was extremely risky. Because the homeless are hard to define, much less to find, the bureau never claimed that its count would be definitive or complete. But this acknowledgement collided with the agency's ever-present preoccupation with producing accurate and authoritative data.[96] And indeed, homeless advocates roundly criticized the bureau for producing a misleadingly low and inaccurate homeless count.[97] While satisfying explanations as to why the Census Bureau undertook S Night are not at hand, there can be no doubt that a "conservative and cautious" agency would simply have avoided the whole business.

Finally, the Census Bureau has revealed itself to be anything but institutionally conservative about statistically adjusting the census. For both the 1990 and 2000 censuses the bureau has demonstrated a willingness to be out in front of Congress, of the Department of Commerce, and of the American public on an undertaking never before attempted. Whatever one's views on adjustment, the bureau has clearly taken huge chances with its advocacy of this untried methodology.

Why this persistent misconception of statistical agencies generally and of the Census Bureau in particular? One reason is that it reinforces the gratifying image of the bureau as an agency capable of resisting external political pressures. Yet the only sense in which the bureau can fairly be called "conservative" is in habitually pursuing the path of least resistance when confronted by such pressures.

Fact-Finders, Professionals, or Scientists?

But I do not mean to suggest that the Census Bureau is irresponsibly passive before the political forces that press on it from all sides. Even though the census is an inherently political undertaking, the Census Bureau—just like any bureaucracy—strives to stabilize its environment and maintain as much independence for itself as possible.

One way the bureau has done this is by presenting itself as "Factfinder for the Nation." This is how it has described itself for some time in official publications.[98] But this is also how others perceive it. Starr's overall description of statistical agencies in liberal democracies captures this ethos at the bureau:

> The public and its officials typically subscribe to a radical empiricism that presumes that statistical inquiry can be theoretically as well as ideologically innocent. These expectations mean that professionals must translate political purposes, cultural presuppositions, and formal social science theories into statistical procedures and data while only seeming to apply their technical skills.[99]

The basic stance of those who work at the bureau toward their political superiors is: "You tell us what to count and we'll count it." I have seldom heard personnel there describe themselves as technocrats, but they clearly see themselves as such.

As President Nixon's Commission on Federal Statistics observed almost thirty years ago, this emphasis on fact-finding allows the Census Bureau "to be 'objective' in the sense of avoiding commitment to explanatory theories of behavior that may generate controversy with users."[100] Indeed, the bureau has successfully presented itself to average citizens as well as congressional overseers as a no-nonsense agency going strictly about the public's business. Moreover, fact-finding has helped it avoid the liability of "doing research," a frequent charge of zealous members of Congress eager to rein in reputedly wasteful and intrusive investigators indulging their curiosity at the taxpayers' expense.[101]

But letting the facts speak for themselves has its downside. Fact-finding may afford the bureau political protection from some critics, but it comes at the price of frustrating and even alienating potential allies. For example, when demographer Ira Lowry refers to the bureau as "our national fact gatherer," he is criticizing it for not adopting a more scientifically rigorous and challenging research agenda.[102] Commenting on the usefulness of the bureau's published material, Jencks makes a similar point: "Bureau publications offer hundreds of millions of numbers, but they offer readers little guidance in interpreting these numbers. Helping readers interpret numbers—or even helping them avoid the most common misinterpretations—evidently threatens the 'objective' image that the bureau cultivates."[103] To sophisticated users of Census Bureau products, the fact-finder stance is annoyingly unpersuasive. It is certainly implausible that bureau professionals do their work without making judgments that have political implications and even direct political consequences. As Judith Innes explains:

> The mere design of a table involves a considerable array of choices each of which affects our perception of the nature of the problem. The statistician chooses the title of the table, the categories to apply and the relationships to feature. Unless we suppose the choices are random, we have to assume that the statistician applies his own perceptions of what is important and his own analyses of the issues.[104]

The point is driven home by none other than former census director Barabba: "Although the bureau cannot afford to give up any of its valuable technical excellence, it needs to broaden its conception of itself. It cannot persist in the quaint notion that technical and social matters can be dealt with separately."[105]

Professionalism is another means the Census Bureau relies on to buffer itself from politics. One particular area where the bureau has resolutely staked its bureaucratic independence and professional autonomy is the confidentiality of census data. Earlier in our history, standards were not only more lax, they were fundamentally different: census results, complete with individual names, were posted in public.[106] In the first decades of this century the bureau shared data on individuals with other federal agencies. For the past fifty years, however, it has consistently refused requests for data from all agencies, public and private, that might allow "any direct or indirect disclosure of information about any individual."[107] As William Petersen confirms: "However improbably, the Census Bureau has established a perfect record, never once accidentally or illegitimately revealing a single datum tied to an individual."[108]

Petersen's conclusion is all the more cogent, since as author of a monograph on Japanese Americans he is well acquainted with the episode that has cast most doubt on the integrity of the bureau's confidentiality policy: its role in the wartime internment of Japanese Americans.[109] Early in 1942 the War Department asked the bureau for the names and addresses of all Japanese and Japanese Americans enumerated in the 1940 census in the western United States. The bureau refused to honor that request, but it did provide small-area tabulations identifying concentrations of Japanese that clearly facilitated the internment effort. The bureau is decidedly uneasy about its role in this affair, for which it has been roundly criticized.[110] Yet the fact remains that the agency did refuse to release the individual names and addresses initially requested by the War Department.[111] Indeed, Petersen describes this episode as "a prime instance of the Census Bureau's probity, even under intense pressure from other government agencies and despite a prevailing mood of hysteria."[112]

Since this episode, there have been other occasions when the bureau has been asked for data and has refused to cooperate. In the late 1940s, for example, the FBI failed to obtain census data on people living in and around Blair House, where President Truman resided while the White House was undergoing restoration.[113]

Confidentiality of census data is now a matter of law as well as professional ethics.[114] Yet it remains at the core of the bureau's understanding of its mission as a federal agency. Indeed, the norm of confidentiality is primarily what permits those who work at the Census Bureau to point to their independence from external political forces and therefore call themselves professionals.

Yet however critical to the agency, these ethics constitute a very restricted notion of professionalism. To be sure, confidentiality is not the only hook on which professionals at the bureau hang their hats. They rightly point out that there are proper and improper ways to undertake enumerations and perform statistical procedures, as well as prudent and imprudent, correct and incorrect ways to tabulate data and conduct surveys. If the decision has been made to do a survey to look at poverty rates, for example, then the professionals might argue that there is a need to oversample in minority areas. A political appointee might well respond, on fiscal or even political grounds, that she does not want to oversample. In such an instance, professional opinion arguably ought to prevail. But such an outcome would hardly be certain.

Such a neat separation of means and ends is seldom readily available. Moreover, although the distinction between professional standards and judgments on the one hand and political opinions and objectives on the other is critical, the dominant professionals at the bureau—demographers and statisticians—do not have the technical and intellectual virtuosity of economists, scientists, or perhaps even engineers. Census professionals typically lack an impressive bag of tricks to keep nonspecialists at bay, and they know it. And because demographers and statisticians—unlike doctors and lawyers, for example—lack the professional authority that comes from well-established canons of practice developed over centuries of addressing problems deemed critical to society, they do not have much clout when they are up against political authorities.

Of course, if it relied on stronger professionals, the Census Bureau would undoubtedly have to contend with, as have other government agencies, strains and conflicts between its bureaucratic goals and incentive structures outside its control.[115] There is no easy or obvious resolution of such bureaucratic tensions. Undoubtedly a stronger shield for the bureau than fact-finding or professional ethics would be science. In our political culture, which is so suspicious of governmental authority, science is frequently turned to as a source of authority that transcends politics. Indeed, this is one reason why government agencies dealing with intractable issues invoke science to defend themselves and to justify controversial policies.[116]

Yet in the recent controversy over the undercount, it has been advocates of statistical adjustment of the census based outside the bureau who have most consistently and energetically invoked the authority of science. While agency executives have on occasion relied on science to defend their policies, the bureau has for the most part eschewed any such characterization of its efforts.[117]

Why is that? One reason may be that by not claiming the mantle of science the bureau forestalls the questions that would arise if it were in fact pursuing its own research agenda. Any such undertaking would obviously involve critical choices about methods and topics, which would inevitably raise concerns, especially from congressional overseers, about the values guiding those choices. Though hardly overwhelming in its own terms, such a prospect would be particularly daunting to an agency that has for so long defined (and defended) itself as a mere fact-finder.

But a more compelling reason why the bureau has not relied on science to defend itself is that its work is not scientific in nature. One of the hallmarks of doing science is the testing of hypotheses in order to build theory. The trained social scientists at the Census Bureau understand this; they further understand that the fundamental direction of their work is not determined by the demands of scientific inquiry but by the various requirements of the political system. As one high-level census professional with a Ph.D. in demography replied when quizzed about his role as a scientist, "Gee, we don't do much science around here. Really, it's mostly glorified accounting."[118] This conception of the work of the bureau helps to explain why, in interviews and public pronouncements, census professionals acknowledge without embarrassment or hesitation the direction they receive from political actors. This particular point has already been made here. But the following examples take on additional significance in light of the persistent view that the census can be cleansed of politics and that science can be the solvent.

Legitimate "Meddling"

According to Paul Starr, "in the United States, institutional safeguards for the most part shield the statistical agencies from meddling by politicians and interest groups."[119] This is hardly the case at the Census Bureau. On numerous occasions, politicians and interest groups have had their way with the bureau. Yet as suggested earlier, it is not always helpful to think of these as "meddling"; they often consist of precisely the kind of boundary drawing discussed above, which is to say that politics was inevitably, even properly involved.

The most salient example is the absence of a religious question on the census form. In the mid-1950s the census director proposed that the 1960 questionnaire contain an item on religious background. This proposal was supported by various Catholic organizations as well as by the Population Association of America and the American Sociological Association. But it was opposed by the American Civil Liberties Union, the Christian Science Church, and various Jewish organizations, including the American Jewish Committee and the Anti-Defamation League. Among other points, opponents argued that including such an item on a questionnaire to which replies are mandatory would violate the First Amendment. The bureau eventually relented and dropped the question from the census. Nevertheless, a religious question was included on the March 1957 Current Population Survey (CPS), on which cooperation was not mandatory.

One volume of summary results was then published, but a second volume of more detailed results never saw the light of day. This time Mormons joined the opposition, and in June 1958 the assistant secretary of commerce canceled the second CPS volume, noting that "it would be inadvisable to pursue any further inquiries on the subject of religion, even in voluntary, sample surveys."[120] Comments William Petersen: "No other statistics have ever been secreted in this fashion, contradicting the norm that all of the bureau's data not pertaining to identifiable individuals are to be open to public scrutiny in full."[121] The Census Bureau is still at pains to avoid any hint of a religious question. On the 1980 self-administered census questionnaire, for example, instructions accompanying the ancestry question warned, "A religious group should not be reported as a person's ancestry."[122]

This example is not typical; usually political pressure is directed toward getting items *on* the questionnaire, not keeping them off. For instance, the ancestry question ("What is this person's ancestry?") first appeared on the census long-form questionnaire in 1980 and then again in 1990.[123] This item, which effectively replaced a century-old question about the place of birth of the respondent's parents, was criticized by social scientists for being vague and uninformative.[124]

It turns out that the Census Bureau itself had similar objections. So why did the ancestry question end up on the questionnaire? According to former deputy census director Louis Kincannon, who was working at the Statistical Policy Division of OMB when the decision was made, "The ethnic desk in the [Carter] White House insisted the ancestry question go on the census."[125] Beyond stating that he and his colleagues at OMB opposed the ancestry question, Kincannon does not elaborate. But it is evident that in the period leading up to the 1980 presidential campaign, politics overrode the objections of both OMB and the Census Bureau.

A more striking example of political pressure involves the Hispanic origin question, added to the census questionnaire in 1970. A clear victory for Hispanics, this was nevertheless one of the Nixon administration's more blatant intrusions on the prerogatives of the bureau.

This episode even involved a bit of drama. The finalized questionnaires for the 1970 census were already at the printers when a Mexican American member of the U.S. Interagency Committee on Mexican American Affairs demanded that a specific Hispanic-origin question be included. The same White House that had recently inaugurated Hispanic Heritage Week was quick to respond.[126] Over the opposition of Census Bureau officials, who argued against inclusion of an untested question so late in the process, Nixon ordered the secretary of commerce and the census director to add the question. But the short form was already in production. So the Hispanic question was hastily added to the long form.[127] As former bureau official Conrad Taeuber recalls: "The order came down that we were to ask a direct question, have the people identify themselves as Hispanics. . . . [T]he 5-percent schedule had barely started at the printers when we pulled it back and threw in the question which hadn't been tested in the field—under orders."[128]

As bureau officials predicted, the data on Hispanics from the 1970 census proved to be of very poor quality.[129] But this only heightened political pressure to get more and better data on this growing minority group. In 1976 Congress passed the Roybal Act, which required the bureau and other federal statistical agencies to produce separate counts of persons of Hispanic origin.[130] The act was then implemented as part of a broader effort to rationalize and coordinate federal statistics on racial and ethnic groups. Following the usual public comment and rule-making procedures, on May 4, 1978, OMB issued Directive No. 15: "Race and Ethnic Standards for Federal Statistics and Administrative Reporting." That directive laid down the five basic categories that are still in use today: "American Indian or Alaskan Native," "Asian or Pacific Islander," "Black," "White," and "Hispanic."[131]

During this same period, political pressure was institutionalized and actually brought into the bureau. As mentioned earlier, after the 1970 census Director Barabba set up a system of racial and ethnic advisory committees to get input from minority organizations and leaders. Whereas committees of outsiders had in the past been composed of experts such as demographers and statisticians, these committees were now composed, in the words of demographer Ira Lowry, "of nine to twelve persons manifestly chosen more for their ethnic political connections than for their knowledge of survey research."[132] Census officials have never claimed that these committees were composed of experts; rather they acknowledge them to be part of a classic strategy of cooptation.[133]

In 1980 the Hispanic-origin question was moved onto the short form, which is mailed to every American household. There it has remained in 1990, 2000, and presumably beyond. Social historian Stephan Thernstrom puts these developments into perspective when he points out that Hispanics are now the one ethnic group offered two chances to identify themselves on the census: either on the Hispanic-origin question on the short form or the open-ended ancestry question on the long form.[134] Demographer Ira Lowry has argued that "from a scientific perspective there has never been a good reason to separate the Hispanic origin from the ancestry question."[135] But from a political perspective there are a couple of reasons. Redistricting requires small-area data that can only be provided with the more intensive coverage afforded by some sort of Hispanic-origin item on the short form. Moreover, the separate question on the short form consistently yields higher counts of Hispanics than does the ancestry question: in 1990, for example, 6.4 percent higher.[136]

At the time these changes were announced, demographers and statisticians denounced the appearance of the Hispanic-origin question on the short form as a "political" decision. The headline on the front page of the *New York Times* on May 14, 1978, declared "Census Questions on Race Assailed as Political by Population Experts."[137] Yet memory on such matters is short. Now deemed integral to the census, the separate Hispanic-origin question is no longer understood to be the result of lobbying efforts, much less the machinations of the Nixon White House. On the contrary, proposals to eliminate the question, or merely to amend it, are today denounced as "political" intrusions on the scientific prerogatives of Census Bureau professionals.

Alternatively, the heat generated by clashing political interests is cooled in the deep freeze of bureaucratic forgetfulness. In 1995 OMB offered this account of the events leading up to the issuance of Directive No. 15 in 1978: "Hence, the population groups identified by the Directive No. 15 racial and Hispanic origin categories reflected legislative and agency needs, and not efforts by population groups to be specifically identified."[138] OMB thus depicts "legislative and agency needs" as denatured of politics. Yet how else were these "needs" defined and placed on the political agenda, except by organized interests concerned about the specific identification of certain "population groups"? By contrast, former Census Bureau officials whom I have interviewed are unequivocal and unapologetic: the Hispanic-origin question is on the census questionnaire because they were told to put it there by their political superiors.[139]

There is a more recent episode in which a critical decision about the census was based not on science but on politics—not because politics intruded improperly but simply because science had no guidance to offer. After the 1990 census, one proposed improvement was to incorporate the separate

Hispanic-origin question into the race question. As a separate item, "Hispanic" was highlighted as an ethnic category distinct from the categories specified in the race question. Amalgamating the two questions would make "Hispanic" one of several items listed under the race question. This change had the virtue of making census racial categories consistent with everyday usage among many Hispanics who define race more in cultural than in biological terms. More to the point, it would make census categories consistent with emergent usage in law and politics, where Hispanics have come to be treated as a distinct racial group with a history of discrimination. Indeed, some advocates argued that categorizing "Hispanic" as a race on the census would overcome the usual black-white dichotomy that leaves Hispanics out of the racial picture.[140] For such reasons, most, though not all, Hispanic advocacy organizations initially supported the proposed change.[141]

This lasted until the results of a massive federal survey were made public. To shed some light on the issue, the BLS undertook a special one-time supplement (in May 1995) to its monthly Current Population Survey. With a sample of about 100,000 individuals, the CPS presented a unique opportunity to see how revised racial and ethnic categories would affect the way all Americans identify themselves.

Those results, released early in 1996, demonstrated that more individuals—from 18 to 30 percent more, depending on the specific format—identified themselves as "Hispanic" when "Hispanic" was a separate ethnic category than when it was one of several racial categories.[142] Hispanic leaders, long concerned with documenting their growing numbers as the nation's "second largest minority," realized that the proposed change would not work to their advantage, and their support for making "Hispanic" a racial category quickly eroded. Soon there was a unanimous demand that "Hispanic" remain on the questionnaire as a separate ethnic category, and the bureau quickly and quietly concurred. Once again, politics prevailed.

As the foregoing suggests, Hispanics are extremely active in census politics. Yet they are hardly the only group that has shaped bureau policy. Indeed, what the GAO describes as "the most controversial change to the race and ethnic questions in the 1990 census" involved the group designated as "Asian or Pacific Islander" (API), the fastest-growing group in the United States today.[143]

This episode is recounted at length by two Census Bureau professionals in a paper for a conference sponsored by the bureau:

Political pressures, primarily from the Asian and Pacific Islander community, and Congress influenced the Census Bureau's final decision on the 1990 Census race question. . . . Based on evaluations of test results, assessment of data needs and consultations with a wide variety of data users, the Census Bureau submitted to Congress for approval a new, shortened race question with only 7 categories for the 1990 Census. The Bureau had determined that this shortened question that required all Asian and Pacific Islanders to write in their individual group performed better for all races than other versions. However, the Asian and Pacific Islander community had strong misgivings about the quality of data for the detailed groups, especially the newer immigrants. After considerable controversy and congressional legislation on the matter, the Bureau reconsidered its original decision and decided to use an untested format with the listing of nine detailed API groups and a residual "Other API" category.[144]

Worth noting again is the matter-of-fact way in which these officials explain how the bureau was overruled by politics. API advocates had legitimate concerns about how non-English-speaking members of their group would deal with the write-in item originally proposed by the bureau. But their involvement went much further. As straightforward as the above account is, it neglects to mention that both houses of Congress passed specific legislation filed by Representative Robert Matsui (Democrat of California) in which the formatting of the API race question was spelled out, even to the point of stipulating that "Taiwanese" be one of the subgroups. It was only President Ronald Reagan's pocket veto that blocked this extraordinary degree of congressional involvement in what is ordinarily considered the technical side of questionnaire design.[145] As for the bureau, it did not even take advantage of this political cover from the White House; instead, it yielded to most of the demands of the API lobby and went ahead with a format that was not only untested but also in contravention of what had been learned from the available test data.[146]

None of this is to suggest that politics improperly intruded on the prerogatives of the bureau. The realism of the Framers would certainly argue against any such understanding of the census. To be sure, Congress specifying the precise formatting of questions might strike many observers as over the line. But the fact is that these are difficult political judgments for which no simple formula can be readily devised.

Nevertheless, we might want to examine the criteria by which such political judgments are made. So, too, we might want to ask whether it is prudent to have racial and ethnic advisory committees lobbying the bureau from the inside. But such questions should *not* be premised on the prevalent assumption that the census is a scientific enterprise suddenly imperiled by politics. In every aspect, but especially with regard to racial and ethnic data, the census is a political undertaking. If we are to resolve the controversies enveloping it, we must do so through—not outside of— politics.

CHAPTER THREE

Creating Racial and Ethnic Categories

A s chapter 2 suggests, the most contentious boundaries the Census Bureau has to deal with are those concerning race and ethnicity. This chapter explores why this is so. In part it is because science has little guidance to offer when it comes to counting racial and ethnic minorities. As demographer Ira Lowry has noted about precisely this aspect of the census: "Where science is weak, politics flourishes."[1]

A related factor is the imprecision of the racial and ethnic data upon which so much public policy relies. This imprecision stems from the inadequacy of our measurement tools as well as from the conceptual vagueness of our racial and ethnic categories. Moreover, these problems are exacerbated by the enormous demographic changes the nation is now experiencing.

Meanwhile, the very nature of racial and ethnic group affiliation has been undergoing a transformation. For a few decades now, the census has, for a variety of reasons, relied on self-identification of racial and ethnic status. Not so long ago such self-identification was a report on an individual's observable social ties to members of fairly well-defined racial or ethnic groups. But in this era of identity politics, self-identification has increasingly become a matter of individual psychology, of an individual's highly subjective feelings of attachment to some group, its culture or language, or perhaps its historical experience.

Yet just when racial and ethnic data have become more susceptible to the vagaries of individual psychology, they have become more important to policymakers. The Census Bureau and other federal statistical agencies therefore find themselves manipulating these data in order to make use of them—which is to say, to make sense of them. But the imposition of such bureaucratic rationality does violence to the principle of individual autonomy and self-expression that has become a fundamental rationale for self-identification. How, then, do the Census Bureau and other federal agencies negotiate this dilemma? What are the implications of their efforts for public understanding and trust in the racial and ethnic data collected by the census?

Categories, Not Boundaries

At the beginning of its widely cited Directive 15, "Racial and Ethnic Standards for Federal Statistics and Administrative Reporting," the Office of Management and Budget (OMB) states: "These classifications should not be interpreted as being scientific or anthropological in nature."[2] Revisiting this issue almost two decades later, OMB is even more emphatic: "The racial and ethnic categories set forth in the standards should not be interpreted as being primarily biological or genetic in reference. Race and ethnicity may be thought of in terms of social and cultural characteristics as well as ancestry."[3] OMB is echoing the prevailing view among scholars. In the National Academy of Sciences (NAS) report on racial and ethnic statistics mentioned earlier, editor Barry Edmonston and his colleagues emphasize: "There is no scientific basis for the legitimacy of race or ethnicity as taxonomic categories. That is, although there clearly are many and varied racial and ethnic distinctions, their multiplicity of sources defies a single-variable classification scheme based on a single individual characteristic."[4] The NAS Edmonston report then elaborates:

> The dominant perspective in social science now views race and ethnicity as social constructions, which develop over time as groups share common social and political experiences. From this perspective, race and ethnicity are dynamic and vary across groups and over time. This view stands in marked contrast to the widespread popular perspective that race is biologically determined and permanent and that ethnicity is culturally determined and equally permanent.[5]

This understanding of race and ethnicity has important implications for census politics. But before exploring these, I must clarify two critical points.

First, it is not the Census Bureau but OMB that in fact bears the bureaucratic responsibility for drawing these boundaries, whether around metropolitan statistical areas or around racial and ethnic groups. This is an important but frequently neglected point that will become increasingly salient as the analysis proceeds.

The second point concerns racial and ethnic boundaries. Although I have been referring to the drawing of such boundaries, neither OMB, the Census Bureau, nor any other federal agency in fact draws any such lines. Rather, the census uses OMB-established *categories* in which individuals place themselves. The boundaries separating these categories are implied but not rigorously defined. Certainly these boundaries are not made clear to the individuals who fill out their census questionnaires and identify their race and ethnicity as they see fit.[6] Yet as already indicated, in order to make sense of these data, OMB must eventually impose boundaries on them, though never quite admitting it.

This curious aspect of how the Census Bureau actually operates is almost universally overlooked. The academic literature certainly focuses on boundary drawing,[7] as shown in this passage from two leading students of the subject, Michael Omi and Howard Winant: "Viewed as a whole, the census's racial classification reflects prevailing conceptions of race, establishes boundaries by which one's racial 'identity' can be understood, determines the allocation of resources, and frames diverse political issues and conflicts."[8] Though seemingly minor, this distinction between creating categories and drawing boundaries has major implications. Indeed, the lack of explicitly defined boundaries between racial and ethnic groups contributes to the controversy over their proper enumeration. It is as if the federal government admitted two new contiguous states to the Union but neglected to establish a boundary between them. The obvious result would be confusion and dissension about the location of the actual boundary, about who lived on either side of it, and about the population of both states.

Of course, we not only lack well-defined boundaries, we also experience high rates of mixing among groups. In such a social context, myriad questions arise about the assignment of specific individuals to appropriate racial and ethnic categories. For example, the apparently simple case of categorizing the children of a white father and a black mother becomes problematic. Yet even with clearly established boundaries between designated categories, difficult determinations as to where specific individuals belong would still be necessary. Thus, when the census did have explicit racial boundaries based on blood quanta, census enumerators still had to decide how to categorize individuals.

The Appeal of Self-Identification

Self-identification has considerable appeal over explicit racial and ethnic boundaries. Most Americans feel uneasy when an individual is assigned to a racial or ethnic category by the government. To the extent that we regard such categories as legitimate at all, we tend to believe that individuals should assign themselves to them. Thus the preferred means of categorizing individuals racially and ethnically, on the census and most other government surveys, is self-identification. As question 4 on the 1990 census questionnaire reads, "Fill ONE circle for the race that the person considers himself/herself to be."[9] OMB, which is responsible for coordinating the activities of all federal statistical agencies, including the Census Bureau, is now thoroughly committed to self-identification: "Respect for individual dignity should guide the processes and methods for collecting data on race and ethnicity; ideally, respondent self-identification should be facilitated to the greatest extent possible."[10] In a recent reference to its landmark Directive No. 15, issued in 1978, OMB emphasized:

> Directive No. 15 does *not* establish criteria or qualifications (such as blood quantum levels) that are to be used in determining a particular individual's racial or ethnic classification. Directive No. 15 does *not* tell an individual who he or she is, or specify how an individual should classify himself or herself.[11]

As an OMB official once shot back in response to a related question: "We don't classify individuals around here!"

Enshrined though it may be, self-identification is a relatively recent methodology. The NAS Edmonston report notes: "The fact that self-identification is taken for granted as the preferred means for classification reflects the social changes that have taken place in US society in recent years."[12] Self-identification was introduced in 1960, when the Census Bureau began to curtail reliance on field enumerators visiting every household to pose questions. One initial reason was cost reduction: the new procedure could take advantage of computer technology capable of quickly reading returned questionnaires.[13]

Self-identification has also taken hold because survey researchers have found it superior to so-called objective indicators. One such objective indicator of ethnic background would be language use. Yet because most Americans speak English (even with today's high levels of immigration), this indicator would shed insufficient light on the ethnicity of millions.

Another objective indicator would be the birthplace of an individual or of his or her parents.[14] But because most Americans are native-born of native-born parents, this indicator, too, would be of limited use. To be sure, the inquiry could be pushed back to the birthplaces of grandparents, but problems arise here as well. In 1970, about 56 percent of the adult population reported that all four of their grandparents were native-born. To obtain more complete information on this large segment of the population, it would then have been necessary to determine the birthplace of each individual's eight great-grandparents.[15] But such "objective" information is readily influenced by highly subjective perceptions. Who remembers exactly where four grandparents, much less eight great-grandparents, were born? Such complications have led Tom Smith of the National Opinion Research Center to conclude: "The measurement of ethnicity . . . involves a strong subjective aspect; . . . a well-crafted subjective question is the best single indicator for most purposes."[16]

Yet in a liberal democracy such as ours, self-identification of race and ethnicity is sustained by more than convenience to bureaucrats or social scientists; it also fits well with American individualism. Amid controversies over group rights, it is hard to imagine even the most zealous advocates of affirmative action arguing for the policing of racial boundaries to ensure that only bona fide members of protected minorities benefit from such programs.[17] Sociologist Stanley Lieberson observes: "In most democratic societies, the forced classification of persons by a government body is generally viewed as repulsive."[18]

One reason why Americans are repulsed by the thought of a government agency assigning individuals to racial or ethnic categories is the nation's past failures to apply its individualistic values to various racial minorities. Slavery, Jim Crow, and the wartime internment of Japanese civilians are just a few examples that come quickly to mind. Because of this historical gap between our values and our practices, self-identification of race and ethnicity has now emerged as a virtual regime principle.[19]

If not always evident in our racial history, self-identification and its ill-defined boundaries have been part of our *ethnic* history. Michael Walzer has depicted the American experience with ethnic groups as "communities without boundaries."[20] Similarly, the social historian John Higham identifies in contemporary America a pattern of "pluralistic integration," such that ethnic groups have both nuclei that "are respected as enduring centers of social action" and boundaries that "are understood to be permeable."[21]

Further entwining self-identification with individualism is the evolving American conception of race and ethnicity. Within the dominant understanding of these as social constructs lies a certain ambiguity, especially as it relates to self-identification. What kind of "self" is doing the identifying? A socialized self attached to some group or groups that influence its choice of identification? Or the self-actualizing self of popular psychology, autonomous and preoccupied with asserting whatever identity or identities the individual desires?

During the thirty years that the census has relied on self-identification of race and ethnicity, our concept of the self has become increasingly psychologized. Indeed, it has virtually become the norm that the individual is the sole and final arbiter of which group or groups he or she is part of. Group ties are understood to be based less on social relationships than on psychological identification with group goals and symbols.[22] The historian David Hollinger suggests that, under the influence of multiculturalism, ethnicity has subtly shifted its meaning from a social concept denoting affiliation to one or more groups to a psychological concept denoting identity.[23] Accordingly, the NAS Edmonston report emphasizes "the increasing recognition that race and ethnicity are subjective, personal characteristics."[24]

All this leaves census-taking in a rather confused state. On the one hand, OMB accepts the received academic wisdom that race and ethnicity are not biological categories but social constructs. Yet before the ink dried on its 1978 regulations, race and ethnicity were being transformed by the wider culture into subjective, psychological categories. The social historian Stephan Thernstrom notes with concern that ethnicity in the census has become "a matter of choice, a state of mind rather than a matter for genealogists to determine: 'It doesn't matter if you don't think I look Chinese. I feel Chinese; ergo I am Chinese.'"[25]

To be sure, these two conceptualizations of race and ethnicity—the social and the psychological—are not mutually exclusive. But neither are they identical. The point is that census experts assert either or both conceptualizations as suits their purposes, without ever acknowledging that an important shift has occurred.

Moreover, to the extent that these categories are becoming more subjective and psychological, they are also becoming more imprecise and volatile. In other words, as the census moves toward counting racial and ethnic *identities,* its task becomes more difficult. At the same time, the shift to a psychological concept of race and ethnicity only further embeds self-identification as a fundamental principle of our individualistic regime.

Administrative Limits on Self-Identification

However congruent with our values it may be, self-identification of race and ethnicity is hardly inviolate. On the census and other federal surveys, it is often constrained or even violated outright. OMB, for example, has made it quite clear that self-identification is not an absolute: "Self-identification is the preferred means of obtaining information about an individual's race and ethnicity, except in instances where observer identification is more practical."[26] One such instance was the nighttime effort to count the homeless described in chapter 2. On that occasion the bureau's admittedly imperfect efforts to find and count the homeless were further complicated by the difficulty of determining their racial and ethnic identities. Instructed to ask the homeless to self-identify, census enumerators found many such individuals asleep or unwilling to cooperate in the shadows of their makeshift quarters. Self-identification consequently yielded to observer-identification, with enumerators making judgments about the race and ethnicity of individuals literally in the dark.[27]

The example may seem exotic, but the bureau has long relied on such methods. In recent censuses, for instance, when a given household has failed to mail back its questionnaire, an enumerator has been sent out to make inquiries. If upon repeated attempts no respondents have been found, the enumerator might well impute answers on the basis of information gathered from inspection of the dwelling and of neighboring households.

While not involving the census, another exception to self-identification occurs so frequently that it deserves mention. Birth and death records, which are maintained by state and local jurisdictions, are routinely based on the observations of physicians and other health professionals who may or may not consult with family members. Because self-identification is rarely feasible in these situations, observer-identification is often unavoidable. Yet it generates inconsistencies in our racial and ethnic data that go largely unchallenged.[28]

The most common exception to self-identification brings us back to the census: the fact that typically only one member of a household fills out the questionnaire. On any number of items, including those pertaining to race and ethnicity, there may well be discrepancies between how the person filling out the questionnaire answers and how others in the household might respond for themselves. Under such conditions, self-identification is a convenient fiction.

Perhaps the most suggestive exception to self-identification involves how the Census Bureau deals with the bewildering array of write-in responses to its open-ended questions on race, Hispanic origin, and ancestry. For the sake of brevity, I will focus here on the race question. But the point applies to the other open-ended questions as well.

On the 1990 census form, the race question permitted respondents to write in, where applicable, (1) the name of the Indian tribe in which they were enrolled; (2) the specific Asian or Pacific Islander group to which they belonged if other than those listed on the form; (3) the race to which they belonged if "other" than the four OMB-approved categories ("white," "black," "American Indian or Alaskan Native," and "Asian or Pacific Islander"). This "other race" category underscores the fact that the census, because of its unique status as the nation's statistical benchmark, is permitted to gather data outside the four basic racial categories that OMB imposes on all other federal agencies. Nevertheless, these census data must eventually be made compatible with the data used by those other agencies.[29]

The Census Bureau received a total of nearly 8 million write-in responses to these various parts of the race question. These had to be reviewed and edited for obviously incorrect or inconsistent answers and then sorted according to 300 coded categories for race and 600 for American Indian tribes.[30] Consolidating these hundreds of coded responses down to the four OMB categories was greatly facilitated by computer automation. Nevertheless, difficult and time-consuming judgments had to be rendered about how to racially classify write-in responses such as "South African," "Guyanese," "Moslem," or "American," which have no clear racial meaning. Even more substantial difficulties were posed by the more than 250,000 multiracial write-in responses received, such as "black/white" or "white/Asian." The Census Bureau reclassified these according to the first race cited, although the significance of order was never indicated to respondents on the census form—an obvious affront to self-identification.[31]

Of these 8 million write-in responses, about 2.5 million indicated some "other race." More than 1 million of these, fully 41 percent, identified ethnic groups such as "Irish," "Arab," "Iranian," "Jamaican," and the like. Obviously incorrect according to OMB categories, these responses were recoded by the bureau as either "white," "black," "Asian or Pacific Islander," or "American Indian or Alaskan Native."[32]

In this instance, the principle of self-identification was arguably not much strained. This could not be said of the bureau's handling of the total of 9.8 million individuals who in 1990 identified themselves as "other race" (either by writing in an answer or simply filling in a computer-readable bubble). Here again, in order to make census data compatible with those of other federal agencies, these 9.8 million people eventually had to be reclassified to the four OMB-approved categories. The bureau did this by means of a complicated algorithm that basically assigned "other race" individuals to the same race as individuals similar to them in other respects. Of this process, the NAS Edmonston report notes, "There is no way to evaluate how this reclassification corresponds to people's self-perceptions or, in fact, to any other basis for classification."[33]

To accommodate the individualism and diversity of contemporary American life, the Census Bureau opts for self-identification and open-ended, write-in questions. Indeed, the bureau does this at the expense of precious time and resources.[34] Yet there are definite limits as to how far the census can move in this direction. After all, self-identification taken to its logical extreme would mean the elimination of all racial and ethnic categories. But apart from the need to make sense of confusing or inconsistent responses, bureau professionals require some framework to impose order on the deluge of data. In this case, OMB imposes such a framework. But if it did not, some other classification scheme would inevitably be called into service, along with rules as to how to place individual responses within it. Try as we might to reconcile them, self-identification eventually collides with the administrative demands of the contemporary state.

Political Constraints on Self-Identification

Other limitations on self-identification are driven less by the requirements of public administration and governance than by the obdurate realities of politics. These are acknowledged, albeit obliquely, in OMB's Directive 15, which stipulates that for persons of mixed racial or ethnic origins "the [single] category which most closely reflects *the individual's recognition in his community* should be used for purposes of reporting"(emphasis added).[35] This suggests that while we get squeamish when the government exercises authority categorizing individuals into racial or ethnic groups, we are more tolerant when those same groups do so.

The extreme if atypical case is American Indians.[36] First of all, the census relies on self-identification to enumerate Indians, just as it does for all other racial and ethnic groups. But OMB's Directive 15 defines an "American Indian" (or an "Alaskan Native") as "a person having origins in any of the original peoples of North America, and who maintains cultural identification through tribal affiliation or community recognition."[37] The phrase "maintains cultural identification through tribal affiliation or community recognition" is at best highly ambiguous, suggesting an effort to combine subjective and objective indicators. So OMB subsequently stipulated that, despite the fact that federally recognized tribal governments have their own formal membership criteria, Directive 15 does not require an individual to be a tribal member to identify himself on the census as an "American Indian."[38] This probably explains why the 1990 census counted 1.8 million Indians, while the Bureau of Indian Affairs (BIA) reported only about 1 million on the tribal rolls around that time.[39] In an effort to minimize such discrepancies, the Census Bureau had shifted away from pure self-identification for Indians by including in the 1990 race question the instruction: "Print name of enrolled or principal tribe."[40]

This shift, however slight, apparently reflects the concern of Indian leaders that tribal recognition be a legal definition not reducible to self-identification.[41] Indeed, Indians seeking hiring preferences from the BIA (which is required by law to provide them) must produce a properly executed "Certificate of Indian Blood."[42] To paraphrase Thernstrom, this is about as far as we can get from: "I feel like an Indian; therefore I am an Indian."[43]

A broader political constraint on self-identification surfaced in the recent debate over whether to include a multiracial question on the 2000 census. Since OMB Directive 15 was issued in 1978, respondents to the census and other federal surveys have not been allowed to identify themselves as belonging to more than one race. If they did so (and in 1990 about 0.5 percent did), then, as noted, their answers were recoded for one race.[44]

In recent years a growing number of multiracial individuals and parents of mixed-race children have argued against this one-race restriction on the grounds that it forces individuals, in particular children, to deny the racial heritage of one parent, thereby adversely affecting their self-esteem, psychological well-being, and family pride.[45] In response to such criticisms, OMB explored the implications of moving to a question that allows individuals to identify themselves as belonging to more than one race. Extensive surveys demonstrated that an extremely small segment of Americans—less than 2 percent—identify as "multiracial" when offered the explicit opportunity.[46]

Yet these test surveys also revealed significant impacts of a multiracial question on specific groups. A multiracial option reduced the number identifying as "American Indian or Alaskan Native" and "Asian or Pacific Islander." On the other hand, there was little impact on the numbers reporting "white" or "black."[47]

The responses to these findings were striking and somewhat surprising. Many Indian tribal governments expressed concern about a multiracial question.[48] Some Hispanic leaders also raised objections. But without a doubt the most vocal and sustained objections were raised by black leaders and organizations, who seemingly had the least to lose from the proposed change. They argued that whatever the test results showed now, a multiracial option on the census would eventually reduce the numbers of those identifying as "black" and, perhaps more to the point, would blur the categories on which hard-won antidiscrimination and affirmative action programs are based. Their allies, including civil rights enforcement agencies of the federal government, similarly argued against any change in the existing racial classification scheme.[49]

In the face of such opposition, OMB decided against creating a separate multiracial question on the 2000 census. Instead, the agency eventually decided to allow individuals to check off more than one of the four existing racial groups. Yet as will be addressed later, this response merely pushes the problem back one step: OMB must still decide how these responses will be classified and then tabulated.

Whatever one's opinion of the merits of the multiracial proposal, it was undeniably consistent with the letter and spirit of self-identification. The advocates of a multiracial question were merely extending the inherent logic of the existing regime. It was the proposal's opponents who were not only defending the status quo but also putting limits on the principle of self-identification. As the NAS Edmonston report has noted: "If self-identification is taken as a basic principle, there are no grounds for recoding a multirace person to a single race."[50]

Yet, as it turns out, civil rights organizations are quite accustomed to non-self-identified data. For example, racial and ethnic enrollment data relied on by the Office of Civil Rights at the U.S. Department of Education are frequently based on observations by school officials.[51] Similarly, racial and ethnic data submitted to the Equal Employment Opportunity Commission (EEOC) for monitoring employment discrimination are typically based on visual observation by employers. In fact, the civil rights enforcement agencies regard self-identification with a certain suspicion.[52] Self-identification is, for example, inconsistent with the EEOC's prohibition on employers inquiring into a job applicant's race or ethnicity until after he or she is hired. Even after hiring, the EEOC discourages employers from making such inquiries:[53] "Obtaining information on the race/ethnic identity of employees directly from employees is not recommended because, first, direct inquiry may raise concerns about the purpose for the data and second, responding employees may be reluctant to classify themselves into one of the five categories."[54] As Deval L. Patrick, assistant attorney general for civil rights, argued to OMB in defense of observer-identification:

> Whether someone is a victim of discrimination often turns on the way in which others perceive the color of the victim's skin, the ethnic origin of his or her last name, or the accent with which the victim speaks. Such issues do not depend generally on the way in which a victim identifies the various components of his or her racial or ethnic background.[55]

One OMB official summed up the logic of the civil rights establishment's position: "Discrimination occurs by observers."

A similar suspicion of self-identification has been voiced by some advocates of affirmative action. Reacting to instances of whites claiming minority racial status in order to obtain affirmative action benefits, lawyer Christopher Ford has actually argued that the federal government should officially classify individuals by race and ethnicity.[56] Though clearly an extreme (and ironic) policy for a liberal democracy to adopt, such a proposal reflects an awareness that in this realm subjectivity has liabilities and that at some point authoritative governmental decisions are necessary.

Popular Misconceptions

Despite their efforts to adhere to self-identification, OMB and the Census Bureau in particular get no credit for their labors. Self-identification may be enshrined in the census and consonant with our political culture and values, but it is not well understood by most Americans. They are either unaware of it or simply do not understand what government officials mean when they explain how it works. Indeed, there is widespread public confusion about how the federal government deals with race and ethnicity.

Consider this remark by a Colombian immigrant interviewed in a recent study of Latino identity:

In the census you're not allowed to write down that you're white. It's so strange. I have a Colombian friend, he's really very white. He looked like an egg-white. He became an American citizen and when they asked him for his skin color, he wrote down "white." But they said to him: "You're not white," and they erased the color. "What color are you going to make me?" "Black," they said.[57]

It is of course difficult to know what actually happened here, or whether it happened at all. That is not important. The point is that this individual *believes* that the Census Bureau decides who is white and who is not.

This is not just the mistaken perception of an unsophisticated newcomer. In 1990 a *Washington Post* reporter observed that Hispanics "must declare themselves either black or white for Census Bureau purposes."[58] A similar, albeit more subtle example emerges in a *Washington Post* editorial on the occasion of the Clinton administration's preliminary decision in July 1997 not to include a specific multiracial question on the 2000 census. As indicated earlier, the administration opted to allow individuals to check off more than one of the four OMB-approved racial groups. The *Post* editorial noted with approval: "After a three-year struggle . . . a federal task force has come up with a novel answer: Let the population describe itself." The editorial then declared that while "self-identification will undoubtedly raise new concerns," OMB was right in "allowing people to identify themselves by whatever categories they choose."[59]

It is striking that not even the *Post* understood that the census had *already* been relying on self-identification for the past twenty-seven years, or that even under the Clinton administration proposal (which has since been finalized) individuals will still be obliged to choose among the racial categories set up by OMB. Even further from the *Post*'s awareness was the fact that OMB will be making the critical decisions about how to tabulate the responses of those who check off more than one racial category. For instance, if 10 percent of respondents classify themselves as "black" and another 2 percent as both "black" and "white," will the latter 2 percent be counted as "black" or "white" or something else? Whatever the tabulation decision, it surely will not be an instance of "letting the population describe itself."

Similar misconceptions abound among academic experts. The sociologist who interviewed the Colombian immigrant quoted above nowhere acknowledges that her informant was mistaken. Nor does she mention that in the 1990 census fully 52 percent of Latinos in the United States identified themselves as "white."[60] In an authoritative and widely cited monograph, *Who Is Black? One Nation's Definition,* sociologist F. James Davis writes: "Although various operational instructions have been tried, the definition of black used by the Census Bureau has been the nation's cultural and legal definition: all persons with any known black ancestry."[61] To the extent that Davis is asserting that in the United States the informal and formal (in the courts, for example) definition of who is black continues to obey the so-called one-drop rule, he is correct. But when he suggests that today's Census Bureau routinely uses the same definition to classify individuals as "black," Davis misleads his reader.

Washington elites similarly fail to understand self-identification. Echoing the complaints of multiracial couples that their children do not fit into any of the government's racial or ethnic categories, writer and former Reagan domestic policy adviser Dinesh D'Souza asserts that his two-year-old daughter, "who has a white mother and an East Indian dad," is classified as "white" by the Census Bureau "because mixed-race children are expected to take the race of their mother."[62] Underlying this assertion is D'Souza's objection to the entire effort to classify individuals by race and ethnicity. Apparently assuming that racial classification is based on a notion of pure racial stocks, he offers the curious argument that his daughter's mixed background puts her "beyond racial classification." Moreover, he links such classification to affirmative action: "For a generation now the U.S. government has been classifying citizens by skin color, a measure necessary to implement affirmative action programs."[63] On the basis of his opposition to affirmative action, D'Souza then condemns all federal efforts at racial and ethnic classification.

Such misconceptions are instructive. In some situations—on birth certificates, for example—children are assigned the race of their mothers.[64] Yet it is profoundly misleading to argue that the Census Bureau routinely assigns children to their mother's (or anyone else's) racial category. Moreover, it is simply not the case that affirmative action requires the bureau to classify individuals by race.

This highlights a curiosity of contemporary racial policies in the United States: while the federal government clearly does establish racial and ethnic categories, it does not typically assign individuals to them. As we have seen, the Census Bureau certainly does not. And although the government does assign some benefits on the basis of membership in designated minority groups, membership in those groups is for the most part determined not by government classification but by individual self-identification.[65] This regime poses many challenges, but not those cited by D'Souza.

Thus the federal government's efforts to abide by liberal individualist principles in the collection of racial and ethnic data meet an intriguing fate. On the one hand, the Census Bureau is unfairly accused of routinely telling individuals what group they belong to. On the other hand, the many subtle ways in which the bureau and other federal agencies do in fact assign individuals to racial and ethnic categories are overlooked. That such disaffection and confusion about a relatively straightforward aspect of the census should be found among struggling immigrants, sober academics, and savvy Washington pundits alike ought to signal caution to those who have more ambitious plans for the decennial count.

Race or Ethnicity?

Not surprisingly, the tendency in contemporary American culture to define race and ethnicity in subjective, psychological terms (as "a state of mind" in Thernstrom's phrase) confounds the actual collection of data.[66] Sociologist Charles Hirschman writes:

> For the area of ethnicity . . . statisticians and others concerned with data collection have begun to doubt the conventional strategies of measurement. Attempts to improve the measurement of ethnic categories in censuses and surveys have been frustrated by the seeming inability of respondents to give consistent or meaningful responses. The examples of "contradictory" responses for measures of race, ethnicity, ancestry, language, birthplace and similar questions are familiar to every statistician and scholar.[67]

The variety of responses that the bureau encounters in its several open-ended, write-in questions on race, Hispanic origin, and ancestry apparently stems from the sheer confusion that inheres in those questions: respondents simply misunderstand what the census is asking.

This was evident in 1990, when a noticeable number of individuals responded to the race question by identifying themselves as "Guamanian" (one of the subcategories listed under "Asian or Pacific Islander") and to the ancestry question by writing in "Guatemalan."[68] Then there were those identifying as "Pakistani" and as "Asian Indian" who also listed their ancestry as "American Indian." Census officials speculated that immigrants from the Indian subcontinent might be trying to indicate that their children were American-born, until it emerged that most of those actually born on the subcontinent also identified themselves as "American Indian."[69]

Similar confusion occurred in 1970, when the number of persons identifying themselves as "Central and South American" was about 1 million higher than the figure projected by demographers. When census officials noted the geographic concentration of these respondents in the central and southern United States, they concluded that "Central and South American" had been given an unexpected literal interpretation by non-Hispanics living in the Midwest and the Bible Belt.[70]

In 1980 and 1990 non-Hispanic whites and blacks, especially in parts of the nation where Hispanics were sparse, indicated on the Hispanic-origin question that they were "Mexican American." Apparently these individuals interpreted this response category to mean Mexican *or* American.[71]

Some misinterpretations are arguably not misinterpretations at all. For example, in 1980 and 1990 a number of individuals of Portuguese or Brazilian descent checked off "other Spanish/Hispanic" on the Hispanic-origin question. This is hardly an unreasonable response, given that Portugal and Spain share the peninsula historically known as Hispania and that former representative Tony Coelho, of Portuguese descent, used to be a member of the Congressional Hispanic Caucus.[72]

But were the 86,224 individuals who on the 1980 census identified themselves as "other Spanish/Hispanic" and also wrote in "Filipino" confused or mistaken? It depends on whether Filipinos are classified as "Hispanic" or as "Asian or Pacific Islander," a question to which there is no definitive answer.[73]

As these examples suggest, misunderstanding of census categories runs deep and cannot always be attributed to a lack of education or unfamiliarity with the racial and ethnic terminology used in the United States. In some instances the census itself contributes to the confusion. Take, for example, the 1990 questionnaire, which lists under the heading "Race"— along with "white," "black or Negro," and "Indian (Amer.)"—several national-origin options under "Asian or Pacific Islander (API)," such as "Filipino," "Korean," "Japanese," "Samoan," and "Guamanian." Is it surprising that respondents often write in their own nationalities (such as "Polish" or "Jamaican") in the box labeled "other race"?[74]

Ultimately, this confusion arises from a fundamental lack of conceptual clarity. Social scientists certainly do not agree about how (or whether) to distinguish between race and ethnicity. Some researchers insist on a sharp distinction between the two, maintaining that ethnicity pertains to cultural and linguistic characteristics, while race pertains to biological traits. Other analysts argue that race is really a subset of ethnicity.[75] No wonder the general public confounds these two concepts.

Validity and Reliability

Social scientists rely on two criteria to assess the accuracy of the racial and ethnic data they collect and analyze: validity and reliability. Validity denotes the degree to which a census or any other survey question actually measures what it is supposed to measure. Given the conceptual ambiguity and disagreement over race and ethnicity, it is not surprising that valid measures have been difficult to come by. The NAS Edmonston report concludes: "Because of the many factors of self-identity and social context discussed throughout this report, there are no commonly accepted methods for measuring the validity of racial and ethnic data."[76]

Reliability, by contrast, denotes the degree to which a survey question elicits the same response at different points in time. A question may exhibit reliability, meaning that it produces highly consistent results,[77] without having much validity, meaning that it does not measure what it is supposed to.[78] Clearly, validity is a more demanding criterion for social scientists to satisfy than reliability.

As it happens, racial and ethnic data from the census and other surveys do not measure up very well in terms either of reliability or of validity. Survey researcher Tom W. Smith comments: "Of all basic background variables, ethnicity is probably the most difficult to measure." One reason is that the intensity of an individual's identification with an ethnic group is highly variable. Smith explains: "Like religion and political party preference ethnicity is not a simple all or nothing proposition. Researchers have long recognized that a person's level or intensity of identification with a particular ethnicity can vary from a weak-nominal association to a strong-committed association."[79]

More to the point, the intensity of one's ethnic or racial identity varies with the context. Survey researchers refer to "the data collection environment," which includes the social milieu and collection methods as well as question wording, format, and placement.[80] The timing of a survey can also powerfully affect responses to racial and ethnic questions. During World War II, for example, there was a decline in the number of survey respondents claiming German descent.[81] Since the end of the cold war there has been an increase in the number of Americans identifying themselves with various Eastern European nationalities. Demographer Reynolds Farley reports that between 1980 and 1990 the number of whites claiming Yugoslav ancestry on the census fell 28 percent, while those claiming Croatian ancestry grew 81 percent. Those identifying as Lithuanian went up 13 percent,

Armenian 44 percent, and Slovak 133 percent, while those claiming Czech ancestry fell 21 percent. Farley concludes: "This did not come about because of immigration, but rather reflects, I believe, . . . governmental changes in those countries which make Americans increasingly likely to identify with such origins."[82] In a similar if more fanciful vein, an OMB official reports an upsurge in survey respondents identifying as American Indian while the Disney film *Pocahontas* was in the theaters.

As for the well-known effect of question wording on survey responses, race and ethnicity are particularly susceptible to what are known as "example effects."[83] These arise when respondents repeat the response offered as an illustration in the question. When in 1980, for instance, 49.6 million persons reported "English" on the census ancestry question (a significantly higher number than was reported in the Current Population Survey four months earlier), researchers surmised that the inflated number was due to "English" having been one of the example responses listed with the ancestry question.[84] A second example effect was traced to the language question immediately preceding the ancestry item, in which the word "English" appeared three times. In 1990 the language question was distanced from the ancestry question and "English" eliminated as an example response. The result? Persons reporting "English" ancestry declined from 49.6 to 32.7 million.[85] Similarly, "Hungarian" appeared as an example response with the ancestry question in 1980 but not in 1990. Over that period those reporting "Hungarian" ancestry declined 19 percent.[86] Finally, those claiming "French" ancestry declined from about 13 million in 1980, when "French" was listed as an example, to 10 million in 1990, when it was not.[87]

A systematic analysis of the reliability of responses to the ancestry question is provided by the Census Bureau's Content Reinterview Survey (the CRS). Relying on highly trained, experienced interviewers using computer-assisted interview schedules that probe more deeply than usual, the CRS is regarded as the standard against which census results are to be measured.[88] After completion of the 1990 census, CRS staff reinterviewed a random sample of about 24,000 individuals drawn from returned questionnaires. The responses to those reinterviews were then compared with those individuals' original census answers.

The results of the 1990 CRS are instructive. The open-ended, write-in format of the ancestry question permits multiple responses ("German-Italian," for example) and therefore complicates interpretation. Nonetheless, the ancestry question clearly lacks reliability. Among those who claimed one or more ancestries on both the census and the CRS, at least one census response matched one CRS response for only 75 percent of all respondents. Reliability was even lower among those who claimed just one ancestry on both instruments. Among these only 68 percent of census responses matched the CRS.[89]

Ancestry data, regarded by the Census Bureau as "moderately inconsistent," are among the least reliable of the racial and ethnic data collected.[90] Responses to the ancestry question are certainly less reliable than responses to the race question. In 1990, for example, 97.6 percent of those identifying as "white" on the CRS did the same on the census. Of those identifying as "black" on the 1990 CRS, 96.3 percent so identified on the census. Finally, 90.1 percent of those identifying as "Asian or Pacific Islander" on the CRS so identified on the census.[91] The Census Bureau regards this as high response reliability, though even here perfect consistency is not to be found.

Yet not all responses to the race question are so reliable. The reliability of census data on American Indians is notoriously poor. In 1990 only 62.8 percent of those who identified as "American Indian, Eskimo, or Aleut" on the CRS so identified on the census. In 1980 this figure was even lower: 58.0 percent.[92]

The disparity between the number of Indians based on the 1990 census race question and on actual tribal enrollments around that time has already been noted. There is an even wider gap between 1990 numbers based on the race question and on the census ancestry question: 1.8 million identified racially as "American Indian" while 8.8 million reported some "Indian" ancestry.[93] Demographers have also been perplexed by a dramatic and seemingly inexplicable increase over time in the number of those identifying racially as "American Indian." From 1960 to 1990 that number tripled, far surpassing natural population growth.[94]

The only race category that has proved less reliable than "American Indian" is "other race." In 1990 just 38.2 percent of those who so identified on the CRS did the same on the census. In 1980 that figure was 36.0 percent.[95] As discussed earlier, the confusion surrounding the "other race" category is so great that on the 1990 census 41 percent of the original write-in responses were obviously incorrect and had to be changed by the bureau.[96]

Like the "American Indian" category, "other race" has been growing. In 1980 about 6.8 million individuals so identified; by 1990 that number had increased 45 percent to more than 9.8 million. In fact, "other race" grew faster than any other race category except "Asian or Pacific Islander."[97]

Moreover, it turns out that 97.5 percent of those identifying as "other race" in 1990 were Hispanics (compared with 95 percent in 1980).[98] The obvious inference is that the low reliability of the "other race" item has to do with how Hispanics identify themselves racially. Indeed, the 1990 CRS found that the majority of unreliable "other race" responses were from Hispanics identifying as "other race" on the census and "white" on the CRS (or vice versa). As the bureau notes: "It is apparent that Hispanics have difficulty in classifying themselves into the race categories presented." The bureau concludes that "the Hispanic population are contributing most of the bias in the race data in the census."[99]

Yet Hispanics are not the only source of bias in the race data. Some low response reliability is traceable to foreign-born individuals generally, as well as to those speaking a language other than English at home.[100] Concludes another NAS panel chaired by economist Charles Schultze: "With some exceptions, it seems to be foreign-born people and both foreign- and native-born Hispanics that had the highest levels of inconsistent reporting on the race questions. Foreign-born people showed considerably more inconsistency on the race item than native-born ones."[101] Not surprisingly, foreign-born people tend to have different conceptions of race from native-born Americans. As the NAS Schultze panel observes: "Foreign-born Hispanics and foreign-born Asians and Pacific Islanders view race in terms of national origin or language."[102]

Still, Hispanics seem to be the group whose understandings of race collide most directly and most frequently with those built into the U.S. census questionnaire. The NAS Edmonston report observes:

> It is clear from census responses and from the investigations of researchers that the conception of race by Hispanics is substantially different than that of non-Hispanic respondents. In part, this is because Hispanics tend to use "race" as a cultural identification and because Hispanics, as a group, are a mixture of blacks, American Indians, and whites.[103]

And among Hispanics the foreign-born and recent immigrants have the most difficulty with census race categories.[104]

Quite aside from how Hispanics identify racially, the very category "Hispanic" lacks reliability. Twenty years ago two Census Bureau demographers analyzed the quality of their agency's data on Hispanics and bluntly observed: "A central problem is the inability of the census data to reflect a clear, unambiguous, and objective definition of exactly who is a member of the Hispanic population."[105] As explained in chapter 2, data on Hispanics from the 1970 census were of exceptionally poor quality. In fact, only 75 percent of persons who identified as "Spanish-origin" in the 1970 CRS had done so in the census.[106] The census has been doing better since then, but Hispanic data remain problematic. In 1980, 88.7 percent of persons identifying as "Spanish-origin" on the CRS answered the same way on the census.[107] In 1990 that figure was essentially unchanged: 88.6 percent.[108] Such numbers certainly exhibit less reliability than the corresponding numbers for whites and blacks in 1990: 97.6 percent and 96.3 percent, respectively.[109] The NAS Edmonston report concludes: "In general, there are higher consistency rates for larger and older categories, such as blacks and whites, and lower rates for smaller and newer categories, such as Hispanics."[110] In a realm where boundaries are fuzzy to start with, the one between Hispanic and non-Hispanic is, as Charles Hirschman notes, among the fuzziest: "For the censuses of the United States, the addition of new questions on Hispanic origin and ancestry has created more data but has given rise to even more uncertainty over the ethnic composition of the population and raised new questions on the meaning of ethnic identity."[111]

Imputing Hispanics

Another problem with the Hispanic-origin question arises when people fail to answer it. This can of course happen with any census question, but the Hispanic-origin question is particularly prone to this, with some surprising results.

When an item goes unanswered on an individual questionnaire, the Census Bureau routinely imputes an answer on the basis of the response of some other member of the same household or of a comparable individual in a neighboring household.[112] A widely accepted procedure to reduce bias in data because of nonresponse, imputation is basically an educated guess that can itself introduce error.[113] Accordingly, those who work with census data view the level of imputation associated with any given question as an indicator of the quality of the data generated by that question. The technical term for the percentage of nonresponses to a specific question (for which missing values are then imputed) is the allocation rate.[114] Thus high allocation rates signal possibly suspect data.[115]

The point here is not to question the wisdom of imputation but merely to highlight that the Hispanic-origin question had the highest allocation rate of any item on the 1990 census.[116] Fully 10.0 percent of those responses

Table 3-1. *Comparative Allocation Rates for Selected Census Questions from the Short Form Questionnaire, 1980 and 1990*

Percent

	1980	1990
Ethnic question		
Hispanic origin	4.2	10.0
Race questions		
Total	1.5	2.0
Black	1.6	2.9
American Indian, Eskimo, Aleut	3.1	2.5
Asian/Pacific Islander	2.1	2.7
White	1.3	1.7
Other race	3.9	6.4
Other questions		
Age	2.9	2.4
Marital status	1.3	2.0
Sex	0.8	1.2

Source: Barry Edmonston and Charles Schultze, eds., *Modernizing the U.S. Census* (Washington, D.C.: National Academy Press, 1995), pp. 382–83.

had to be imputed, which is substantially higher than the allocation rate for any other census questions (see table 3-1). Moreover, the allocation rate for the Hispanic-origin question more than doubled since 1980. And while other census items had allocation rate increases from 1980 to 1990, that exhibited by the Hispanic-origin question was by far the greatest. One bureau analyst concludes with characteristic understatement, "Persons may have had more difficulty answering the Hispanic-origin question in the 1990 census than in the 1980 census."[117] Or as the GAO puts it, "The results from the 1990 census showed that the Hispanic-origin item continues to pose one of the more significant data quality challenges for the bureau."[118]

Some of those who fail to respond to the Hispanic-origin question are Hispanics who confound race and ethnicity. They respond to the race question by turning to the "other race" category, where they write in "Hispanic" or, more likely, a national origin (for example, "Mexican"). When these individuals come to the Hispanic-origin question a few items later, they skip over it, believing it to be superfluous.[119]

Yet most of those who fail to respond to the Hispanic-origin question are actually *non*-Hispanics who mistakenly assume that it does not apply to them, even though the first listed response is "No (not Spanish/Hispanic)." As it happens, the allocation rate on this question for non-Hispanics is higher than for Hispanics: in 1990, 10.2 percent compared with 7.2 percent.[120]

But why should we be concerned if non-Hispanics are failing to answer the Hispanic-origin question? One reason is that such high nonresponse rates can be costly to deal with, requiring follow-up phone calls and in-person interviews. And if such follow-up is not done, data quality will suffer.

Another reason is that the bureau's imputation procedures may actually lead to *overestimates* of the total number of Hispanics. An analysis by Arthur Cresce and his Census Bureau colleagues of how this might occur provides a fascinating glimpse into the complicated and often counterintuitive dynamics of census-taking. As indicated earlier, when the bureau imputes a response to an unanswered question, it relies either on the response of another member of the same household or, if there are no such responses, on that of an apparently similar individual drawn from a neighboring household. It so happens that in 1990 the Hispanic-origin question was the most likely to go unanswered by entire households.[121] Therefore imputations for this question relied to an exceptionally high degree (81 percent) on responses from neighboring households.[122]

Demographers and statisticians refer to this specific procedure as "hot-deck" imputation.[123] In this instance, the hot-deck method relies on the assumption that individuals living in neighboring households are of the same race and ethnic origin. As Cresce and his colleagues point out, this assumption works well in relatively homogeneous neighborhoods, even when nonresponse rates are high. But in areas that are racially or ethnically heterogeneous, it does not work well, especially if nonresponse rates for a particular question are high *and* if one group is more likely than another to answer it. Under such conditions, hot-deck imputation overestimates the size of the group more likely to report its race or ethnicity.

How does all this affect the count of Hispanics? Since they frequently reside in racially and ethnically heterogeneous neighborhoods,[124] *and* since they are more likely to respond to the Hispanic-origin question than are non-Hispanics, the hot-deck method may well impute Hispanic values to non-Hispanic individuals, resulting in upwardly biased counts of Hispanics.[125] The outcome is exactly the opposite of a minority undercount, underscoring a richly ironic point: because non-Hispanics are less responsive than Hispanics on the Hispanic-origin question, the latter are overcounted!

There is one more twist of logic to be untangled here. Such overcounting from hot-deck imputation coexists with the more widely acknowledged undercounting of Hispanics in the decennial census. I address the latter issue in chapter 4.

One final point: these nonresponse problems are exacerbated as the geographical scope of the data becomes smaller. The allocation rates cited here are at the national level; local rates may be much higher. In certain census tracts in Los Angeles County in 1990, allocation rates for the Hispanic-origin question approached 20 percent. Some local allocation rates for the race question were similarly high. This means that small-area analyses relying on racial and ethnic data from the census, such as assessments of residential segregation, can be particularly fraught with error.[126]

The Inevitability of Ambiguity

Given these persistent problems, are there better methods of obtaining racial and ethnic data? As committed as the federal statistical system is to self-identification, there are instances, mentioned earlier, when agencies rely on observer-identification to ascertain an individual's race or ethnicity. Would increased reliance on such third-party identification reduce the volatility and inaccuracy of racial and ethnic data collected by the Census Bureau and other federal agencies?

The short answer is no. The GAO concludes: "Observer-identification can lead to incorrect classification of individuals."[127] Perhaps the best evidence on this point comes not from the census itself but from studies comparing the information on birth and death certificates.

In the United States today, the race and ethnicity of a newborn is recorded as that of its mother on the basis of how she identifies herself on the birth certificate. If she does not identify herself, the infant's race or ethnicity is based on how the father identifies himself.[128] Though not pure self-identification (since the parents, not the infant, are doing the identifying), this is the norm for birth certificates.

On death certificates, by contrast, individuals tend to be classified by third-party observers, usually physicians or funeral home directors. One study comparing infant birth and death records reveals substantial discrepancies. Of those infants whose parents both identified themselves as "black" on the birth certificate, 3.0 percent were not classified as "black" at the time of their death. Of those infants whose parents both identified as "American Indian," 9.7 percent were not so classified at death. And of those whose two parents identified as "Chinese," the figure was 38.6 percent.

For infants of mixed-race parentage, misclassifications are dramatically higher. In the same study, 37.9 percent of such infants identified as "black" at birth were classified otherwise at death. Among mixed-race infants identified as "American Indian" at birth, 71.2 percent were subsequently classified otherwise. And for such infants identified as "Chinese," the figure was 78.3 percent.[129]

Another study reports similarly high misclassification of Hispanic infants. Of infants identified as "Mexican American" at birth, 11.4 percent were identified as "non-Hispanic white" on their death certificates. Of infants identified as "Puerto Rican" at birth, 20.0 percent were subsequently identified as "non-Hispanic white." The comparable figure for those identified at birth as "Cuban" was 36.7 percent.[130]

Studies of the racial and ethnic classification of adults reveal similar discrepancies between self-identification and observer-identification. An important consequence of such misclassification is that reported mortality rates for Hispanics, American Indians, and Asians are to varying degrees underestimated.[131]

Such inaccuracies are further compounded when racial and ethnic data based on observer-identification are used with data based on self-identification. This problem arises frequently in the civil rights area, where, it will be recalled, enforcement agencies prefer observer-identification. Thus schools or firms produce numbers on minority students or employees based on observer-identification. But these are then typically compared with local demographic data from the census, which of course relies on self-identification.[132]

The larger point is that the subjectivity of race and ethnicity affects the observers as well as the observed. Moreover, possible remedies for this problem are likely to collide with our liberal democratic principles. As the NAS Edmonston report concludes:

> The only way to ensure that the reported race on a person's death or birth certificate is the same as in the census would be to have some kind of requirement for consistent individual identification. Such identification, tantamount to an individual race identification system, would be antithetical to the nation's history of individual privacy and would contradict current understanding about the fluidity of racial and ethnic identity.[133]

There simply is no terra firma here. British statistician Sir Josiah Charles Stamp exaggerates but surely has a point when he reminds us:

> The government are very keen on amassing statistics. They collect them, raise them to the nth power, take the cube root and prepare

wonderful diagrams. But you must never forget that every one of these figures comes in the first instance from the village watchman, who just puts down what he damn pleases.[134]

Or as Stanley Lieberson puts it succinctly: "We have to live with ambiguity in our census data on ethnic and racial groups."[135] As the evidence from birth and death certificates suggests, this ambiguity will only increase with the continued intermixing of groups.

So, too, with the sustained influx of immigrants the nation is experiencing. Recent immigrants pose the challenges already indicated. But even as they assimilate, new sources of ambiguity arise. Here again, the breakdown of group barriers and intermarriage will result in the blurring of established racial and ethnic categories. This is undoubtedly good news for our society, but it definitely complicates the work of the Census Bureau. Demographer Jeffrey Passel, formerly with the Census Bureau and now at the Urban Institute, concludes: "Group boundaries are becoming 'fuzzier.' There are more and more individuals who could claim to be a member of two or more racial/ethnic groups. This situation makes the data more volatile."[136]

Once again, the need for realism in what can be expected of racial and ethnic data is evident. Moreover, the ambiguity and volatility of these numbers highlight the enormous incentives for groups to manipulate existing racial and ethnic categories to their advantage or to press for the creation of new ones.[137] Yet these same factors mean that such efforts are fraught with uncertainty. Hispanic groups realized this when, as explained in chapter 2, they backed off their original demand that the separate Hispanic-origin question be made part of the race question, once they realized that doing so would have reduced their census count. All of this underscores the fact that increasingly volatile racial and ethnic data will lead to increasingly volatile census politics.

The Need to Impose Order

As we have seen, self-identification results in such a profusion of racially incorrect or simply idiosyncratic responses (and nonresponses) that federal bureaucrats must impose enough order to make sense of the data. Sooner or later, government officials must make critical decisions about racial and ethnic categories that most Americans, if fully appraised, would regard as infringing on a deeply personal area. In spite of its own declared aversion to doing so, this liberal regime has no choice but to exercise authority in this realm.

Of course, the recoding, reclassification, and imputation discussed so far are obscure technical procedures that escape public notice. But there are more visible examples of the authority exercised by the Census Bureau and other federal statistical agencies. In some cases, these may be self-evident. Yet they merit attention because federal officials typically downplay their importance.

The most obvious example is the recognition and legitimation that a group secures simply by being listed on the census questionnaire. For some groups this may mean a stronger claim on government resources; for others, the ability to document discrimination and other grievances, or merely the gratification of group pride.[138] Front-row seating at the "national ceremony" of the census comes with a powerful imprimatur that can be bestowed only by the state.[139]

A more compelling example is Directive No. 15 from OMB, which in 1978 first issued the four "standard classifications" for federal statistics on race ("white," "black," "American Indian or Alaskan Native," "Asian or Pacific Islander") and one on ethnicity ("Hispanic"). David Hollinger has noted that this "ethno-racial pentagon . . . is an implicit prescription for the principles on which Americans should maintain communities; it is a statement that certain affiliations matter more than others."[140]

Yet Hollinger understates the case: the directive's authority is hardly "implicit." As the NAS Edmonston report notes, "features of Directive 15 are not permissive."[141] The directive explicitly defines "the basic racial and ethnic categories for Federal statistics and program administrative reporting." Federal agencies may collect data that do not conform to these five categories as long as those data "shall be organized in such a way that the additional categories can be aggregated into these basic racial/ethnic categories." The directive further states that in no case may the term "nonwhite" be used, and that Hispanic origin data must always be separable from race data. And until recent revisions, the directive did not permit multiple responses. Finally, it stipulates that "the categories specified above will be used by all agencies . . . for civil rights compliance reporting and equal employment reporting . . . for federally sponsored statistical data collection where race and/or ethnicity is required."[142]

Whatever its formal authority, Directive 15 has been, again according to the NAS Edmonston report, "influential far beyond its original intent."[143] Few federal agencies other than the Census Bureau (which, as we have seen, created its own "other race" item) have taken advantage of the directive's permission to elaborate on the five basic categories.[144] Indeed, these categories have, in the words of the NAS Schultze panel, "become reified as absolute standards."[145] Nor has Directive 15's impact been confined to the federal government. The NAS Edmonston report concludes: "Although Directive 15 was originally promulgated solely for the use of federal agencies, it has become the de facto standard for state and local agencies, the private sector, the nonprofit sector, and the research community."[146]

Not surprisingly, few data users have the time or money to go back to original survey tapes and retabulate the numbers using their own categories. In many instances this would not even be possible, since Directive 15 categories are embedded in response codes. "Although nongovernment researchers don't have to use official government categories," says one OMB official, "things are a lot easier when everyone is speaking the same language."[147] Because public and private agencies use Directive 15 categories to organize data that they must report to the federal government, those categories wind up as the template for all racial and ethnic data. Citing this "trickle-down effect," the NAS Edmonston report observes: "Although Directive 15 was never intended to establish a national standard for race categories, it has come to function partly in that way."[148]

It is scarcely news that the federal government has, through the force of its example and resources, come to dominate still another policy arena. The important question is why federal statistical agencies like the Census Bureau and especially OMB downplay the authority they wield. Chapter 2 highlighted OMB's denial that political pressures figured into the inclusion of an Hispanic-origin question on the census questionnaire. And the closer one cuts to the regime principle of self-identification, the more intense such denials become. OMB and the Census Bureau are both extremely reluctant to admit that they exert any influence over the racial and ethnic identities that it is their responsibility to count.

This reluctance shows up clearly in the byplay between OMB and the Census Bureau about who is responsible for what. The bureau is prone to remind Congress and other interested parties that OMB is responsible for creating the racial and ethnic categories that appear on the census questionnaire. While strictly accurate, this claim overlooks the fact that, as the preeminent federal statistical agency, the bureau can bring considerable influence to bear on OMB's determinations. It is the bureau, for example, that directly undertakes or sponsors the research on which OMB bases many of its decisions. And as noted above, the bureau can obtain waivers to collect data outside the basic categories (such as "other race") established by Directive 15.

For its part, OMB is reluctant to own up to the authority it wields over the bureau and other federal statistical agencies. In congressional testimony and *Federal Register* notices, OMB officials invariably emphasize their agency's role as coordinator of a highly decentralized federal statistical system. These officials repeatedly stress that the Directive 15 standards were "developed in cooperation with the Federal agencies" to "provide a *minimum* set of categories for data on race and ethnicity,"[149] and that "in no case should the provisions of this Directive be construed to limit the collection of data to the categories described."[150] Such declarations contain no hint of the NAS Schultze panel's observation that OMB's categories "have become reified as absolute standards."

OMB officials are also at considerable pains to emphasize that (as cited earlier) "we don't classify individuals around here." Though literally true, this claim is misleading. While OMB has never told individual Americans what their racial or ethnic identity is, the agency has not, at least until quite recently, permitted individuals to claim multiple or overlapping identities.

OMB's reluctance to acknowledge responsibility even for the creation of its own categories emerges with striking clarity from the following explanation offered by Suzann Evinger, policy analyst with OMB's Office of Information and Regulatory Affairs: "OMB's role is not to define categories of race and ethnicity but rather to facilitate the measuring and reporting of information on the social and economic conditions of our nation's population for use in formulating public policy."[151] In the same vein, OMB avoids acknowledging that those categories actually deal with race and ethnicity. Its various documents and publications routinely avoid the term "racial and ethnic groups" in favor of "population groups," as in the following passage from a 1997 *Federal Register* notice: "The standards also permit the collection of more detailed information on population groups provided that any additional categories can be aggregated into the minimum standard set of categories."[152] One OMB official inadvertently summed up his agency's perspective when he urged me not to use the phrase "racial and ethnic groups" because "race is too loaded."

Did Someone Say Federal Benefits?

Whenever possible, OMB also emphasizes that its authority to coordinate the racial and ethnic categories used by federal agencies does not extend to determinations of which, if any, groups are eligible for government benefits. Most recently the agency has asserted: "The categories in Directive No. 15 do *not* identify or designate certain population groups as 'minority groups.' As the Directive explicitly states, these categories are *not* to be used for determining the eligibility of population groups for participation in any Federal programs."[153] The NAS Edmonston report concurs: "OMB's Office of Statistical Policy, which is responsible for Directive 15, does not and cannot decide which groups should benefit from governmental policies and programs."[154]

Again, these statements are literally accurate. Yet the matter cannot be left there. Beyond the symbolic value mentioned above, being listed on the census is a tangible political resource for any racial or ethnic group. As political scientist Kenneth Prewitt wrote some years ago, before his current assignment as census director, "Resource-poor social interests turn to a statistical description of their plight in order to generate political pressure and to mobilize adherents to their cause."[155] And the NAS Edmonston report itself emphasizes that the Census Bureau's use of the term "Hispanic" not only antedated popular usage but actually "bolstered the growth of Hispanic or Latino/a identity." The report further concludes: "There is a symbiotic relationship between categories for the tabulation of data and the processes of group consciousness and social recognition, which in turn can be reflected in specific legislation and social policy."[156] Counting racial and ethnic identities is not like picking apples off trees. Try as it might for understandable political reasons, OMB has difficulty avoiding the reality that its own operations affect the statistics for which it has responsibility.

Nevertheless, OMB is justified in contending that it has no authority to create specific beneficiary categories. As noted in chapter 2, the Hispanic-origin question was developed first at the behest of the Nixon White House and then of Congress. More to the point, any federal benefits that may be afforded Hispanics derive not from OMB's decisions but from those of Congress and the courts.

Yet as the coordinator of a classification scheme in which some groups and not others receive benefits, OMB's routine administrative authority inevitably involves the agency in decisions about who will and will not continue to receive those benefits. Several instances of OMB's indirect authority in this area have already been touched upon. Recall the proposal to incorporate the separate Hispanic-origin item into the race question for the 2000 census. After concerns were aroused that this change would reduce the count of Hispanics, OMB rejected this idea. Similarly, OMB decided against creating a multiracial question amidst objections that it would lead to a reduction in the group totals of American Indians and black Americans.[157]

There are other examples. One recent proposal was to divide the "Asian or Pacific Islander" category into two separate items on the 2000 census form. Here, the argument was that Asians and Pacific Islanders are two distinct groups with divergent socioeconomic profiles. Specifically, with Pacific Islanders constituting only 365,000 of the 7.3 million Asian or Pacific Islanders counted in 1990, it was argued that their relatively disadvantaged situation had been masked in the combined category.[158]

Around the same time, OMB was urged to separate out Native Hawaiians from the "Asian or Pacific Islander" category and to include them in the "American Indian or Alaskan Native" category. Here again, the argument was that the socioeconomic plight of the smaller group (Hawaiians) was obscured by inclusion in the "Asian or Pacific Islander" category.[159] But this proposal was also based on a normative claim: that Native Hawaiians are not immigrants and therefore ought not to be classified with Asians.

In response to these proposals, the 2000 census questionnaire has eliminated the "Asian or Pacific Islander (API)" heading that appeared on the 1990 questionnaire, but still offers essentially the same check-off opportunities (including "Asian Indian," "Chinese," "Filipino," and "Samoan") that appeared ten years ago. The 2000 questionnaire also offers two new write-in opportunities: "Other Asian" and "Other Pacific Islander." In other words, OMB refused to create a single, overarching, and distinctly new "Pacific Islander" category.

The 2000 questionnaire does have a new "Native Hawaiian" check-off that replaces the 1990 "Hawaiian" check-off. Thus OMB rejected the notion of combining Native Hawaiians with American Indians and Alaskan Natives. This was partly for technical reasons.[160] But just as important was the objection raised by Indian tribal organizations that such a change in classification would artificially enhance *their* socioeconomic profile. In addition, these organizations expressed concern that to share a census category with Native Hawaiians would undermine the unique claims and status of Indians in the American polity.[161]

These examples are particularly revealing of how proposed changes in OMB's racial and ethnic categories can draw the agency into decisions that are in fact determinations of eligibility for federal benefits. To be sure, it now remains to be seen whether their new categories will afford Pacific Islanders and Native Hawaiians benefits even remotely comparable to what the creation of the Hispanic-origin question thirty years ago has bestowed on Hispanics. OMB would clearly like to avoid such situations, but it is evident that seemingly innocuous technical changes can subtly implicate the agency in problematic distributional issues. The point is that *any* change in OMB's existing classification scheme is likely to have implications for racial and ethnic groups afforded specific federal protections or benefits, even though OMB does not in the first instance make such determinations.

The Reasons for Reticence

It is not difficult to fathom why OMB and federal bureaucrats generally avoid calling attention to the authority they wield in this realm. Nevertheless, their reasons for doing so are worth reviewing.

OMB is at the center of a decentralized statistical system in which myriad federal agencies jealously guard their prerogatives. And while its authority as coordinator of this system is clearly restricted, OMB is ever at pains to at least appear not to be overstepping its bounds.[162]

The Census Bureau has its own bureaucratic reasons for exercising extreme caution. As discussed in chapter 2, the bureau has long regarded itself as "factfinder for the nation." But as a fact-finder the bureau is uncomfortable with the necessarily subjective nature of self-identification. As Lieberson notes, there is

a general disposition of censuses to avoid asking attitudinal questions or other "subjective" questions. Census organizations are resistant to them since it is not part of the traditional orientation of census takers. The census asks what year were you born in, how much money did you earn, what is your occupation and where do you live. The census usually does not ask whether you think you are old or not, whether you would call yourself poor or rich, what occupation you would like to have or where you prefer to live.[163]

Self-identification of race and ethnicity may be the accepted methodology among survey researchers and even the general public. But by drawing the Census Bureau into a realm where facts are few and far between, self-identification undermines the very fact-finder stance that provides the agency cover during times of political turbulence.

Beyond such bureaucratic concerns loom larger challenges. As we have seen, race is sufficiently "loaded" that OMB officials actually avoid using the word when discussing their racial and ethnic classification scheme and opt for the seemingly neutral "population groups" instead. To a large extent OMB and the Census Bureau are reacting to public opinion. After all, the racial and ethnic data in question are used (and for the most part have been generated) in order to administer a controversial set of race-conscious policies.

Yet the controversial nature of affirmative action programs is only part of the problem. The poor quality and outright inaccuracy of the data that these programs must rely on cannot help but raise the anxiety levels of risk-averse bureaucrats. Federal officials are also aware that their efforts to count racial and ethnic identities significantly shape what they are counting. At a minimum, they would rather not acknowledge this publicly.

The success OMB and the Census Bureau have had downplaying this aspect of their work is all the more remarkable in light of the scholarly consensus that race is not a biological category but a social construct. Despite this consensus, scholars have not paid much attention either to the increasingly psychological basis of race and ethnicity or to the role of politics and government in the fabrication of this construct. Michael Omi and Howard Winant are the notable exceptions. They specifically mention the role of the census in "racial formation" and argue that "the determination of racial categories is thus an intensely political process."[164]

Thus the ongoing public policy debate has really failed to acknowledge the "intensely political" nature of the census. One reason why may be that academic experts, as well as their counterparts at OMB and the Census Bureau, are concerned that their understanding of race as a social construct will undermine support for embattled affirmative action efforts. Advocates of affirmative action are certainly not eager to admit that the high political and moral ground on which they stand rests on a foundation of fuzzy categories and squishy numbers.

"It's Not Affirmative Action, Stupid"

The controversy over affirmative action may contribute to bureaucratic uneasiness about the political nature of the census. Yet this does *not* mean (as many who argue that the government should not be collecting racial and ethnic data appear to believe) that affirmative action offers incentives for individuals to identify themselves on the census as protected minorities.

Thoughtful analysts of affirmative action (critics and supporters alike) have noted the anomaly that it affords benefits to individuals who may have a choice about claiming membership in designated beneficiary groups. Demographer Ira Lowry explains: "From the perspective of civil rights enforcement, there is something fundamentally wrong with the notion that ethnic status is elective. If one can gain advantages by claiming membership in a particular ethnic group, surely some of us will make unwarranted claims."[165] Thernstrom cites the case of two white brothers who were denied jobs in the Boston Fire Department, only to get hired when they subsequently identified themselves as black. The brothers were later determined by the Supreme Judicial Court of Massachusetts to be white, a bizarre proceeding that prompted Thernstrom to make the rhetorical point:

> If benefits are to be provided to people on the basis of the ethnic identity they claim, it may follow that we need gatekeepers to check credentials and accept or throw out the claim. If what group one belongs to determines what is a passing score, it seems anomalous to leave it to the individual to choose that group.[166]

Thernstrom, an outspoken critic of affirmative action, is being ironic. But Christopher Ford, a legal scholar and supporter of affirmative action, cites the same case and ends up advocating something very close to Thernstrom's gatekeeper suggestion.[167]

The salient point here is that episodes like this are fundamentally different from what occurs with the census. An individual may well increase her chances of gaining a benefit when she checks the box marked "Hispanic" on a college application. But for so identifying on the census questionnaire, there are no such direct or tangible incentives *for individuals*.

To be sure, *someone* benefits when more rather than fewer individuals claim minority status on the census. Judges and administrators certainly rely on census data to determine affirmative action goals and quotas. Minority leaders understand this and are therefore concerned about the census undercount. As Lowry notes: "The larger the minority's count, the greater advantage all its members have in affirmative action programs."[168] Higher census counts do translate, albeit indirectly, into more benefits to individuals *as members of designated minority groups*. But *as individuals* minority group members are free riders: the benefits they derive from affirmative action programs do not depend on how they identify on the census.

Such details are lost on critics like D'Souza, who is nevertheless correct to focus on census questions about race and ethnicity as part of the administrative apparatus of affirmative action, which he so vehemently opposes. One suspects that a similar misconception about the connection between affirmative action and the census lurks in the minds of many who argue against statistical adjustment of the census. Yet such critics overlook a telling irony: if there were some tangible reward for identifying as a protected minority on the census, then individuals would be self-identifying as minorities in much greater numbers—and the minority undercount would be much lower.

Bureaucratic Dilemmas

Such ironies reflect a larger dilemma confronting both OMB and the Census Bureau. As sociologist Mary Waters notes: "There is a tension between public policy categories, the categories that we need to do the work of government, and the principal [sic] of self-enumeration that people don't come in neat categories, people come in blended packages."[169] This is more than a problem of fuzzy categories colliding with bureaucratic rationality, however. The interesting question is how these tensions are negotiated.

The maneuvering by OMB and the Census Bureau that has been described here is an understandable response to a fundamental conflict between increasingly subjective, psychologized notions of race and ethnicity on the one hand, and the demands of contemporary public policy on the other. One's racial and ethnic "identity" is increasingly defined as just that: a matter of private self-definition that has less than ever to do with socially negotiated status or membership. But the salience of ethnic and racial data in politics and public policy has grown. Omi and Winant note:

> How one is categorized is far from a merely academic or even personal matter. Such matters as access to employment, housing, or other publicly or privately valued goods; social program design and the disbursement of local, state, and federal funds; or the organization of elections (among many other issues) are directly affected by racial classification and the recognition of "legitimate" groups.[170]

Indeed, racial and ethnic identity are of such importance that the government is reluctant simply to leave them up to the preferences of respondents. Hence the countless ways in which self-identification is stretched, contorted, or—in the case of civil rights enforcers—actively resisted and rejected. Yet such policies obviously strain liberal democratic principles of individual autonomy and rights. And when racial and ethnic counting are structured so as to maximize the numbers of designated minorities, that strain is intensified.

At the same time, the changing nature of race and ethnicity makes measuring them all the trickier. As the Census Bureau wades into increasingly subjective attitudinal phenomena, its self-conscious mission as objective "fact-finder" makes less and less sense. Yet precisely because the uses to which these numbers are put are so controversial and politically explosive, the bureau must cling ever more tightly to the mantle of objectivity.

The dilemma facing agencies such as OMB and the Census Bureau reflects broader currents in contemporary American politics. Lowi has long argued that the post–New Deal state is premised on an unwillingness to acknowledge, first, that government is about making difficult moral choices and, second, that these choices must be enforced by a state apparatus that is fundamentally coercive. To avoid confronting this reality, Lowi argues that the federal government has come to rely on broad, vague delegations of authority by Congress to bureaucrats in executive agencies and independent regulatory bodies. Struggling with their unenviable task, these bureaucrats typically try to make sense of what Congress intends by calling upon the private interests whom they have been charged with overseeing. In Lowi's view, the outcome is a complicated bargaining process that results not only in confused public policy but, more important, in undermining the crucial distinction between private power and public authority.[171]

At the heart of the matter lies the delegation of congressional authority. As Steven Holmes of the *New York Times* comments about OMB's enormous influence in the proposed revisions of Directive 15, "Congress has been reluctant to insert itself into the issue of racial classifications."[172] In the same vein, the Interagency Committee for the Review of the Racial and Ethnic Standards recently noted: "Generally, the statutes that require collection of data on race and/or ethnicity do not specify the exact categories that Federal agencies must use. Most of these laws simply require that data on race and ethnicity be collected."[173] Even when Congress has mandated the collection and dissemination of data on specific groups (which it did for "Americans of Spanish origin" in the 1976 Roybal Act), it has left critical details up to OMB.[174] Characterizing the heavy responsibility shouldered by her agency in clarifying loosely defined terms in legislation requiring racial and ethnic data, chief OMB statistician Katherine Wallman concludes: "The tail is wagging the dog."[175]

Deepening the dilemma facing OMB and the Census Bureau is the wave of regulatory reform that occurred during the 1960s and 1970s. Political scientist Sidney Milkis has explained that during those decades a public interest movement dedicated to "participatory democracy" sought to remake the administrative state fashioned by the New Deal. Yet, as Milkis notes, the outcome of these reforms was other than intended. Indeed, another layer of bureaucracy was added on top of the old one:

> Whereas the reformers of the 1960s and 1970s rejected the New Deal instrument of progressive government—the modern presidency—as undemocratic, they devolved public authority to a less visible coalition of bureaucratic agencies, courts, congressional subcommittees, and public interest groups that defied meaningful discourse and broad-based coalitions.[176]

Hence the political environment in which OMB and the Census Bureau operate is an arcane realm dominated by activists and insiders who know every twist and turn in the corridors of administrative power. Needless to say, this political environment is one that leaves the mass of ordinary Americans very much on the outside. The experts and professionals at OMB and the bureau find themselves in the uncomfortable position of having to make critical decisions about racial and ethnic statistics without the support, or knowledge, of a broad segment of the public.

Torn between the regime principle of self-identification and the bureaucratic requirements of the contemporary administrative state, OMB and the Census Bureau have up to now maneuvered rather successfully. But there should be no doubt that these agencies are negotiating a political minefield of misapprehension and distrust, among minorities and the general public alike, of the government's ability to deal fairly with racial and ethnic issues. And the novel conceptions of race and ethnicity that record numbers of immigrants are bringing to these shores will only exacerbate the problem.

It may be tempting to attribute this confusion and distrust to the highly technical nature of the census. Yet this fails to explain why so many Americans mistakenly believe that the Census Bureau preemptively assigns individuals to racial categories. After all, most Americans have at one time or another been exposed to a census questionnaire and they have seen for themselves how questions about race and ethnicity are phrased. In any event, the persistence of these misperceptions should serve as a caution to those with ambitious plans to remedy the persistent census undercount of minorities. It is to that topic that I turn in chapter 4.

CHAPTER FOUR

The Undercount: Some Causes and Proposed Remedies

Census demographers refer to the errors discussed thus far as "classification errors." These arise when an individual is counted but is nevertheless misclassified according to race, ethnicity, income, or another of the census's many categories. A different problem, "coverage error," arises when an individual is counted more than once or is not counted at all. Jeffrey Passel has noted that "coverage error . . . can often be smaller than classification 'error.'"[1] Yet in the continuing controversy over the census, it is coverage error—specifically, the racial minority undercount—that has been the exclusive focus of attention. Chapter 5 will consider the sources of this curious imbalance. The present chapter examines some of the causes of the undercount, not all of them directly attributable to the Census Bureau.

A largely untapped body of ethnographic research sheds light on these causes, which range from literacy and language barriers to cognitive differences to noncooperation, outright misrepresentation, and evasion. The source of this evidence is the bureau itself. Sponsored by the bureau as "alternative enumerations," scores of studies were undertaken by social scientists who did field research in various hard-to-count neighborhoods around census time. These results, alongside those of the actual enumeration, go a long way toward explaining why certain individuals are not counted.

After examining this body of evidence, I conclude this chapter by setting forth the technical aspects of the proposed remedy for the differential racial undercount: statistical sampling and adjustment. While I pay a good deal of attention to potential problems with the adjustment process, I acknowledge that conventional enumeration also has its weaknesses. When it comes to the census, accuracy is nowhere easily attained.

The Overall Undercount

There are many ways to look at the census undercount—or more accurately, census undercounts. The most obvious is the overall undercount of the nation's population. Because the true population of the United States is unknown, the undercount can only be estimated. Two such estimates are available for 1990: 4.7 million (1.8 percent) and 4.0 million (1.58 percent). These were derived by two methods: demographic analysis and a postenumeration survey. Each has its strengths and weaknesses.

Demographic analysis (DA) relies on official records, including birth and death certificates, as well as immigration and emigration data. DA's virtue is that it provides undercount estimates going back to 1940. Yet data from administrative records are of uneven quality, particularly with regard to race and ethnicity. Emigration data are notoriously inadequate, while immigration data miss many illegal aliens. In addition, DA produces undercount estimates only for blacks and nonblacks, and only at the national level.[2]

By contrast, a postenumeration survey (PES) yields undercount estimates down to the local level. Yet such data go back only as far as 1980. As its name suggests, a PES relies on a huge sample survey conducted after the actual census. Those results are then matched against the census to determine who was missed.[3] As will soon be evident, this method is extremely complicated and, depending on the uses to which its results are put, subject to challenge.

Over the past several decades, the undercount, according to DA, has been declining (see table 4-1). To be sure, the 1990 undercount was higher than that for 1980: 1.8 versus 1.2 percent. Yet 1980 was an anomaly. Although it registered a very low undercount, the 1980 census involved considerable double-counting such that most experts regard it as a near fiasco. At the bureau the old hands say: "In 1970 we made sure everyone was counted *only* once, but in 1980 we made sure everyone was counted *at least* once." So if 1980 is treated as an outlier, then the 1990 undercount,

Table 4-1. *Population Totals and Net Population Undercounts in the Census by Demographic Analysis (DA), 1940–90*

	1940	1950	1960	1970	1980	1990
Total						
Population (millions)	131.7	150.7	179.3	203.3	226.6	248.7
Undercount rate (percent)	5.4	4.1	3.1	2.7	1.2	1.8
Blacks						
Population	12.9	15.0	18.9	22.6	26.7	30.5
Undercount rate	8.4	7.5	6.6	6.5	4.5	5.7
Nonblacks						
Population	118.8	135.7	160.5	180.7	199.9	218.2
Undercount rate	5.0	3.8	2.7	2.2	0.8	1.3
Difference:						
Black–nonblack undercount rate	3.4	3.7	3.9	4.3	3.7	4.4

Source: Barry Edmonston and Charles Schultze, eds., *Modernizing the U.S. Census* (Washington, D.C.: National Academy Press, 1995), p. 32.

the second lowest in census history, can be seen as consistent with a steadily declining undercount stretching back over the past half-century. Research indicating pre-1940 undercounts of 6 to 7 percent suggests that this encouraging trend goes back even further.[4] That this impressive record is rarely acknowledged reflects the extraordinary expectations that we have of the census. Certainly compared with most surveys, the census has an outstanding coverage rate. Former census director Barbara Bryant observes: "Coming from academic and private-sector research, where 70 to 90 percent response rates are cause for celebration, I consider the Census Bureau's record phenomenal. Neither the academic nor the private sector ever even attempts to survey one-quarter of a billion people."[5]

The Differential Racial Undercount

The overall undercount has never been the focus of controversy, however. What has received all the attention is the undercount of blacks, Asians or Pacific Islanders, American Indians/Eskimos/Aleuts, and Hispanics in relation to non-Hispanic whites. For a variety of reasons explored below, the undercount of blacks and Hispanics has been the most visible and contentious.

There is no gainsaying this "differential racial undercount." As table 4-2 reveals, in 1990 the undercount for non-Hispanic whites was 0.7 percent, compared with 2.33 percent for Asian or Pacific Islanders, 4.43 percent for blacks, 4.96 percent for Hispanics, 4.52 percent for American Indians/Eski-

Table 4-2. *Estimated Net Undercount of Demographic Groups according to the Postenumeration Survey (PES), 1990*

Demographic group	Net undercount (percent)
Total population	1.58
Residents of	
Owner-occupied housing	0.07
Rental housing	4.31
Race	
Nonblacks	1.18
Males	1.52
Females	0.85
Blacks	4.43
Males	4.90
Females	4.01
Asian/Pacific Islanders	2.33
Males	3.44
Females	1.25
American Indians, Eskimos, Aleuts	4.52
Males	5.18
Females	3.86
American Indians on reservations	12.2[a]
Non-Hispanic whites	0.7[a]
Ethnicity	
Hispanics (of any race)	4.96
Males	5.51
Females	4.39

Source: Committee on Adjustment of Postcensal Estimates, *Assessment of Accuracy of Adjusted versus Unadjusted 1990 Census Base for Use in Intercensal Estimates* (Census Bureau, August 7, 1992); Howard Hogan and Gregg Robinson, "What the Census Bureau's Coverage Evaluation Tells Us about Differential Undercount," *1993 Research Conference on Undercounted Ethnic Populations* (GPO, October 1993), p. 18.

a. Special CAPE estimates cited by Hogan and Robinson.

mos/Aleuts, and a whopping 12.2 percent for American Indians living on reservations. And this pattern has endured over the decades. Table 4-1 presents the available time-series data for blacks and nonblacks (recall this limitation of DA). From 1940 to 1990 there has been a persistent undercounting of blacks. More to the point, the black-nonblack differential has widened, from 3.4 percent in 1940 to 4.4 percent in 1990.

Table 4-1 shows another trend worth highlighting. Despite the growing differential, the black undercount has actually been diminishing: from 8.4 percent in 1940 to 5.7 in 1990. Yet over the same period, the nonblack undercount has diminished even more dramatically, from 5.0 in 1940 to 1.3 in 1990. The result, as noted, is that the black-nonblack differential increased, but not because of a complete lack of progress.

Minorities are not the only demographic groups that are undercounted. In fact, anywhere from two-thirds to three-fourths of the 1990 undercount were nonblacks, mostly whites. More than half were children, a substantial proportion of whom were undoubtedly minorities.[6] Clearly there are many perspectives from which to view the census undercount.

Housing tenure appears to be as important in explaining the undercount as minority status. As table 4-2 indicates, in 1990 the undercount for all renters was 4.31 percent, compared with 0.07 percent for all homeowners. The renter-homeowner undercount differential was actually larger than the black-nonblack differential.[7] Now, it is not clear whether the census had more difficulty counting renters because they change residence more than homeowners, for example, or because renters are disproportionately minorities.[8] Whatever the answer to this question, the differential racial undercount will doubtless continue to be the focus of public controversy. In American politics, race trumps socioeconomic differences—never mind housing tenure—as a basis of social cleavage, political mobilization, and policy debate.

This is all the more reason to note that the undercount is not uniform within specific minority groups. For example, the undercount for black Americans in 1990 (based on demographic analysis) was 5.7 percent, which is actually a weighted average of strikingly divergent rates for various black subgroups. Black males aged twenty to sixty-four had an undercount of 11.2 percent; black males thirty to thirty-four a rate of 14.0 percent. For black children (male and female, aged birth to nine) the undercount was 8.0 percent. And for black females the undercount in 1990 was very low: the highest was 4.9 percent for those aged twenty-five to twenty-nine, and for those fifty-five to fifty-nine it was zero. For black females sixty to seventy-four there was a substantial *overcount*.[9] This 1990 pattern essentially repeats those from 1960–80, underscoring the fact that the black undercount primarily involves adult black males.

A similar pattern emerges with other groups. As table 4-2 reveals, in 1990 Hispanics experienced a higher undercount than blacks, and Hispanic males experienced a higher undercount than Hispanic females (5.51 versus 4.39 percent). So did Asian or Pacific Islander males and American Indian males.

Such findings should caution against the notion of any global discriminatory mechanism working to exclude minorities from the census. Diverse minority groups encounter the census in different contexts and with different attitudes and interests. Similarly, different members of a given group experience the census in disparate ways.

Table 4-3. *Error in the 1990 Census*
Millions of persons

	Estimate 1	Estimate 2
Omissions	9.7	15.5
Erroneous inclusions	4.4	10.2
Net undercount	5.3	5.3
Gross error (omissions plus erroneous inclusions)	14.1	25.7

Source: General Accounting Office, *1990 Census: Reported Net Undercount Obscured Magnitude of Error*, GAO/GGD-91-113 (August 1991), p. 5.

Before scrutinizing those differences, I want to highlight an important aspect of census undercounts. The figures cited above are all *net* undercounts. Actual undercounts are in fact higher. These net rates are calculated by taking the total number of individuals omitted in the census and subtracting those erroneously included. The latter might include persons counted more than once, nonexistent persons for whom enumerators falsified data, persons counted but assigned to the wrong location, or persons incorrectly included because they died before the day of the census or were born after it.

The General Accounting Office (GAO) estimates that there were anywhere from 4.4 to 10.2 million erroneous inclusions in the 1990 census. It further estimates that total omissions ranged from 9.7 to 15.5 million persons. As table 4-3 illustrates, subtracting the former from the latter leaves a net undercount of 5.3 million persons, regardless of which set of numbers is used.[10] A moment's reflection on table 4-3 will confirm that it is possible to reduce the net undercount by increasing the number of erroneous inclusions. Or as the GAO declares: "A focus on the *net* undercount obscures the true magnitude of the error in the census because, while millions of persons were missed by the census, millions of other persons were improperly counted."[11] For this reason, the GAO focuses on gross error (the sum of omissions and erroneous inclusions).

Yet the precise implications of this point remain unclear. Some argue that the Census Bureau has reduced net undercounts by increasing erroneous inclusions—in other words, by increasing gross error.[12] Many of these erroneous inclusions may be, for example, affluent individuals who get counted a second time at vacation homes or in college dorms. We also know that census omissions are disproportionately poor minorities. As a result, it has been argued that net undercounts obscure the fact that the census compensates for minority undercounts by double-counting nonminorities. On the other hand, the extra efforts exerted by the bureau to find and count minorities may also result in double-counting some of them. In any event, the National Academy of Sciences (NAS) panel chaired by Charles Schultze suggests that "for the nation as a whole and for large geographic areas, many of these errors cancel out." In 1990, according to the NAS Schultze panel, 40 to 50 percent of erroneous inclusions were individuals who were also counted as omissions.[13]

Unfortunately, we do not know enough about who is being erroneously counted to determine the full implications of this problem. But the problem itself is another reminder of the limitations of census data, especially for small geographic areas where the likelihood of such errors canceling out is greatly diminished. We are also reminded that even though the controversy focuses on net undercounts, the problem of gross census error looms in the background as another potential political dispute.

Causes of the Undercount

Why does the differential racial undercount persist? The reasons are many and range from the bureaucratic politics discussed in chapter 2 to factors quite beyond the Census Bureau's control. Some of these problems antedate the current controversy, but several others are traceable to it. However one assesses the relative importance of each factor, the bureau has clearly been experiencing problems accomplishing its mission.

As discussed in chapter 2, the bureau has had enormous difficulty keeping pace with innovation and change in survey research, and especially in computer technology, both of which industries it ironically helped to launch.[14] Aside from this fundamental challenge, which confronts the government in general, the main problems affecting the internal operations of the bureau have been, in the broadest sense, political. Indicative of these have been budget cutbacks and reorganizations beginning in the late 1970s during the Carter administration and continuing into the 1980s under Ronald Reagan.[15] Here again, we are reminded that the Census Bureau produces a public good that has few organized interests willing or able to defend it.

More important have been the scrutiny and involvement of the legislative and especially the executive branches chronicled in chapter 2. Given the inherently political nature of the census, it is difficult to see how such intrusions can be curtailed or eliminated. Yet it is also clear that these episodes have increased as the census has found itself at the center of high-stakes political maneuvering in the wake of the 1960s one-person/one-vote court decisions. These intrusions have also been driven by the perceived importance of census data in federal formula grants.

Recall former census director Bryant bemoaning the "takeover" of the bureau by political appointees at the Commerce Department. She attributes this development to the various lawsuits challenging census undercounts and warns of the increased influence and authority that lawyers have gained over the process. As a result, litigation advocating adjustment and predicated on the view that the census ought to transcend politics has not only resulted in a more politicized census but has also apparently hindered the bureau's ability to accomplish its mission. As one former high-level bureau official recounted to me, lawsuits launched against the 1980 census distracted him and his colleagues to the point of jeopardizing the quality of the decennial count.[16]

Beyond such bureaucratic political dynamics lie the many difficulties highlighted in the bureau's own extensive body of ethnographic research on the causes of the undercount. Such studies are particularly valuable because conventional survey research on census nonresponse is plagued by . . . nonresponse! Not surprisingly, individuals who do not cooperate with the census tend not to cooperate with surveys about the census.[17] Indeed, the kinds of problems unearthed by the bureau's ethnographic research are likely to go undetected by any of its other evaluation programs.

These studies reveal a mind-boggling variety of reasons why certain groups are disproportionately undercounted. Nevertheless, a number of clear patterns can be discerned and valuable lessons learned. I will extract these from the studies, but first I want to present some of the findings.

Unusual Households

The most obvious problems relate to the "irregular housing" in which many minorities live. Residences in makeshift subdivisions may not have doorbells that work, doorbells at all, identifiable address numbers, or mailboxes with names on them.[18] Or if there are names on the mailboxes, they may not be reliably matched to the tenants. Such arrangements are likely to be found in illegal units in subdivided buildings or in converted garages often inhabited by immigrants. Compounding the difficulty is the fact that such units may be hidden from public view in backyards or on rural roads.

In an ethnography of a San Diego barrio populated mostly by illegal aliens, the research team consisted of bilingual social service providers who had been working in the neighborhood for years. Yet even they had a difficult time identifying all the housing units and were able to do so only after multiple visits.[19] An old mansion overlooking San Diego Harbor that had been subdivided into twenty-two apartments on four floors required four visits before the team could put together a map revealing every unit in the building. Even then, ten visits were required to complete the study's alternative enumeration. Not surprisingly, census enumerators had missed eight residents living in four households in this building.[20]

Another example from this San Diego barrio involves four owner-occupied bungalows in front of a building containing eight housing units. The bungalows appeared to be single-family homes but actually had upstairs rental units. This arrangement was sufficiently confusing that five visits were necessary to map all the units. The census had missed three of the bungalow units in which thirteen individuals lived. As for the building behind the bungalows, it was not visible from the street. Even after it was identified, gaining access to it required the researchers to negotiate an obstacle course consisting of the bungalows, assorted strangers, abandoned automobiles, and watchdogs. Again, it is not surprising that the actual census had missed four entire households and twelve individuals counted in the alternative enumeration.

In San Francisco's Mission District, a researcher describes what had once been a hotel but was subsequently converted to an apartment building:

> The two story building has nineteen apartments and three different addresses. One apartment on the first floor has its own entrance and address number. Fourteen apartments on the second floor have another entrance and share the same street address. Four apartments . . . have yet another separate entrance and a separate street address. . . . There are no individual mail boxes.[21]

It took two weeks of fieldwork before the research team was able to identify all nineteen units.

On the North Shore of Long Island, in a community populated mostly by undocumented Salvadorans, anthropologist Sarah Mahler describes "a flourishing underground housing market."[22] Along with "mother-daughter houses" (one built first and the other squeezed in behind it) that share the same mailboxes, Mahler notes the following:

> One specific case of unusual housing which was not detected by the census is that of 4 apartments located above an old factory which now serves as a small clothing store. The entrance to the apartments (one of which is an attic studio) is from the rear of the building and, as such, conceals their existence. The census housing list did not include these apartments which is why they were missed.[23]

Finally, Ansely Hamid describes some apparently abandoned buildings in Harlem occupied by drug users:

> The building was formally abandoned in late 1988. . . . The stairway indoors collapsed between the second and third floors and subsequently, more sections fell off. Visitors got upstairs by negotiating sharp-edged ruins of concrete by the light of a dim naked bulb, and passed by landings where psychiatric [*sic*] homeless men would rear up suddenly from beneath shelters made of cardboard boxes, muttering curses and offering fierce gestures.
>
> Nevertheless, eight apartments remained occupied. Residents continued to have electricity, but fetched water from the fire hydrant at the curb. They were principally women, as many as six to each apartment, which they maintained as a locale for using crack.[24]

Hamid reports that in this neighborhood the census counted fifty-two fewer housing units and seventy-one fewer persons than his alternative enumeration.[25]

A different challenge facing the census is what demographers refer to as "complex households." As the following examples reveal, this syndrome is related to irregular housing but tends to have different consequences. Whereas irregular housing is difficult to locate and typically results in the omission of entire households, complex households are identified by the census but specific individuals within them are often overlooked.

A good example of such a complex household is what Martin Montoya, in his study of Mexican migrant workers in rural Oregon, calls the "Ad Hoc Household":

> The most important byproduct of the Ad Hoc Household arrangement is the generation and maintenance of relationships which can only be described as loosely tied, ephemeral, and alienated (no responsibility to household) because each slot in the household is allocated by money and not necessarily kinship. Housemembers come and go as they please with little concern for the housing unit itself, individual household members or groups.[26]

This kind of living arrangement is hardly limited to Mexican migrant workers in rural areas. It is associated with Hispanic immigrants more generally: among Mexicans in San Diego, Dominicans in the South Bronx, and Salvadorans in Long Island. For example, the San Diego study describes a backyard shed converted into a one-bedroom apartment: "A total of eleven men, all undocumented Mexican immigrants, lived in this unit. These men were all employed and worked different shifts, thus not all of them were in the housing unit at the same time. Their work schedule permitted them to sleep in shifts."[27] Such shift-sleeping is the classic pattern for unattached immigrant males with meager resources intending to return home with as much savings as possible.[28]

Yet similar arrangements are also evident among nuclear families. In San Francisco's Mission District an ethnographer describes a three-bedroom apartment rented by a Salvadoran man and woman in their thirties, who worked in low-wage service jobs and had lived in the United States for three years. This couple, their eleven-year-old daughter, and their eight-year-old son shared one bedroom, while the two remaining bedrooms were rented out to nine other Salvadorans: one to a woman in her thirties with her twenty-one-year-old partner, their six-month-old child, her two young sons from previous relationships, and her partner's nineteen-year-old brother. The third bedroom was occupied by three men: a twenty-five-year-old and a sixty-five-year-old recently arrived in the United States, and a forty-five-year-old who was the father of the woman in the first couple. The actual living arrangements are described thus:

> The residents have organized the apartment into three internal apartments with each bedroom representing a separate unit. Each bedroom has a lock. The bathroom and kitchen are shared; however, each group has a separate section in the refrigerator and much of the dry and canned food is stored in their rooms.

Located in the aforementioned hotel that had been converted into a maze of substandard apartments, this unit and its thirteen residents were not discovered by the ethnographers until they had been doing fieldwork in the building for two weeks.[29]

In Houston, Nestor Rodriguez and Jacqueline Hagan identified fifteen types of complex household arrangements among Central American and Mexican immigrants (mostly undocumented) living in a 645-unit garden-style apartment complex on the city's west side.[30] And in Fort Lauderdale, Haitians have built complex households around a nuclear core with peripheral individuals constantly coming and going—including weekend residents, boarders, fellow villagers saving up to start their own households, visitors "just passing through" (in Creole, "pase li pase"), and recently arrived illegals.[31] In Miami's Little Haiti, sociologist Alex Stepick describes how households routinely take in "just comes" as well as the children of relatives, friends, and fictive kin on a "temporary" basis that can last from two weeks to four years.[32]

Among impoverished black Americans, household arrangements are similarly "irregular."[33] At one extreme Hamid describes Harlem's "freak houses":

The salient characteristic of these households was contained in the "freak" part of the word: they appealed to male crack users who wanted to "freak," or to enjoy the sexual services of many women in an ensemble. Crack using women flocked to them to receive cash or crack, and their proprietors received crack and cash for mediating the exchange.[34]

One household was

maintained by a young woman and her transvestite brother. Co-resident with them were four other male transvestites and a young former crack dealer escaping surveillance by the probation officers. The five transvestite males work every night at a nearby "strip," and return with their earnings to the household to consume crack.[35]

Of such living arrangements in general, Hamid observes: "Although resident in the respective units on Census Day, these households are very frangible, and are vulnerable to internal fissions as well as pressures from the police, landlords, and fellow non-drug-using residents."[36]

Mobile People

As suggested by the foregoing, residential mobility is another factor, often associated with irregular housing and complex households, that tests the ingenuity of the Census Bureau. Residential mobility certainly characterizes the poor black communities studied by these ethnographers. But while it clearly complicates the job of the bureau, mobility in such neighborhoods does not necessarily result in outright omission from the census. In immigrant neighborhoods, by contrast, residential mobility appears to figure more prominently among the causes of undercounting.[37] For example, it is cited as contributing to an undercount of Cambodians in Long Beach, California.[38] And as just noted, there is considerable movement in and out of Haitian households in Florida. This is especially true of recent immigrants who have not yet secured a steady job and a place of their own. But as we have also seen, even Haitians who have been in the United States for some time have various peripheral individuals moving in and out of their households.

Among more settled immigrants, other reasons for high mobility include avoiding crime, seeking better schools, or visiting relatives back home for weeks or months at a time.[39] Of Haitians in Miami, Alex Stepick and his colleagues report: "Since 1983 we have conducted two large-scale longitudinal surveys which included the sample site. In each, over a two-year period 40 to 50 percent of our sample had moved at least once with many, many households moving twice or more. With each move the probability of household composition change increases."[40] Among Dominican and Mexican immigrants in the South Bronx, movement occurred in and out of a research area but also within it:

> Many boarders would move from apartment to apartment on a near-monthly basis. For example, one family which had been evicted from their apartment in another area lived with a sister's family for one month in one of the buildings that comprise the AE [alternative enumeration] site. This family then moved into another apartment and, shortly thereafter, moved out of the building completely. All this occurred during the six weeks of the AE. This was not typical of families, but certainly was typical of single boarders and some relatives.[41]

About a second apartment building in the same neighborhood, these researchers remark: "The superintendent's apartment was utilized as a kind of 'way station' for new arrivals. These people would often stay a few weeks until they found more permanent housing within the building or elsewhere."[42]

In her study of Salvadorans on Long Island, Mahler reports that many of them move as often as three times a year in search of jobs, cheaper housing, or larger apartments to accommodate newly arrived family members. Although most of the census omissions in her study area occurred because enumerators missed entire housing units, Mahler notes: "It is not too difficult to speculate that many would have been missed anyway, even if their units had been identified. They would have been missed precisely because they are so mobile and difficult to find attached to a given housing unit."[43]

In their study of Central American and Mexican immigrants in Houston, Rodriguez and Hagan found an even more "transient population" than they had anticipated. They identify residential mobility as the principal reason for the many omissions in the actual census—either because the individuals Rodriguez and Hagan located were not living in Houston on the day of the census or because the census simply missed them.[44] These researchers identify several factors contributing to immigrant transience:

the continual arrival of newcomers, the return migration of others, rent increases, and local economic fluctuations.

Negotiating the Form

Compounding these concrete, physical challenges to census-taking are an array of cognitive and motivational factors.[45] Among the cognitive factors is the minor but suggestive finding that recent immigrants from Latin America are not familiar with computer-readable forms. Accustomed to filling out "important" and "official" documents in ink, such individuals become flustered by the notion of penciling in circles on census forms.[46]

Undoubtedly more problematic is the fact that immigrants routinely throw away mail not directed to any specific person but addressed to "resident," which is how census forms are sent out. Non-English-speaking immigrants also routinely throw away mass mailings written in English, which again include census forms.[47] Of course, the lack of English-language skills is a real barrier to filling out census questionnaires, assuming they are not summarily thrown away. Non-English versions were available in 1990, but ethnographers report that individuals who tried to obtain them were rarely successful.[48] Even when such forms are readily available (as the Census Bureau intends for the 2000 census), many immigrants are not literate in their native language.[49]

A more fundamental cognitive challenge has to do with divergent notions of what constitutes a "household." Among Latino immigrants, "household" is taken to mean family, which means that boarders and unrelated individuals residing in the housing unit are typically not listed on census forms.[50] Among recently arrived Mexican, Guatemalan, Salvadoran, and Peruvian immigrants living in Long Beach, California, "visitors" may be routinely accepted into homes, but just as routinely not reported on the census, even among those who reliably fill out their questionnaires.[51] Haitian households appear to be more inclusive of nonfamily members, but the larger point is that the bureau's definitions of "family" and "household" often conflict with on-the-ground realities.[52]

Meanwhile, in New York City's Chinatown, elderly Chinese reported their adult children on their census form even though the latter had been living on their own for some time.[53] This pattern was also noted among Chinese in San Francisco's North Beach area. As ethnographers there noted: "In Chinese culture, family members can be dispersed geographically but still be thought of as constituting a household as long as they contribute all or part of their income to get managed by the family head."[54]

One need not focus on such relatively exotic neighborhoods to encounter similar problems. Among black Americans, there are notions of family and of residence that definitely depart from Census Bureau assumptions. Anthropologist Joyce Aschenbrenner notes in her ethnography of a predominantly black neighborhood in St. Louis:

> Individuals were missed in both middle and lower-income Black families in greater number than in White families. I attribute this to a different concept of "household" and "family" than in the case of White social organization, stemming from different historical and cultural backgrounds, in which a household functions in a social milieu of related households whose fortunes are tied together. In such an organization, the question of where one is actually sleeping and eating at the moment is not vitally important to one's identity and well-being; what is important is that one is a part of a network in which one's needs can be met from the time one is born until one dies. . . . Under the circumstances, the attempt to characterize the household makeup at a point in time is contrary to realities in Black family life.[55]

Such complicated living arrangements can result in overenumeration—for instance, when individuals, especially males, are counted in two different households, their mother's and their girlfriend's.[56]

Reasons for Avoidance

Motivational factors are probably the most important in contributing to the undercount.[57] These might be as innocuous as Koreans not reporting boarders in their apartment out of shame at the consequent overcrowding.[58] But literally being afraid to open the door is a more common reason why many individuals do not cooperate with census enumerators. In the South Bronx, Boanerges Dominguez, a male ethnographer of Dominican origin, spent two weeks knocking on doors in two apartment buildings occupied by Dominicans, Mexicans, and Puerto Ricans. For the most part, tenants would simply not respond or would refuse to open the door to someone they did not know personally. The only way Dominguez began to gain access was to pay the building superintendent to accompany him. Even then, "many apartments had to be visited and revisited several times in order to gain the confidence of the residents."[59] During the two and a half months that Dominguez was working in the area, drug-dealing was "ever-present and open," and there were drug raids by police, a fire, and several assaults, including shootings and a murder. Dominguez was even approached by a tenant known to be a contract killer, who threatened to kill him if he did not cease his activities in the neighborhood.[60] Elsewhere in New York City during the 1990 census, regular enumerators were reportedly shot at by residents.[61] Is it any wonder that so-called enumerator fear is an important factor in the undercount of such neighborhoods?

These difficulties led Dominguez to conclude that women would be more successful enumerators in such neighborhoods, albeit at high risk to themselves.[62] In a similarly troubled San Francisco neighborhood, however, a female ethnographer was unable to get residents in a dangerous single-room occupancy hotel to speak with her.[63]

Yet not all poor or minority neighborhoods are so troublesome. In Miami's Little Haiti, residents patiently answered and reanswered the questions of several successive census enumerators who did not realize that their respondents had already been interviewed. In this case, the result was not an undercount but, once again, an overcount.[64]

These two vignettes represent extreme situations; far more typical are the challenges facing the Census Bureau in neighborhoods characterized by pervasive distrust and lack of cohesion. Quite aside from the dramatically deleterious impacts of violent crime and drug-dealing, many hard-to-count areas are populated by highly transient individuals or groups of individuals who, far from wanting to get to know their neighbors, focus on minding their own business. In such neighborhoods residents may not even know their neighbors' names.[65] This situation is typical of low-income private as well as public housing projects, but also of immigrant areas.[66] Of the latter, economist Michael Piore has observed that immigrants, especially recent arrivals, resemble the "atomized utility maximizer" of economic theory, so intent are they on working hard, saving as much money as possible, and returning home.[67] In sum, such neighborhoods are not very accurately described as "communities." It is not surprising that in such areas ethnographers, who were more familiar with them than census enumerators ever could be, were typically avoided or lied to. Even those who hired local residents to assist them encountered resistance.[68] Indeed, one ethnographer reports that one of the local residents she paid to conduct interviews withheld information from her.[69]

In such neighborhoods atomization and distrust are pervasive on both sides of the apartment door. Particularly among immigrants, individuals may share physical space but little else. The image of the complex household described earlier (with locks on each bedroom door) is a powerful reminder of the social dynamics here. In such situations, fellow apartment dwellers either do not know much about one another or, if they do, choose to keep such knowledge to themselves.[70]

Such behaviors often reflect experiences or values immigrants carry with them from their homelands. In Queens, for example, Korean women living with or married to non-Korean men did not report their partners to the census out of concern that they had violated a Korean norm.[71] Or an immigrant mother may misrepresent her family to the U.S. census because in her country of origin, the census was associated with identifying youth old enough for military conscription or with cataloguing personal property for taxation. As a proverb among Korean farmers warns: "Don't let the government know how many sons and how many cows you have."[72] Finally, Salvadorans living in overcrowded apartments in Long Island avoid conversations with one another out of concern not to reignite old battles from their recent civil war.[73]

The immediate situations in which individuals find themselves can also generate quite rational reasons for avoiding intrusive questions from census-takers or other strangers. Among these the most obvious is concealment of criminal or illegal activities such as drug use, parole violation, or welfare fraud.[74] The last is a persistently cited factor in almost thirty years of research on why minority males are undercounted. Welfare recipients simply do not believe that welfare rolls will not be checked against census records. Anthropologist Mercer Sullivan concludes that "fear that Census Bureau information will be cross-checked with welfare records is probably the single largest source of error in counting young adult males who are black and non-Latino or who are Puerto Rican."[75]

Yet welfare fraud is hardly the only reason why individuals evade the census. Among immigrants, welfare dependence is likely to be less entrenched and therefore less salient as a cause for noncooperation. More typical of immigrants are, as we have seen, myriad irregular arrangements that lead to secretiveness and evasion of public authorities. Those living in rental housing are likely to be concerned that reporting additional occupants could lead to rent increases or even eviction.[76] For example, Korean tenants in a Queens building who used their apartments for garment subcontracting sought to conceal their activities and the income from it.[77] Similar in-home, underground economic activities among Cambodians and Latinos in Long Beach, California—whether preparing desserts for ethnic restaurants, sewing and tailoring, renting wedding outfits, or processing wedding videos—led residents to evade census enumerators and other inquiring officials.[78] Or when leaseholders sublet portions of their apartments, they typically fail to report all the residents to the Census Bureau out of concern that the arrangement and especially the additional income will be revealed to the landlord or other government agencies.[79]

Often noncooperation is traceable not to tenants but to resident managers and landlords to whom census questionnaires are frequently mailed directly. Typically benefiting from overcrowding and other irregular arrangements, such individuals might not fill out census forms truthfully for fear of alerting those, especially housing inspectors, who might expose substandard or illegal conditions.[80] In such environments where many residents have (or believe they have) something to hide from officialdom, the result is a pervasive lack of trust, not just of public and private authorities but of neighbors who might turn information over to them.

Perhaps most striking in the ethnographic research on census noncooperation and evasion is the relative unimportance of being an illegal immigrant. Mahler explains how this finding ran contrary to her initial expectations in studying illegal Salvadorans on Long Island: "In general, individuals were more reticent about declaring boarders who might make them susceptible to eviction from their apartments than they were about discussing their legal status for fear of government officials."[81] A similar point is made about illegal Mexican immigrants in the South Bronx. Dominguez reports that these were among the most forthright individuals encountered in a rather hellish environment: "When I asked them why they were so open, they would say something like the following: 'We don't even care if you are from the government. If the Migra [immigration authorities] comes and deports us we'll just jump back across the border the next day.'" Attempting to make sense of this surprising finding, Dominguez writes: "Most of these illegal Mexicans had arrived in the U.S. within the past year or two and had come explicitly to earn some money and return. Although they were hoping to avoid deportation, this was *not* a big issue for them."[82]

By contrast, the undocumented Dominicans were "much more concerned about their immigration status." Dominguez speculates: "Perhaps this is because travel from the Dominican Republic to the United States is relatively more difficult and costly than travel from Mexico to the United States." Because these Dominicans tended to live with family members who were legal residents, Dominguez concludes that the census overlooked

Dominican immigrants "not because of their immigration status but because their families were afraid to lose public assistance."

The point here is not that undocumented immigrants are completely unconcerned with their illegal status. There is evidence that recently arrived illegals as well as illegals working in rural areas are quite anxious about their situation. Yet it does appear that the longer undocumented immigrants reside here, the less their responses to government agencies such as the Census Bureau are influenced by their immigration status and more by other irregular or illegal activities in which they may be involved.[83]

A different but related point to be gleaned from this research is that the lack of cooperation with the census reflects distrust and fear of neighbors and local officials as much as of anonymous bureaucrats in Washington. This is underscored in an ethnography of a multiracial public housing project in San Francisco. Though not untouched by drug and alcohol abuse, teenage pregnancies, crime, and violence, this project was considered by tenants to be one of the more desirable such facilities in the city. In any event, many of these tenants misrepresented their incomes and household sizes to local housing officials in order to avoid rent increases and evictions. Like their counterparts in other projects, these residents had things to hide.

When the research team went into this project, anthropologists Tom Shaw and Patricia Guthrie anticipated that—on the basis of the team's personal contacts in the project, their familiarity with the neighborhood, language skills (including Khmer and Chinese), and racial backgrounds (a white male, an African-American woman, and two Chinese)—they would gain the residents' trust and therefore obtain more accurate information than census enumerators. But as Shaw and Guthrie acknowledge: "We were surprised to learn that residents in many instances had been more honest with the census enumerator than they had been with us."[84] They go on to explain:

> In the Projects it makes more sense and is more practical to suspect the motivations of your neighbor than it does to suspect an official representing the distant authority of the federal government. Guthrie and Shaw did have close acquaintances with key Project residents, but our relationships with residents and association with the Projects' staff made us appear to be even more of a risk to those with whom we were not in such close communication. From many residents' perspective, a friend of their neighbors was no more trustworthy than the neighbor himself or herself, and in many (but not all) cases neighbors were not to be trusted.[85]

In this instance residents apparently believed census enumerators who told them that their responses would be kept confidential, at least more than they believed the researchers. Although a few other researchers have also found themselves being lied to, this is still a surprising outcome, for in most cases researchers have obtained more accurate counts than the census enumerators.

Though hardly consistent or definitive, these findings suggest that individuals refuse to cooperate with the census on the basis of rational calculations about concrete interests (ranging from housing benefits to personal safety) that they believe to be at risk. To be sure, these individuals may misjudge the risks and interests at stake, but that hardly distinguishes them from the rest of us. Hard-to-count populations may also include a disproportionate number of irrational souls trapped in various social pathologies.[86] Nevertheless, the Census Bureau is clearly not paying attention to its own research when it attributes noncooperation with the census to Americans "becoming alienated from society in general and more mistrustful of government in particular."[87] Indeed, such trendy nostrums obscure the important insight that noncooperation is rooted not so much in mass psychology as in the interest calculations of individuals.[88]

Moreover, these calculations focus on local actors understood to have influence over goods or services of direct importance to the hard-to-count. Granted, such locals might be perceived (mistakenly) to pass on information from the census to federal officials capable of sanctioning respondents. But again, to construe this simply as "fear of government" is to overlook the local culture of distrust in which hard-to-count populations are enmeshed. This distrust is not directed simply or even primarily toward remote formal institutions (public or private) but toward individuals close at hand and immediately familiar.

Policy Implications

This research has sobering implications for efforts to address the census undercount. For instance, during recent censuses federal officials have sought to promote cooperation by reducing the profile of agents of the Immigration and Naturalization Service (INS) in immigrant neighborhoods. Yet these ethnographies indicate that such efforts premised on immigrants' presumed anxiety about their legal status will not be very effective.

Another proposal seriously challenged by these findings is the notion of hiring local residents as census enumerators, either for their knowledge of the environs or for the racial or ethnic background they share with their neighbors. Yet as noted, local hires may misrepresent census results to their supervisors. More to the point, such local knowledge comes with local baggage that can exacerbate noncooperation. As for shared backgrounds, several of these ethnographers indicate that being minorities themselves or relying on minority assistants did not help them very much.[89] The distrust among residents of undercounted neighborhoods is apparently stronger than any trust that might be derived from shared ethnic or racial origins.

For similar reasons, appeals to group interest or identity, which were emphasized with the 1980 and 1990 censuses, are not likely to have much impact either. At least, it is doubtful that such appeals would be weighty enough to counteract the individual interest calculations that lead to avoidance of the census in the first place. More generally, these studies underscore that when it comes to cooperating with the census, the interests of individuals are different and much more strongly felt than those of the groups or communities of which those individuals are members.

This research also suggests that racial and ethnic groups are undercounted for different reasons. Thus the undercount of black Americans appears to have somewhat different causes from that of Hispanics. For example, concern about losing program benefits seems to be most prevalent among blacks.[90] Among Hispanics and other immigrants, language and cultural barriers contribute to the undercount. Certainly, the cognitive problems discussed earlier add to the confusion that immigrants, especially Hispanics, experience when responding to the racial and ethnic questions.[91] But perhaps the most salient factor among Hispanics and immigrants generally is their extremely high residential mobility.[92] So, while we tend to talk of "the differential racial undercount" or merely of "the undercount," there seem to be different undercounts with distinctive dynamics.

Finally, this research challenges the very way we conceive of census undercounts. Implicitly or explicitly, the typical formulation is that "the census undercounted x percent" of a specific group. Yet in addition to highlighting the array of true challenges facing the census, these findings dramatize that an undetermined but clearly significant component of the undercount is traceable not simply to the bureau's failure to accomplish its mission, but to the duplicity and active resistance of individuals who do not want either to give the census accurate information or to be counted at all. There are a good number of individuals in the United States who, in the words of rock singer Sting, "don't ever want to play the part of a statistic on a government chart." In an individualistic society such as this, where many are jealous of intrusions into their privacy by the state (quite aside from any of the more specific calculations examined here), it is hardly fair or accurate to assign all responsibility for the undercount to the Census Bureau.[93] Nor under these circumstances is it prudent to regard the undercount as, in the words of the *New York Times* editorial page, a "national injustice."[94]

What Are Sampling and Adjustment?

Given the persistent, even growing differential racial undercount, various proposals have emerged to address the problem. Not all of these have necessarily involved statistical sampling and complex estimation procedures, but the most controversial certainly have. Thus the 1990 census was followed by a postenumeration survey (PES) whose results were, according to a court-supervised agreement, to be considered for adjusting the headcount. But in July 1991 Secretary of Commerce Robert Mosbacher decided against using the PES results for any such purpose.

Almost immediately, pressure began building to statistically adjust the 2000 census. For most of the 1990s the Census Bureau was planning an ambitious program that originally would have involved two sampling programs. The less visible was an unprecedented effort to use sampling to obtain information on the growing number of census nonrespondents. The standard practice in such cases has been to send out enumerators to households that failed to mail in their questionnaires. With some households receiving as many as six visits before the bureau gives up and imputes data from other sources, this intensive follow-up has been time-consuming, costly, and not always accurate. Accordingly, for 2000 the bureau proposed a truncated follow-up that would stop at some predetermined point, after which a sample survey of nonrespondents would be taken in order to draw inferences about the remaining nonrespondents.

This so-called sampling for nonresponse follow-up (SNRFU) has many variants. In February 1996 the Census Bureau proposed a SNRFU plan that would rely on traditional follow-up methods, with personal visits by enumerators to nonresponding households, *until* at least 90 percent of households in each county were tallied. At that point a one-in-ten random sample of the remaining nonresponding households would be taken. Data for the nonsampled households would then be estimated on the basis of that sample.[95]

Yet in the event, SNRFU was obviated by the January 1999 Supreme Court decision enjoining the Department of Commerce from using any form of statistical sampling to produce population counts for purposes of congressional apportionment.[96] Since the Court's decision meant that traditional follow-up had to be relied on for apportionment, it made no sense to undertake SNRFU for any other purpose.

Because the Court did not rule out census sampling for purposes other than apportionment, the second sampling program remains part of the 2000 census, albeit somewhat altered. Integrated coverage measurement (ICM) was intended to be a bigger, better version of 1990's PES. As its name suggests, ICM was originally designed to produce one set of census numbers into which had been built the sample-based adjustment results. Whereas the 1990 census culminated in two sets of census numbers—the traditional headcount and the adjusted numbers—ICM was to result in "the one-number census."

But in the wake of the Supreme Court's decision, the one-number census was abandoned by the Census Bureau. ICM has been scaled down to something much closer in size to the 1990 PES, which is now called the accuracy and coverage evaluation (ACE) survey. As with the 1990 census, there will be two sets of numbers issuing from the 2000 enumeration. First will be the results of the traditional headcount that will be reported to Congress by December 31, 2000, for the purpose of apportionment. Some months later a set of adjusted census numbers based on the ACE will be available. How and whether these will be used remains unresolved. What is clear is that there will be considerable controversy, as was the case after the 1990 census.

In the following exposition of the procedures developed to statistically adjust the census, it should be remembered that despite differences among the PES, ICM, and ACE, each is a variant of the same basic methodology. Because there is a wealth of information and research on the Census Bureau's experience with the PES in 1990, I necessarily focus on it in order to shed light on the as yet unrealized ACE.

At various points in this exposition, I emphasize that unadjusted as well as adjusted census data are subject to error. When it comes to the census, absolute accuracy or certainty is nowhere to be found. This important point becomes lost in the technical and scientific polemics over adjustment. As will be evident, adjustment proponents are prone to focus almost exclusively on the nonsampling error in the census, while critics focus on the nonsampling error in statistical efforts to improve the census. With a few exceptions, the two sides simply talk past one another. This nonexpert review of the technical aspects of sampling and adjustment aspires to overcome this aspect of the debate. Yet while striving to be fair, I do not pretend to be neutral. I believe the critics of adjustment have the better of the argument, even though at times they neglect the problems with the census that have brought us to this controversy.

The actual ACE survey will begin about eleven weeks after Census Day, April 1. Toward the end of June, specially trained enumerators will be sent out to a random sample of 10,000 census block groups drawn from the approximately 5 million inhabited blocks in the nation. Stratified to ensure that all relevant demographic groups are adequately covered, this sample will comprise about 300,000 housing units and 750,000 individuals.[97]

In 1990 this phase of the postcensus survey was followed by what is referred to as dual-system estimation (DSE). This is the process by which the results of the census are compared with those of the postcensus survey in order to deduce an estimate of the true count.

The first and most difficult step in DSE is matching the names and addresses gathered by the survey against those names and addresses gathered by the original census from the same sample blocks. For each person found in the survey, it is necessary to determine where the census reported that individual residing on census day, assuming the census found him or her.

Conversely, for each census record in the sampled block groups, it is necessary to determine whether each individual is in the survey. For the names and addresses that do not match up directly, an investigation must be undertaken. Was the person found by the census but missed by the survey because he or she moved out of the block group right after census day? Or did the survey simply miss the person? If a person is found by the survey but not by the census, is this because the census counted the person but put him or her at the wrong address, outside the correct block? Or perhaps there is a nonmatch because the census counted this person twice, because he sent in two forms? Or was this person an infant who was included in the census but was actually born right after census day?

There are four possible outcomes of this matching process: (1) the census and the survey correspond, a match; (2) the survey identifies an individual for whom no record can be found in the census, referred to as a gross omission; (3) the census identifies an individual not found by the survey, referred to as an erroneous enumeration; (4) an individual is missed by both the census and the survey. This last outcome is the most problematic. Of course, it should be no surprise that elusive individuals not found by the census also get missed by the survey. But the number of such "unreached individuals" is extremely difficult to estimate reliably, although a figure can be inferred from the results of the three other possible outcomes.[98]

Movers pose a particular challenge for DSE. Over a four-month period about 5 percent of the U.S. population moves, which is roughly three times the 1990 estimated undercount.[99] Yet people who change address between census day and the survey, several months later, cannot be matched unless they are so identified, which depends on getting accurate information from respondents or their neighbors on where they were living at census time.[100] Even when individuals cooperate with the census, they may not remember such details accurately. More to the point, cooperation, as noted, is most problematic among those populations whose transience is itself an important cause of their being undercounted.

Thus even when a match is made, which is to be sure fairly common, it is often only after considerable effort. Typically, searches of blocks nearby but not actually in the sample need to be conducted. If clerical as well as computer processing does not yield a match, enumerators are sent out into the field to reinterview specific households. Even then, there are unresolved cases, for which data may then have to be imputed on the basis of information gathered elsewhere.[101] None of these procedures is made easier by the obvious fact that data clearly get recorded incorrectly, both by the census and by the survey. Matching is further complicated because the census, for confidentiality reasons noted earlier, cannot collect unique identifiers such as social security numbers.[102]

As a result, at each of these junctures the possibility of error is substantial. Moreover, the relatively small numbers in any such sample survey means that the consequences of mistakes are magnified enormously in the final adjustment results. Thus in the 1990 PES one unmatched family of five contributed 45,000 to the final undercount estimate.[103]

Of course, it is also the case that many of these same problems plague conventional census enumeration. The passage of time certainly works against traditional follow-up efforts, by which enumerators are repeatedly sent out into the field to seek out nonrespondents. As one adjustment advocate has noted: "When you are knocking on doors in August in Harlem, asking who lived in that apartment on April 1 [Census Day], the likelihood of getting accurate information about that household is less and less and less as times go on."[104] Under these circumstances the information retrieved is often highly unreliable. So we are again reminded that census accuracy is nowhere easily attained.

The results of this matching process are then used to calculate the net undercount, which is approximately the difference between the numbers of gross omissions and erroneous enumerations. But this calculation is not done for the sample as a whole. Because the propensity to be undercounted varies across demographic groups, the Census Bureau calculates separate undercounts for many different, relatively homogeneous groups. In 1990 the Census Bureau identified 1,392 such groups: for example, Hispanic males, aged twenty to twenty-nine, living in owner-occupied housing in central cities in the states of California, Oregon, Washington, Alaska, and Hawaii.[105] The results of the matching process for each of the approximately 400,000 individuals in the PES sample were then assigned to one of these 1,392 groups, called poststrata because they were created after the original stratified sample of block groups was drawn.

The next step in the process was to compare the estimated true population count to the actual census count for each poststratum. This is the raw adjustment factor. For example, if the estimate for a particular poststratum is 1.05 million and the census count is 1 million, then the adjustment factor is 1.05, reflecting a 5 percent estimated net undercount. Because, as we have seen, the census counts some people more than once as well as misses others completely, this raw adjustment factor can either exceed 1 (indicating an undercount) or be less than 1 (indicating an overcount).[106] In either case, in 1990 these raw factors were then subjected to a series of complicated statistical manipulations, explored below, that produced final adjustment factors for each of the 1,392 poststrata.

Finally, these adjustment factors were reintegrated into the census at the block level. The original census total for each poststratum represented on a given block was multiplied by the appropriate adjustment factor. These results were then added up to produce an adjusted block total. Estimates for all larger areas—census tracts, voting districts, cities, counties, states—were then based on these adjusted block counts.[107]

Sampling Error and Its Problems

This adjustment methodology is subject to two broad types of problems: sampling error and nonsampling error. I will deal first with sampling error.

Like any survey, the PES attempts to represent the whole (the population) with a part (the sample). Simply on account of chance, any sample may be wide of the mark and may not be representative of the population from which it is drawn. Sampling error refers of course to the range of values that samples take on when drawn randomly from a population. But such random variation is something that statisticians are quite used to dealing with. They certainly have been rather confident with regard to the sampling error associated with the PES. Nevertheless, there are definite problems to be considered.

One concerns the small size of the PES. This may seem curious, since the PES is by most standards a huge random sample, including several hundred thousand individuals. Yet with approximately 400,000 individuals divided up among 1,392 poststrata, each one contains on average less than 300 people. With such small sample sizes, the raw adjustment factors calculated from them displayed significant sampling error.[108] Berkeley statisticians David Freedman and Kenneth Wachter report that in 1990 only about 13 percent of the poststrata had adjustment factors that differed from 1.00 (which value indicates no net undercount or overcount) by a statistically significant amount. They conclude: "In other words, at the poststratum level, the measured undercounts and overcounts are mainly noise."[109]

For example, the raw adjustment factors for twelve different age-sex poststrata of Asians living in New York City ranged from 1.51 for males twenty to twenty-nine years old to a low of 0.66 for females sixty-five and older. Such disparate results within one racial group struck even adjustment advocates as implausible and indicative of troublingly high sampling error.[110] With the PES sampling, for example, only ninety blocks in all of Los Angeles (out of more than 25,000), such sampling error could wreak havoc with the final adjustment figures.[111]

One means of dealing with such sampling error is a procedure known as "smoothing." Smoothing uses a multiple regression model, composed of variables correlated with being undercounted, to predict an undercount for each poststratum. This predicted value is then averaged with the raw adjustment factor to produce a final adjustment factor for each poststratum.[112]

In 1990 smoothing was used to reduce the wide swings in raw adjustment factors. But as with many such statistical models, the assumptions on which the smoothing model are based have been subsequently challenged by other statisticians for lack of justifiable rationales. Such critics also argue that the model is unstable, with small changes in procedures and assumptions producing very different results.[113] Indeed, they maintain that smoothing introduced new types of error into the very census data it was supposed to correct.[114]

An alternative to such complicated statistical manipulations to reduce sampling error might be to increase the sample sizes of the poststrata. This could be achieved by creating fewer poststrata, with commensurately more individuals in each of them. In 1990 this approach could have been pursued, for there was no technical reason why the Census Bureau had to create 1,392 poststrata. Yet there was an important *political* reason why it had to do so: a court-supervised agreement between parties to a suit over census adjustment stipulated that all procedures in a possible adjustment would be "prespecified."[115] This required the Census Bureau to decide on the number and type of poststrata it would create *before* it saw any 1990 census data. Faced with this constraint, the bureau created as many poststrata as believed necessary to produce reliable adjustment factors, knowing that it would not be possible to add any poststrata once the census was under way. It was under these conditions that the 1,392 poststrata were decided on and then etched in stone.[116]

In this connection, it is intriguing to note that once the secretary of commerce decided against adjustment in July 1991, the Census Bureau, no longer bound by the litigation's prespecification agreement, restratified the original sample and came up with only 357 poststrata. With the size of each poststratum much larger, the raw adjustment factors had much less sampling error, and smoothing was deemed unnecessary.[117] Of course, by then adjustment of the 1990 data was moot.

One other way of dealing with such sampling error would be simply to expand the size of the overall postcensus survey. This was in fact the Census Bureau's goal for census 2000's ICM, originally designed to increase the size of the 1990 PES by a factor of four, with a sample of 750,000 housing units and 1.7 million individuals.[118] Of course, this option has the liability of increasing the cost of census adjustment. Moreover, as surveys increase in size, they are more difficult to manage administratively and to process statistically. Under ever-present money and time constraints, this means that the likelihood of errors also increases with the size of the postcensus survey.[119]

Nonsampling Error

Such issues bring us to nonsampling error. In the ongoing controversy over adjustment, sampling error has tended to get most of the attention. No doubt this is in part because sampling error is what statisticians are more comfortable dealing with. Yet when it comes to postcensus surveys such as the PES and ACE, nonsampling error actually looks to be a much bigger problem.[120] Nonsampling error may not only have a larger overall impact on adjusted census totals, but it is also much harder for statisticians to control or even measure.

One obvious type of nonsampling error is processing error, precisely the kind of error to which the matching component of dual-system estimation is prone.[121] An example is the computer coding error that added 1 million people to the 1991 undercount estimate. This was the result of a complicated mismatching of individuals who had moved into PES-sampled blocks after census day.[122] Involving only 2 out of 5,290 block clusters, this single error was not picked up by the bureau's usual evaluation studies and went undiscovered for more than a year.[123]

The usual assumption is that specially trained postcensus enumerators do not make mistakes. But they do, for example, when they get confused by which of two homes owned by a family is its principal residence; or when they confront the complicated household arrangements among the poor and immigrants highlighted earlier in this chapter. Moreover, postcensus enumerators encounter the same lack of cooperation and resistance among the hard-to-count as do ordinary enumerators.

Then, too, not all such processing error is the result of mistakes. Again like conventional census enumerators, postcensus personnel can and do falsify data to make things easier for themselves. During the 1990 PES in Atlanta and Denver, falsifications increased when those cities experienced severe heat waves.[124]

Such problems are only exacerbated by the time pressures under which a postcensus survey is executed. On the one hand, it cannot be launched until the actual census has been substantially completed. Yet to minimize the error that comes with the passage of time, the survey has to be under way as soon as possible and completed so that adjusted data are available to policymakers in a timely manner. The consequences of the inevitable processing errors that arise under such conditions are greatly magnified by the logic of sampling, which relies on small numbers to make inferences about large populations. So, as we have seen, even relatively small errors at the sample stage translate into huge errors in estimated net undercount.

One final and important consideration is that because the undercount is relatively small, so, too, are the proposed adjustments. But this in turn means that adjusted census numbers can be overwhelmed by nonsampling error. Indeed, adjustment programs actually introduce substantial new error into the census results they are intended to improve. The Census Bureau itself estimates that about 45 percent of its revised (1992) undercount estimate (of 1.58 percent) is such processing error.[125] David Freedman suggests that between 60 and 80 percent of the estimated undercount in 1990 was processing error![126] Though experts clearly disagree over exactly how much such error was introduced by the 1990 PES, there is no disagreement that it was substantial.

Postcensus surveys such as the PES and ACE suffer from other types of non-sampling error that are even more difficult to assess than processing error. To examine these, it is necessary to scrutinize the very assumptions underlying the dual-system estimation methodology. The basic idea of doing a conventional census and then following it with a massive survey draws on a technique known as capture-recapture, which has been used for more than a century to estimate wildlife populations.[127] Yet as will be seen presently, assumptions drawn from wildlife research do not necessarily translate to human population issues.

Let us begin by looking at how capture-recapture works in the wild. To estimate the number of fish in a pond, we would start by catching some fish, tagging them for identification, and then releasing them. After waiting enough time to ensure that the tagged fish mixed with the other fish in the pond, we would catch a second lot of fish and count the number with identification tags. Because the fraction of tagged fish in the second catch would estimate the fraction of the whole population caught the first time, we could then deduce an estimate of the total fish population in the pond.

This procedure clearly rests on certain assumptions: (1) one must be able to count the first catch perfectly; (2) the number of the fish in the pond must be constant between catches; (3) the marks on the fish must be indelible and impossible to misread; (4) all the fish must have the same propensity to be caught; (5) the fish must mix randomly between catches—in other words, the second catch must be a random sample of the fish in the pond and not affected by the first catch.[128]

The parallels between this example and sample-based census adjustment should be evident. The actual census is the first catch, the postcensus survey the second. And the same logic is necessary to deduce the estimated population total from these two "samples."

Nevertheless, problems arise with regard to the critical assumptions underlying the capture-recapture method. As noted earlier, the census has "erroneous enumerations," which violate the first assumption. The second assumption is undermined by the significant population movements between census day and the postcensus survey, which have also been noted. And the third assumption, that people can be "marked"—even with a social security number—in order to minimize confusion about who was missed by the census or the survey is not something our society is willing to tolerate.

As for the fourth assumption, it should be clear by now that all people definitely do not exhibit the same propensity to be "caught." As we saw earlier in this chapter, some individuals deliberately avoid the census as well as special ethnographic enumerators. We have no reason to believe that they would not avoid postcensus enumerators as well.

One way that statisticians address this problem is by creating poststrata, which, it will be recalled, are intended to be relatively homogeneous groups of individuals by sex, age, geographic residence, race/ethnicity, and other key variables. More specifically, the individuals in each poststratum are assumed to be homogeneous with respect to their propensity to be undercounted. Indeed, this is referred to as "the homogeneity assumption."

Yet this assumption also proves to be problematic. Several statisticians argue that in 1990 the poststrata displayed considerable heterogeneity, which in turn biased the adjustment results. A particular point of contention has been that these poststrata were constructed by pooling individuals of specified age, sex, and race/ethnicity from across wide geographic areas on the assumption that all the individuals in each poststratum had the same probability of being undercounted. To take the same example cited earlier (Hispanic males aged twenty to twenty-nine, living in owner-occupied housing in central cities in California, Oregon, Washington, Alaska, and Hawaii), it is not at all clear that such young Hispanic males in Seattle are equally likely to be undercounted as their counterparts in Honolulu.[129]

But how much did failure of the homogeneity assumption actually contribute to error in the 1990 adjusted census figures? Answers to this question are not easy to come by. Adjustment critics argue that the Census Bureau seriously underestimated the impact of heterogeneity on the accuracy of its adjusted numbers.[130] Other statisticians appear less troubled. Yet even the Census Bureau describes itself as "concerned" about the validity of the homogeneity assumption for the 1990 adjustment.[131] Director Barbara Bryant, who in 1991 publicly opposed her superiors at the Commerce Department and advocated adjustment, has noted: "It is possible that errors due to heterogeneity in fact could be larger than all other sources of error in the adjustment."[132]

One more type of nonsampling error that appears to affect adjustment results is "correlation bias." This arises because some persons are missed by both the postcensus survey and the census. Dual-system estimation anticipates this problem and produces an estimate of those missed by both efforts—under the assumption that there is no correlation between the two events. But when this assumption is violated and these misses *are* corre-

Table 4-4. *Net Undercounts by Race and Sex, according to the Postenumeration Survey (PES) and Demographic Analysis (DA), 1990*

	Postenumeration survey	Demographic analysis	Difference: PES – DA
Blacks			
Males	804,000	1,338,000	– 534,000
Females	716,000	498,000	+ 218,000
Nonblacks			
Males	2,205,000	2,142,000	+ 63,000
Females	1,544,000	706,000	+ 838,000

Source: Lawrence D. Brown and others, *Statistical Controversies in Census 2000*, University of California at Berkeley, Department of Statistics Technical Report 537 (April 30, 1999), p. 12.

lated, then the result is correlation bias and the number of such missed individuals is systematically underestimated. Statisticians refer to these as "unreached people," and they are analogous to what wildlife researchers call "wily trout," the ones that really got away. Unreached by both the census and the postcensus survey, such individuals are completely unaccounted for in adjustment data.[133]

In the opinion of various statisticians, including those serving on the Census Bureau's Committee on Adjustment of Postcensal Estimates, correlation bias was a problem for the 1990 adjustment process.[134] The PES apparently missed many of the same people as the census. Presumably, this was because the same people who were not counted in the census avoided the PES, or continued to reside in the same hard-to-find places, or maintained the same confusing, nontraditional households.

Yet by its very nature, correlation bias is difficult to measure. How do we determine how many individuals we have been unable to find? One means is demographic analysis (DA), which provides independent, though not definitive, evidence of the extent of correlation bias in the 1990 PES. Table 4-4 compares net undercounts for specified sex and race categories estimated by the PES and by DA. Because DA relies on administrative records, it is not subject to correlation bias, and at the national level at least, its results are assumed to be more accurate than those of the PES. Accordingly, table 4-4 indicates that while the 1990 PES overadjusted for black females, it actually underadjusted for black males—534,000 fewer of whom were captured by the PES than by DA.[135]

Again, because of the difficulty of determining the number of unreached people, we cannot be certain that these discrepancies between the PES and DA result from correlation bias. Yet several statisticians certainly believe this to be the case. Moreover, they point to the surprising effects PES-based adjustments would have had on critical states (if the secretary of commerce had decided to use them). Adjustment would have in fact reduced the population shares (the percentage of the total U.S. population) of Pennsylvania, Ohio, Massachusetts, Michigan, Illinois, New Jersey, and New York. And it would have increased the shares of California, Texas, Florida, Arizona, and New Mexico. To statisticians Freedman and Wachter, these results indicate that the unreached were probably concentrated in the big cities of the Northeast and Midwest and that correlation bias almost certainly resulted from the PES doing a better job finding Hispanic males in the urban areas of the Southwest than black males in the ghettoes of the North.[136]

Uncertainty—and Disagreement

There are several points to be drawn from this exposition of the technical aspects of census adjustment. Perhaps the most salient, to quote demographer Nathan Keyfitz, is that adjustment is "a gamble." Although Keyfitz was specifically remarking here on the randomness of sampling error, his point is obviously true more generally.[137] The outcomes of census adjustment are simply difficult if not impossible to predict. This is due not only, or even primarily, to sampling error but to the various biases introduced by nonsampling error, including the capture-recapture assumptions that are violated.

Nor is it just laymen who are surprised by these outcomes. As former census director Bryant points out, the experts anticipated that in 1990 DA would show a higher undercount than the PES, in great part because DA does not get ensnarled in correlation bias and unreached people. Yet DA actually came up with a *lower* net undercount estimate (1.8 percent) than the PES (2.08 percent). The subsequent discovery of errors in the PES led to a downward revision in its estimate (to 1.58 percent), which put it lower than DA's estimate and therefore in line with expectations.[138] As will be explored in chapter 5, this unpredictability of census outcomes—with or without adjustment—has important political implications.

The second point is that census adjustment involves much more than just sampling. Too often the ongoing debate has been characterized as between the enlightened proponents and benighted opponents of "scientific sampling."[139] To be sure, there is a science of statistical sampling, and it obviously figures in the adjustment process. Yet the process also relies on dual-system estimation, a methodology that involves elaborate, error-prone matching procedures and statistical manipulations that have nothing to do with what is commonly understood as sampling. Those procedures certainly do not partake of the reliability and objectivity suggested by the phrase "scientific sampling." Political scientist Thomas Brunell puts it well: "The problem with the census adjustment process is not conducting a survey of 780,000 people; the Bureau is well equipped to conduct large-scale surveys. Rather, the problem is matching these 780,000 records with the correct records from the first phase of the census."[140] Undoubtedly this is why the principal opponents of adjusting the 1990 census within the bureau were not the statisticians but those responsible for the operational side.[141]

Moreover, adjustment does not rely on any ordinary form of sampling. Typically, sampling is used to draw inferences about average properties of the whole from its parts. But this is not the case with sampling for census adjustment. As the term "dual-system estimation" indicates, there are two samples: the original census and then the postcensus survey. For statistician Stephen Fienberg this means that "two sources of information [are used] to arrive at a better estimate of the population than could be obtained from one source alone."[142] But as statistician Lawrence Brown observes: "Ordinarily, samples are used to extrapolate upwards, from the part to the whole. Census adjustment extrapolates sideways, from 60,000 sample blocks to each and every one of 5 million inhabited blocks in the U.S."[143] Of course, statisticians are hardly daunted by this aspect of dual-system estimation. Indeed, they have risen to the challenge and developed numerous techniques to perfect it. But as noted, these techniques rely on various constraining assumptions and statistical models that are challenged by other statisticians. These complexities sharply distinguish census adjustment from the routine sampling familiar to many Americans.

A related point is that despite the connotation of phrases such as "statistical adjustment," this is not some precisely controlled test-tube procedure performed by white-coated technicians in a laboratory. Adjustment advocates argue that because postcensus surveys are smaller than an actual census, they can be more carefully planned and executed. It is true, for example, that postcensus enumerators can be particularly well trained, supervised, and evaluated.[144] Nevertheless, we should not lose sight of the fact that statistical adjustment relies ultimately on human beings prone to the same failings and facing the same obstacles as ordinary census enumerators. As pro-adjustment statisticians Thomas Belin and John Rolph point out: "Both census and PES enumerators can fabricate the existence of people, and both sets of interviewers miss residents."[145] In light of the evidence reviewed above, this seems a reasonable caveat.

But beyond these considerations, other analysts emphasize that adjustment of the census involves complicated logistical and statistical procedures that are error-prone even when not subject to severe time pressures. To mount a postcensus survey while trying to finish the actual census and then to report the results in time for apportionment at the end of that same calendar year turns out to be a massive challenge. This is why some argue that adjustment is at least as complex an undertaking as a conventional head-count, if not more so.[146]

A final point is simply that statisticians do not agree about census adjustment. Writing in *Statistical Science,* Belin and Rolph conclude: "We are far from sure that consensus is attainable on census adjustment."[147] This lack of consensus transcends the immediate issue and reflects an ongoing, fundamental disagreement among statisticians over the policy uses to which sophisticated, assumption-driven statistical models can be put.[148]

Yet this split among statisticians has been obscured in the continuing public controversy over adjustment. There has been a tendency among some adjustment advocates and certainly among the media to portray census adjustment as a matter on which the experts agree. *New York Times* reporter Steven Holmes recently wrote: "Statisticians say sampling is much more accurate than traditional means."[149] Yet not all statisticians say this. A more accurate assessment of the state of scientific opinion on adjustment has been offered by Robert Fay, a Census Bureau statistician who supported adjustment in 1991: "I told the Secretary [of Commerce] that . . . reasonable statisticians could differ on this conclusion."[150] But then in a 1996 report, the Census Bureau itself boldly and misleadingly claimed: "Statisticians agree that incorporating widely-accepted scientific statistical methods into Census 2000 will produce a better census at less cost."[151]

To be sure, a consensus in favor of adjustment has developed among those statisticians working under the aegis of the National Academy of Sciences (NAS). Since 1990 three different panels (not all of whose members were statisticians or even social scientists) convened by the NAS have studied and then approved of the Census Bureau's plans to statistically adjust the 2000 census.[152] Not surprisingly, the bureau has advertised this fact whenever and wherever possible, reporting to Congress in 1997 that one of those panels "concluded that scientific sampling was not just *a* solution to the cost and accuracy problems, it was the *only* solution."[153] Yet neither the bureau, adjustment advocates, nor the media have pointed out that other statisticians strenuously oppose adjustment.

During this period a consensus in favor of adjustment has developed among policy experts working on census issues. Again, this consensus has been afforded much attention by the Census Bureau, adjustment advocates, and the media. And again, this consensus has obscured fundamental disagreements about adjustment among statisticians. There is a subtle but crucial distinction between "expert consensus" and "scientific consensus." As Marc Landy and Martin Levin point out about policy disputes over technical and scientific issues:

> The existence of such [expert] consensus should not be taken to imply that the merits of these and other expert-endorsed reforms are unassailable. The achievement of consensus within the relevant reform professional community is not the same as 'scientific' consensus. It is less an intellectual than a political and cultural phenomenon.[154]

It is precisely such a politically and culturally shaped *expert* consensus—not a *scientific* consensus—that has emerged in favor of adjustment.

What Is Error? What Is Accuracy?

Scientists disagree about census adjustment in part because it involves practical judgments that do not depend fundamentally on any scientific training or expertise. Such disagreement can certainly be entwined with technical or scientific issues that do draw on specialized knowledge. Yet the resolution of such disagreement ultimately lies outside the expertise of statisticians themselves.

Nor is it always clear what these scientists are disagreeing about. An important source of confusion is how "error" is defined. As noted earlier, there is a tendency among statisticians generally, but especially among those favoring adjustment, to focus on sampling error. Yet as also noted, nonsampling error is arguably of much greater significance in the adjustment process.

There is a critical difference between sampling and nonsampling error. Because it is random, sampling error tends to cancel or average itself out over large aggregations of data. Nonsampling error does not behave this way. Because it is not random, nonsampling error is referred to as systematic error, or bias. Statistician P. B. Stark describes the difference in the context of adjustment:

> Estimating from a sample is like shooting a rifle. Each shot hits the target in a different place. Sampling error is the scatter in the shots.

> Bias is a tendency for all the shots to be off in the same direction. One can fix bias in a rifle by sighting it in. That is possible, because one can see where the shots land. Fixing statistical bias in a census adjustment is hard: there is only one shot, because there is only one sample, and the bullseye [sic] is not visible, because the true undercount is unknown.[155]

Nonsampling error is *not* self-correcting, and its effects are compounded over repeated trials. That is why, when adjustment advocates address "error" in the adjustment process, they tend to focus on sampling error; and why critics focus on nonsampling error.[156]

Similarly, the term "accuracy" is used in different ways by the various participants in the adjustment controversy. More specifically, the disputants have different levels of aggregation—census blocks, municipalities, states, the nation—in mind when they talk about the accuracy of adjustment. Virtually all statisticians agree that at the block level adjustment involves substantial sampling error, simply because at that level sample sizes are very small. Statisticians also agree that such block-level error, as noted above, cancels out at higher levels of aggregation. But there the agreement ends. Adjustment advocates focus on accuracy at those higher levels of aggregation. As Stephen Fienberg writes: "It is not the accuracy of the block level data that matters but rather the accuracy of the aggregates of large numbers of blocks that make up voting districts."[157]

Such comments are true as far as they go, but they do not address the nonsampling error that looms so large for adjustment critics. Nor do they address the concerns of analysts unconvinced that the consequences of sampling error can be so easily dismissed.[158] In this vein former director Bryant has acknowledged concerns expressed by the bureau's redistricting specialist that block-level sampling error would have caused "disruption" to the 1990 redistricting.[159]

Upon closer scrutiny, adjustment of the 1990 census would not necessarily have been more accurate even at levels of aggregation much higher than census blocks. The Census Bureau acknowledges that adjustment would have left eleven states with less accurate shares of the national population.[160] Bryant had this to say in her recommendation *in favor* of adjustment: "Adjustment, while improving counts for a majority of states and communities, may not improve the count for every community; it may even reduce accuracy for some. There are places where the count, as enumerated, is closer to the truth."[161] In response to such confusing hedging over which levels of aggregation would be more accurate under adjustment, Belin and Roth declare:

> If the choice of a level of aggregation at which to evaluate census numbers is not decided in advance, it will be extremely difficult not only to build consensus around a particular set of census numbers but to even design an undercount evaluation program like the 1990 PES that would be broadly acceptable.[162]

Yet disagreements over adjustment are not always quibbles over which level of aggregation produces the most accurate results. When pressed, adjustment advocates acknowledge the problems identified here, including the daunting implications of nonsampling error. Their considered response is that adjustment would not improve accuracy in all jurisdictions but would do so on average, in most cases. As the bureau's Undercount Steering Committee made the case: "The majority [of the nine member committee] judges that the improvement in counts *on the average* for Nation, States, and places over 100,000 population outweighs the risk that the accuracy of adjusted counts might be less for small areas" (emphasis added).[163] Or as Fienberg observes: "The dual-systems estimates move the raw counts in the correct direction."[164]

In one very important sense, these references to adjustment doing better on average or getting closer to the truth are highly misleading. The real concern of adjustment advocates after all is to improve results for a few specific groups. This concern is no secret, but it does become obscured in the technical justifications for adjustment advanced by statisticians.

Consider the rationale for adjusting the 1990 census articulated by Rolph:

> The Bureau's analysis clearly demonstrated that the adjusted counts were an unambiguous improvement on the original enumeration. Put another way, even if it is difficult to choose between several different versions of an adjustment, and any one of these adjustments will move the counts closer to the truth, that is no basis for preferring the original enumeration. Making some correction is clearly superior to doing nothing.[165]

In this clear formulation we see the essence of the statisticians' disagreement over adjustment. Rolph and other adjusters focus on getting closer to "the truth," which is defined (not always explicitly) in terms of improving the undercount of minorities. Yet this ignores the issue most saliently raised by their critics within the statistical profession: namely, that because adjustment results are not robust and therefore significantly affected by whatever assumptions are invoked, science is not driving the process. In other words, there is no *scientific* means of deciding which set of "better" adjusted numbers should be chosen. Moreover, each set of these numbers produces different winners and losers, making any choice among them necessarily political. Rolph and his colleagues not only sidestep basic issues of fairness to those who lose under various adjustment scenarios, they also (as explored in chapter 5) overlook that sooner or later adjustment would require choices to be made *among* minorities, whose interests do not always coincide. And if the criterion is simply benefiting "minorities," there will be no firm ground on which to choose among conflicting minority interests.

Statisticians favoring adjustment often caution skeptical colleagues against being finicky and, as renowned statistician John Tukey puts it, letting "the best be the enemy of the good."[166] But as the passage from Rolph highlights, there would be many "goods" here among which to choose. And because the choice would be inherently political, it is not one for which statisticians have any particular expertise.[167]

Counts or Shares? Races or Places?

There are other political choices lurking in the technical aspects of adjustment. The first has to do with whether census accuracy is defined in terms of absolute population *counts* or relative *shares* of total population. The discerning observer will have noted that the debate over adjustment oscillates (usually unannounced) between both measures. Since the census is involved with the distribution of resources and benefits that tend to be fixed, population shares are generally considered to be the more relevant measure of accuracy.[168] Nevertheless, the adjustment debate still becomes bogged down in absolute counts. This is in part because these have a certain threshold value, especially for aspiring cities. But it is also because adjustment, though it makes overall counts more accurate, tends to make shares less so. Thus adjustment advocates find it convenient at times to focus on counts rather than shares.

The second set of political choices embedded in the adjustment process concerns how census accuracy is defined in relation to geographic places or to demographic groups, especially racial and ethnic minorities. Once again, the careful observer will have noted that the debate slips back and forth between analyses of data on cities, counties, or states and of data on blacks or Hispanics.

Since adjustment has been driven by concern over the differential racial undercount, it is not surprising that the focus has been on accuracy in relation to minority groups. Yet since census data are used to apportion funds and representation among geographically defined districts, there has also been a tendency to focus on accuracy in relation to jurisdictions.

Whether one focuses on "races or places," in Wachter's formulation, turns out to have enormous implications for how one evaluates census adjustment.[169] For example, assuming that adjustment adds otherwise uncounted minorities to the census, it would improve overall minority counts. But if those additional individuals were assigned to the wrong places (because, as noted earlier, the census is not just about numbers of individuals in the abstract but in relation to temporal, social, and geographical boundaries), then adjustment would cause the counts of jurisdictions to be less accurate.[170]

This appears to be what the 1990 adjusted census numbers would have done if actually implemented. Or such is the thrust of Wachter's critique, which finds that while adjustment would have undeniably increased the shares of undercounted minorities, it would also have suspiciously reduced the shares of states expected to gain under adjustment. Relying on Wachter and Freedman's analyses of the evidence, Secretary of Commerce Mosbacher decided against adjustment in 1991 in part because it would have, in his opinion, improved census accuracy in relation to minority groups at the expense of reducing accuracy in relation to geographic places.[171]

Mosbacher's focus on place-oriented outcomes reflects the innate bias of a political system based on the representation of geographically defined jurisdictions.[172] Because they are elected from districts, politicians tend to think of census results, whether adjusted or unadjusted, in terms of places, especially their own districts. Naturally, Secretary Mosbacher would have been attuned to such concerns. And just as naturally, such concerns about place outcomes would be less salient to statisticians caught up in the adjustment controversy.

This insight about the likely perspective of politicians is important but can nevertheless be pushed too far. After all, many elected officials are in favor of adjustment. And geography has never been the only dimension along which interests have been defined in our political system; pressure groups have certainly been an alternative means of defining interests in which geography may not figure importantly, if at all.[173] More to the point, in recent decades race-conscious initiatives such as affirmative action and the Voting Rights Act have led to increased emphasis on the representation of minority group interests abstracted from geographic place. In such a regime it is hardly irrational for minority leaders to focus on group shares over place shares of the census count.

Granted, group shares are typically defined within the context of some jurisdiction. In day-to-day politics, races and places are not so easily abstracted from one another, as will be evident in chapter 5. Not surprisingly, many minority elected officials keep one eye on their group's share and the other on the relevant geographic shares of the count. But not all minority leaders are elected officials from districts; nor are geographic shares the only way of defining minority interests.

Thus, defining error or accuracy is not as obvious or as straightforward as *any* of the participants in the undercount debate would have it. To quote one Capitol Hill staffer: "If you are a minority, does it help you if adjustment results in New York City gaining population, but New York State loses and its Congressional delegation gets smaller?" An important part of the political battle over the census is fought over which frames of reference are going to be relied on: counts or shares, races or places. It cannot be emphasized too strongly that these are *political* choices that are far too often misrepresented as technical or scientific in nature.

CHAPTER FIVE

The Politics of Census Adjustment

By now there should be no doubt that the differential racial undercount is real. Nevertheless, the implications of the undercount, and of adjusting it, have been misunderstood, in fact exaggerated. While the various participants in this continuing controversy argue as though their interests were clear-cut and substantial, a careful review of the evidence reveals those interests to be ambiguous and even minimal. Moreover, these interests are highly contingent and thus hard to predict.

This critique pertains both to the fiscal implications of the undercount and to its political implications for apportionment and redistricting. For example, when a member of Congress from Georgia argued that adjustment of the 1990 census would mean an additional $18 million per year in federal funds for his state, he was dead wrong: Georgia would almost certainly have lost funding on account of adjustment. The mayor of Denver was also wrong when he insisted that his city would gain $350 annually for each person added by adjustment of the 1990 census. A much better, though still probably high, estimate would have been $56 annually for each uncounted person.[1]

Similarly misunderstood are the partisan stakes. When journalist T. R. Reid points to "a basic fact of demographic life: undercounts hurt Democrats more than Republicans," he too is mistaken.[2]

If this analysis is correct, then what is driving the controversy? Are the participants—the Census Bureau itself, Republican Party leaders, their Democratic counterparts, minorities, local elected officials—deceiving themselves? Or are they simply misinformed? Both explanations have some merit, but here the emphasis is on other factors: first, that the controversy is in part rooted in the lack of any standards by which to gauge the extent of the undercount; second, that the participants are responding to specific incentives that are not always evident from a distance.

I also argue that while the implications of the undercount have been overblown, the risks of adjustment have been underestimated.[3] Specifically, adjustment is likely to discourage participation in the census and thus to contribute to public cynicism toward still another facet of government.

Finally, I scrutinize the assumption that persistently undergirds the argument for census adjustment: that the census can and should be, in the words of a *New York Times* editorialist, "a politically neutral government task."[4] This view rests on two pillars, both of which have been briefly mentioned: science and rights. Americans have long relied on both to get around the untidiness of politics.[5] But when it comes to the census, the invocation of rights claims and appeals to the authority of science are particularly wrongheaded.

Fiscal Implications of the Undercount

The debate over the undercount has focused on specific contexts where it seems to have significant effects. Among these, the fiscal implications are the most straightforward and widely noted. But even these are not what they appear to be.

To be sure, census data are critical in the allocation of substantial sums of federal dollars. In fiscal year 1998, for example, federal grant programs relying on census population data totaled $185 billion. In 1999 the General Accounting Office (GAO) analyzed fifteen such programs, which together account for about four-fifths of this dollar total. The GAO concluded that using adjusted 1990 population counts would have reallocated among the fifty states and the District of Columbia $449 million, which represents only 0.33 percent of the funds apportioned by the grant formulas of these fifteen programs.[6]

This is merely the latest in a series of similar findings that stretch out over two decades of such research by the GAO and other investigators. Earlier in the decade, for example, the Schultze panel of the National Acad-

emy of Sciences (NAS) cited research that in 1989 the total federal allocation for grants involving census population counts was $58.7 billion, or
about $236 per capita to state and local governments. Yet this did not mean
that census adjustment would have afforded those jurisdictions an additional $236 for each uncounted individual.[7] Rather, the NAS Schultze panel
emphasized that the overall amount per net uncounted person (among
those jurisdictions gaining funds from adjustment) would have been about
$56. At most, 40 percent of local and state jurisdictions would have gained
because of adjustment. Other jurisdictions with modest undercounts would
not have gained additional federal grant funds. Many other jurisdictions
would have lost funding. Thus the overall effect would have been relatively
modest: if the 1990 census had been adjusted, $190 million (0.32 percent)
of that $58.7 billion annual allocation would have shifted.[8] As the author
of this study concluded: "Contrary to the expectations of many government officials, I find that adjustment would decrease federal disbursements
to most jurisdictions; even the jurisdictions receiving increases would benefit less than is commonly believed."[9]

About the same time that these findings were published, a similar though
less ambitious study by the GAO reported that adjustment of the 1990 census would have redistributed among the states less than half of 1 percent
of the total funding for three key programs.[10] Earlier studies reported similarly small fiscal effects from the undercount and adjustment.[11]

How are such findings to be explained? One must begin by pointing to
the convoluted interaction of population data with complicated grant formulas. As a knowledgeable Commerce Department official has noted: "The
complexity of the formula issue is incredible. . . . People are always talking
as if population determines how much federal aid they're going to get without knowing how the formulas work. Usually, they're wrong."[12]

Because population is only one of several factors in most federal grant
formulas, increases in population do not necessarily result in commensu-
rate increases in funding. For example, Highway Construction and Planning Grants, the largest nonentitlement grant program, allocated $22.6
billion to states in 1998. But only $1.7 billion, or 8 percent, was appor-
tioned on the basis of census data.[13] A major program, Community Development Block Grants (CDBG), designed to aid distressed communities,
actually reduces funding when a jurisdiction experiences population
growth.[14] Other things being equal, most programs increase grants in
response to a population increase. But as discussed earlier, the critical factor for a given jurisdiction is not absolute population gain, but gain in rela-

tion to other jurisdictions: its share of the total population. This means that an absolute population increase from adjustment could leave a jurisdiction worse off than before. Yet even changes in population shares, up or down, are not necessarily reflected in grant amounts, because of the ceilings and floors that are typically built into program formulas. Many programs have "hold-harmless" provisions ensuring that states and localities will receive at least as much funding as previously.[15] Finally, funding for federal grant programs is typically fixed. Census adjustment would consequently mean more people among whom to divide up a fixed pie. In other words, adjustment would result in an overall per capita reduction in federal formula grants.

Of course, undercount effects are often concentrated in particular jurisdictions. In the 1999 GAO study just highlighted, four states (California, Texas, Arizona, and New Mexico) account for more than a third of the adjusted population and would receive 75 percent of the funds reallocated under an adjustment. California alone accounts for 20 percent of the adjusted population and would receive nearly half of the reallocated funds, $223 million in 1998.[16]

Now $223 million annually is not an insignificant amount of money. Yet this sum represents only 1.62 percent of the total $13.7 billion California received in fiscal year 1998 from the fifteen federal programs analyzed by the GAO.[17] Moreover, this $223 million represents an even smaller proportion of California's annual budget, approximately 0.22 percent of the $100.2 billion spent in 1998.[18]

The program managers and clients who feel the direct impact of such fiscal shifts undoubtedly do not regard these as negligible sums, especially if specific programs are disproportionately affected. And as it happens, 90 percent of all reallocated funds across the nation would be in one program, Medicaid.[19] Thus adjustment would have afforded California an additional $198 million annually in Medicaid funds. Yet even this figure represents only 2.33 percent of California's total federal Medicaid allotment of $8.48 billion (and just 0.20 percent of the state's annual budget).[20]

One limitation of this GAO study is that it focuses on programs like Medicaid that apportion federal grants among the states. Not included in its analysis is the small but visible number of programs that make grants directly to local governments. Because the variation in undercounts is greater among the myriad local jurisdictions than among the fifty states, adjustment would probably have greater impact on the former.

Yet once again, these effects are not large, certainly not as large as the political rhetoric would indicate. The most authoritative study, cited by the NAS Schultze panel, concluded that "census adjustment [of 1990 data] will not alter appreciably the distribution of federal transfers to state and local governments."[21] Focusing on CDBG (the most visible such federal program at the local level and the one most sensitive to adjustment), this research reported that the percentage of total CDBG funds reallocated because of adjustment would have been small—0.97 percent, or $21.3 million annually. Among jurisdictions gaining from adjustment, the average CDBG increase would have been $13.47 per miscounted person per year. Other jurisdictions would have experienced CDBG decreases, but 90 percent of all gains or losses would have been small, within a range of plus or minus 4.5 percent.[22]

New York Times economics writer Peter Passell relied on this research to estimate the overall gain to New York City from an adjustment of the 1990 census. He came up with an annual figure of $10 million. One might quibble with this number, but it is probably on target. The more important point is Passell's conclusion that this was "a nice piece of change, surely, but hardly enough to dent the city's budget for filling potholes."[23]

An earlier (1982) study by Arthur Maurice and Richard Nathan came to a similar conclusion. Examining an array of locally targeted federal grant programs, including CDBG, they reported that for a handful of large cities adjustment could mean as much as an additional $20 per uncounted person annually. But "for the majority of cities, the total change in allocation resulting from an undercount adjustment of population is in the range of plus or minus $5 per uncounted person."[24] Indeed, Maurice and Nathan were at pains to point out that such adjustment effects were dramatically lower than the $200 per uncounted person that the New York City planning office had been citing: "An adjustment of census population figures for the undercount in the decennial census, contrary to what some have suggested, would not dramatically affect federal grant allocations to cities."[25]

Census adjustment would also have impacts within states—for example, on the funding that municipalities and counties receive from their own state governments. And because adjustment-induced population changes would be more volatile for smaller geographic areas, such intrastate impacts could be significant. Yet there is virtually no systematic evidence on this question.[26] My research suggests, however, that states exercise an option that the federal government does not: they routinely alter grant formulas to make allowances for undercounts and other problems. My research also indicates that whatever the intrastate effects of the undercount, exaggerated claims are again the order of the day.

In sum, there is virtual unanimity among researchers that the fiscal impacts of the undercount, though not insignificant, are relatively minimal. Knowledgeable analysts understand this. The interesting question, to be taken up later in this chapter, is why these well-known research findings are not reflected in the political debate.

These fiscal stakes are not only comparatively small but also extremely contingent and hard to predict. So too are the underlying population changes. This emerged most clearly when the Census Bureau published proposed (but never implemented) adjustments to the 1990 count. According to former census director Barbara Bryant, the players and interests in census adjustment changed in the spring of 1991, when those adjusted data were published.[27]

The adjusted numbers simply did not work out as anticipated. Specifically, many of the northeastern and midwestern states that had been assumed to suffer from the undercount actually lost ground. As table 5-1 illustrates, states such as California, Texas, Florida, Georgia, and Arizona had their population shares increased by adjustment. But states such as Pennsylvania, Ohio, Massachusetts, Michigan, Wisconsin, New York, Illinois, and New Jersey lost population shares, even though adjustment would have afforded them absolute population gains. One of the many ironies was that New York and New Jersey were among the plaintiffs in the then pending lawsuit seeking to force the Census Bureau to adjust! After these 1991 figures were published and it became evident that adjustment would cost Wisconsin a congressional seat, Senator Herbert Kohl, the Wisconsin Democrat who chaired the subcommittee overseeing the census, came out against adjustment. On the other hand, Republicans Newt Gingrich and Pete Wilson both supported adjustment, which would have afforded California one additional congressional seat and prevented Georgia from losing one.[28]

The complications and anomalies continue. While adjustment would have hurt many midwestern and northeastern states, in many cases it would have helped large cities in those states. For example, adjustment would have increased the nation's population by 2.08 percent and New York State's by only 1.72 percent. But it would have increased New York City's by 3.04 percent (see tables 5-1, 5-2). In other words, adjustment would have helped New York City but not New York State.[29] Similar outcomes were evident with Chicago and Detroit: these cities would have benefited from adjustment; their states would have lost. More recently, this city-state dynamic

Table 5-1. *Net Undercount in Selected States, 1990*
Percent

	1991 PES[a]	1992 CAPE[b]
National	2.08	1.58
Southwest/South		
California	3.65	2.73
Arizona	3.30	2.37
Texas	3.22	2.76
Louisiana	2.59	2.17
Florida	2.56	1.96
Georgia	2.33	2.12
Northeast/Midwest		
New York	1.72	1.49
Illinois	1.40	0.99
New Jersey	1.35	0.57
Michigan	1.16	0.71
Ohio	0.79	0.69
Wisconsin	0.65	0.61
Pennsylvania	0.63	0.29
Massachusetts	0.38	0.48

Source: Committee on Adjustment of Postcensal Estimates, *Assessment of Accuracy of Adjusted versus Unadjusted 1990 Census Base for Use in Intercensal Estimates* (Census Bureau, August 7, 1992).
a. 1990 postenumeration survey (PES) data, released by the Census Bureau in 1991.
b. Revised PES data, generated by the Committee on Adjustment of Postcensal Estimates (CAPE) in 1992.

developed into an intriguing scenario. Even though officials in Phoenix believed that their city would benefit from adjustment of the 2000 census, they opted out of litigation at the insistence of state officials who believed that adjustment would be harmful to the interests of Arizona.

As for the 1990 census, some cities would have lost outright under adjustment. Boston, for example, would have gained absolute population but would have lost relative population share. This was particularly ironic since Ray Flynn, the city's Democratic mayor and chairman of the National Conference of Mayors, was a nationally prominent advocate of adjustment.

Yet the statistical merry go-round did not stop there. About a year after the Census Bureau published these adjusted numbers in 1991, it announced a computer coding error that had improperly added about 1 million persons to the original undercount estimate. Revising this and some other, minor errors reduced the undercount estimate from 2.08 to 1.58 percent. Undercount figures for the nation's states and localities were also revised, at which point it became clear that the effects of the error were not uniform across jurisdictions (see tables 5-1 and 5-2). With some exceptions, the computer error had systematically benefited jurisdictions in the Southwest and South and put those in the Northeast and Midwest at a disadvantage. Although

Table 5-2. *Net Undercount in Selected Cities, 1990*
Percent

	1991 PES[a]	1992 CAPE[b]
National	2.08	1.58
Southwest/South		
Atlanta	5.10	3.41
Los Angeles	5.06	3.83
Houston	4.96	3.93
Dallas	4.80	3.55
Miami	4.75	4.99
Jackson	4.49	2.94
San Diego	3.95	2.84
New Orleans	3.42	3.31
Las Vegas	3.01	2.41
Phoenix	2.97	2.03
Northeast/Midwest		
Detroit	3.46	2.67
New York	3.04	3.23
Chicago	2.58	2.32
Minneapolis	1.76	1.64
Buffalo	1.51	1.84
Cleveland	1.36	2.13
Philadelphia	1.29	1.45
Milwaukee	1.23	2.30
Pittsburgh	1.10	1.04
Boston	0.94	2.78

Source: Committee on Adjustment of Postcensal Estimates, *Assessment of Accuracy of Adjusted versus Unadjusted 1990 Census Base for Use in Intercensal Estimates* (Census Bureau, August 7, 1992).
a. 1990 postenumeration survey (PES) data, released by the Census Bureau in 1991.
b. Revised PES data generated by the Committee on Adjustment of Postcensal Estimates (CAPE) in 1992.

the revised figures did not fundamentally alter the regional advantage that a census adjustment would have originally afforded the Southwest and South, they would have transformed losses into gains for some midwestern and northeastern cities. Prominent among these was Boston, whose undercount went from well under the national average to well above it. Other cities—such as Cleveland, Buffalo, Milwaukee, and New Haven—would have been pushed from just below the national average to just above it by the "revised adjusted" figures. On the other hand, cities such as Philadelphia and Pittsburgh would have remained losers under either set of adjusted numbers. This unforeseen reshuffling of the deck highlights not only the fallibility of statistical adjustment but also the volatility and unpredictability of adjustment outcomes—making the merry-go-round look more like a roulette wheel.[30]

On the basis of this revised undercount estimate, one member of the bureau's nine-person Undercount Steering Committee testified in court that had he known the undercount was this low, he would have opposed adjustment. Then-director Bryant, who publicly advocated adjustment in opposition to her superiors at the Commerce Department, has intimated that on the basis of the 1.58 percent undercount figure she, too, might have changed her position. "The lower the undercount," she commented, "the harder it is to be sure you're doing the right thing on adjustment."[31]

Congressional Apportionment

Compared with fiscal outcomes, the gain or loss of legislative seats because of the undercount and adjustment may seem more clear cut. Yet these political stakes are perhaps even more unpredictable than the fiscal stakes.

Consider the apportionment of Congress, which is after all the constitutional rationale for the decennial census. In January 1999 the Supreme Court ruled that the Census Act does not permit adjusted census numbers derived from statistical sampling to be used to apportion congressional seats among the states.[32] Because the court did not reach the constitutional question at issue, Congress could still amend the Census Act and permit the use of adjusted numbers for apportionment. However unlikely that scenario may be, it is still useful to review the research that demonstrates the sensitivity of apportionment outcomes to the relatively small demographic shifts associated with adjustment.

After each census, Congress has faced the task of equitably apportioning its membership (fixed at 435 since 1910) among the states without ending up with any fractional seats. A subject of substantial contention during much of our national history, the apportionment formula that Congress has relied on since 1940 is "the method of equal proportions." This formula first awards one seat to each state (as prescribed by the Constitution) and then assigns the remaining 385 seats sequentially, on the basis of a list of descending "priority values." These values are calculated by dividing each state's population by the square root of $N(N-1)$, where N equals the Nth seat (whether the second, fifth, or fiftieth) in a given state's congressional delegation.[33] Thus, the higher a state's population, the higher its priority values.

This relatively straightforward formula has several less than straightforward implications. For example, in 1990 California was assigned its 52d congressional seat before Texas received its 30th seat, and Texas was assigned its 30th seat before Mississippi got its 5th seat. This is because the priority value for California's 52d seat, driven by the state's huge popula-

Table 5-3. *Population Change to Lose or Gain a Seat in Congress,*
1990 Apportionment (unadjusted census data)

Seat in House	State	Apportionment population	Population change required to gain or lose seat[a] Amount	Percent
Possible losers				
428	Calif. (52)[b]	29,839,250	-236,002	-0.79
429	Tex. (30)	17,059,805	-104,241	-0.61
430	Miss. (5)	2,586,443	-15,648	-0.61
431	Wis. (9)	4,906,745	-29,004	-0.59
432	Fla. (23)	13,003,362	-72,490	-0.56
433	Tenn. (9)	4,896,641	-18,900	-0.39
434	Okla. (6)	3,157,604	-9,036	-0.29
435	Wash. (9)	4,887,941	-10,200	-0.21
Possible gainers				
436	Mass. (11)	6,029,051	12,607	0.21
437	N.J. (14)	7,748,634	22,698	0.29
438	N.Y. (32)	18,044,505	98,765	0.55
439	Ky. (7)	3,698,969	34,258	0.93
440	Calif. (53)	29,839,250	401,972	1.35
441	Mont. (2)	803,655	11,002	1.37
442	Ariz. (7)	3,677,985	55,242	1.50
443	Ga. (12)	6,508,419	109,885	1.69

Source: Jeffrey S. Passel, "What Census Adjustment Would Mean," *Population Today*, vol. 19 (June 1991), p. 7.
a. All other factors remaining constant. The entry for each state is based on the assumption that the populations of all other states remain unchanged—a necessary but not realistic premise.
b. Total members of a state's delegation to the House of Representatives.

tion, was greater than the priority value for Texas's 30th seat, and so on (see table 5-3).

Table 5-3 highlights another critical point: minor shifts in state population totals can result in the loss or gain of congressional seats. For example, if in 1990 Massachusetts had had a mere 12,607 additional residents—and if the population of the other states remained constant— the Bay State would have held on to the congressional seat it forfeited in that year's apportionment. Or if New Jersey had had an additional 22,698 residents (0.29 percent of its unadjusted population), again with other factors remaining constant, it would have held on to the seat it lost in 1990. Conversely, if Washington state had had 10,200 fewer residents or Oklahoma 9,036 fewer, each would have ended up with one less congressional seat than it did. Indeed, any of the last seven seats assigned in 1990 would have been forfeited with a loss of 0.61 percent or less of a given state's population. The volatility of apportionment outcomes is underscored by the fact that with small percentage shifts in its 1990 population, California would have lost its 52d or gained a 53d congressional seat. Again, what makes these outcomes so unpredictable is that adjustment would not impact just one or a handful of states but would impose myriad, often marginal changes on all state population totals that would in turn interact with the apportionment formula in complicated ways.

To be sure, this volatility is confined to that handful of states with priority values hovering around the 435th-seat cutoff. Yet it is difficult to know which states will be among that handful *before* the actual census numbers are released. In part this is because apportionment outcomes are so sensitive to small changes in the counts. But it is also because projections of future population figures are notoriously unreliable. Thus, in the period leading up to the 1990 census, the bureau was able to correctly predict less than three out of five of the eventual seat changes.[34] This means that before the 1990 census, there was even greater uncertainty about which states would lose or gain seats than can be discerned from table 5-3, which is based on actual census results.

A similar level of uncertainty has been evident over the last decade. In 1997 the Congressional Research Service (CRS) used Census Bureau projections to predict apportionment outcomes after the 2000 census. At first CRS reported that Colorado, Florida, Montana, Nevada, and Utah would each gain one seat in Congress; Arizona, Georgia, and Texas would each gain two seats. Losing one seat each would be Connecticut, Illinois, Michigan, Mississippi, Ohio, Oklahoma, and Wisconsin. New York and Pennsylvania were projected to lose two seats.[35] Notably, as late as 1997 California was not projected to gain (or lose) any seats.

More recent projections have indicated, however, that Michigan would not lose a seat and that neither Utah nor Montana would gain one. More important, California is now assumed to be in line for one new seat after the 2000 apportionment.[36] But these projections, too, are tentative. As their authors acknowledge, Montana misses gaining a seat only by several hundred people, while the 435th seat that Indiana is projected to get is also not very secure. Moreover, these projections do not include the substantial but presently indeterminate number of federal employees stationed abroad (over 918,000 in 1990) that has typically been included in state totals used for apportionment.[37]

All of these uncertainties arise quite independently of census adjustment. But adjustment would not make apportionment outcomes any easier to predict. It is to that topic that I now turn.

Table 5-3 illustrates what both history and mathematics confirm: those states with priority values near the 435th-seat cutoff tend to be the more populous states. And because high population states tend to be where minorities are concentrated, these tend to be high undercount states (for example, California, Texas, and Florida.)[38] So adjustment would definitely affect apportionment. But once again, that impact and its concomitant uncertainty would be confined to a handful of states that typically stand either to lose or gain one congressional seat. As several analysts have pointed out, the impact of adjustment would be much smaller than that resulting simply from population shifts—as in 1990, when apportionment without adjustment led to nineteen seats shifting among twenty-one states.

In 1980 census adjustment might have afforded California, Texas, and Indiana one more congressional seat each—at the expense of Ohio, Pennsylvania, and Tennessee.[39] In 1990, according to an early analysis relying on preliminary data, adjustment would have meant an extra congressional seat each to Georgia, California, and Montana—the last by a margin of only 510 persons. The losers would have been Oklahoma, Pennsylvania, and Wisconsin.[40]

A subsequent, more definitive analysis determined that the impact of adjustment would have been more confined, with an extra seat for Arizona and California, at the expense of Pennsylvania and Wisconsin.[41] At least, this is how it looked in July 1991, when Commerce Secretary Robert Mosbacher decided against adjustment. About a year later, the impact narrowed even further when the Census Bureau released revised data indicating that adjustment would have meant a shift of only one congressional seat, from Wisconsin to California.[42]

A further note of ambiguity would be introduced by the sampling error associated with adjusted numbers. As demographer Jeffrey Passel puts it: "The precision of the PES [postenumeration survey] estimates falls far short of what is needed to guarantee that an apportionment based on adjusted data is more accurate than the one based on the unadjusted counts."[43] Passel points out that in 1990 sampling error was large enough to affect apportionment outcomes.

Pursuing a similar line of inquiry about the method to adjust the 1990 census, Berkeley statistician Kenneth Wachter found that equally plausible but different procedural details and assumptions produced different sets of numbers, which would have resulted in divergent apportionment scenarios. In other words, adjustment in 1990 would not have led to outcomes that statisticians call "robust." Wachter concluded: "These results lead me to think that an apportionment based on adjusted counts could be easily contested."[44]

What of the partisan implications of apportionment with adjusted census data? It is routinely assumed that adjustment would help Democrats and hurt Republicans. Yet the evidence presented here points to a far more ambiguous outcome.

If we look at one of the scenarios anticipated for 1990, California and Arizona would have each gained one congressional seat, at the expense of Wisconsin and Pennsylvania. At the time most observers assumed that such an outcome would benefit Democrats, while a few perspicacious souls, including director Bryant, maintained that it would aid Republicans.[45] Yet no one could be sure, because any gain from apportionment depends on who within a given state controls the redistricting process. During the 1990 apportionment and redistricting, no one party dominated both legislative branches and the governor's mansion in any of these four states, making it anyone's guess which party would have garnered those additional seats.

Unless Congress abruptly and unexpectedly decides otherwise, there will be no apportionment with adjusted census data in 2000. Nevertheless, if we ponder what might have been, the results are again too ambiguous to support the conventional view.

Consider the case of Mississippi. Using the 1997 CRS projection of 2000 apportionment outcomes, independent analyst Clark Bensen predicted that adjustment would result in one seat shifting to Mississippi from Indiana.[46] But would this benefit Democrats? Under Bensen's scenario Mississippi would hold on to the five congressional seats it has had since 1960, whereas without an adjustment the state will probably lose one seat after the 2000 census. But three of the present five seats are held by Republicans, two by Democrats, one of whom is black. Because the black Democratic seat is protected by the Voting Rights Act and neither party controls the state outright, it is not clear which party in Mississippi would gain from an unadjusted apportionment. With adjustment, on the other hand, the outcome is clear: Mississippi would hold on to its five congressional seats, and the status quo, which in this case favors Republicans, would be reinforced.

Like any analysis based on such projections, this one is hardly definitive. In fact, the specific population projection on which it was based has since been amended, although not drastically.[47] But this 1997 scenario, released when the congressional debate over adjustment was at its peak, was at the time widely accepted as plausible by all participants in the debate—even though none was persuaded to change his position by it.

Redistricting Is the Wild Card

As indicated above, assessing the partisan implications of census adjustment requires analysis not only of apportionment but also of redistricting. And while apportionment will almost certainly not rely on adjusted census numbers, the Clinton administration does intend to release adjusted numbers for congressional redistricting by the states. Whether and how the states will use those adjusted numbers remains unclear.

In the case of apportionment, reliance on a fixed formula has obviated many political conflicts and allowed the process to be driven by demographic change. Redistricting, by contrast, is driven more directly and powerfully by politics. Thus it is all the more curious that the debate over adjustment has reinforced the mistaken notion that there is a direct correlation between population counts and seats in Congress and other legislative bodies. As with apportionment, virtually all participants in the debate have assumed that to redistrict with adjusted census data would be to the advantage of Democrats and to the disadvantage of Republicans. Yet as Passel emphasizes:

> The drawing of legislative boundaries is inherently a political enterprise. A myriad of factors can affect the outcome, including the geographic distribution of the population, the size and distribution of minority populations, the location of jurisdictional boundaries, residential locations of incumbents, and the party affiliations and relative political power of different groups.[48]

The interaction of these many political factors makes redistricting outcomes extremely unpredictable.

Equally misleading is the way the debate over redistricting (like that over the fiscal impacts of adjustment) has focused almost exclusively on Congress. The redrawing of district lines occurs at all levels of government, and the smaller size of state and local districts means that they would be more affected by adjustment than congressional districts—and just as difficult, or more difficult, to predict. Here, too, analysis suffers from a lack of research.[49]

Quite aside from the question of adjustment, census numbers have only a limited impact on redistricting outcomes. According to David Butler and

Bruce Cain, "The excitement over redistricting sometimes leads people to exaggerate the possibilities that a new census will bring."[50] Butler and Cain emphasize in particular that the partisan outcomes of congressional redistricting are greatly exaggerated: "Virtually all the political science evidence to date indicates that the electoral system has little or no systematic partisan bias and that the net gains nationally from redistricting for one party over the other are very small."[51] They add that the conditions for partisan redistricting, defined broadly as "whether the parties disagree over the new lines," are relatively rare.[52] First, one party must be in control of both legislative chambers and the governor's office; otherwise the parties must compromise on redistricting. Second, the two parties in a given state must be in close electoral competition. Third, demographic change must lead to the addition or subtraction of seats from the state congressional delegation.[53] During the 1980 redistricting, only 11 out 50 states had any serious partisan disagreement over congressional redistricting.[54] Even in states under the control of one party, partisan redistrictings did not always occur.[55]

Butler and Cain report further that even partisan gerrymanders do not always work out as intended. Particularly with today's weak partisan ties, redistricting is at best an inexact science: "In an era in which party loyalty has been steadily declining, it is hard to predict whether a change in district composition will necessarily lead to a change in partisan composition."[56] In the 1992 and 1994 House elections, Democrats fared better under redistricting plans devised either by divided state governments or by courts or commissions than they did under Democrat-controlled state governments.[57]

Finally, Butler and Cain make the important point that the decentralized nature of American politics tends to neutralize whatever partisan outcomes do emerge in the states:

> Discussions of systematic redistricting tend to ignore how the federal structure and other more powerful factors in the electoral system dampen its impact. It is inaccurate to think of one overall congressional redistricting at the beginning of each decade. Rather, there are fifty congressional redistrictings and thousands of state and local redistrictings, each conducted under different conditions and constraints.[58]

Much as the Framers intended, broad national ties—of ideology, of interest, or of partisanship—are mediated and attenuated by myriad state and local bonds.

None of this is to deny that the partisan stakes in redistricting can be enormous, whether in the battle over who controls the U.S. House of Representatives or in individual states such as California. And the parties behave accordingly. But before assuming that an adjusted census would be a boon to Democrats, even in California, it is worth recalling that the interests of Democrats have frequently conflicted with those of minorities—particularly when it comes to redistricting.[59]

In the first place, it is not clear that more minorities counted by the census translate into more Democratic voters, as is typically claimed. Quite aside from the Republican leanings of many Hispanics, low registration and voting rates among minorities generally belie this assumption. Second, even if we do not focus on voters but on sheer numbers of minorities, we cannot assume that they will necessarily benefit Democrats. Certainly when it comes to redistricting, additional minorities can threaten the seats of nonminority Democratic incumbents. In the past, it was precisely this threat that led to the dispersion and dilution of minorities across several electoral districts. Such maneuvers are now constrained by the Voting Rights Act. Consequently, to the extent that more minorities in the census result in more minority officeholders, the demands made by those officeholders are likely to alienate nonminority voters, as Democratic party leaders are all too aware.

Conversely, where Republicans have significant influence or control over redistricting, they do not necessarily feel threatened by additional minorities resulting from adjustment. After all, it was Republicans who during the 1990 redistricting cycle perfected the art of packing minorities into "majority-minority" districts, a tactic that has had the dual effect of weakening or even eliminating incumbent nonminority Democrats and fostering the creation of more homogeneously white, Republican-leaning districts.[60]

This point will carry even more weight in the 2000 redistricting, because Republicans will almost certainly be in a stronger position then than they were after the 1990 census. In 1991 Democrats controlled both legislative chambers and the governor's office in nineteen states; Republicans exercised comparable control in only three states. (The remaining twenty-eight were under divided government.) But as the 2000 census approaches, Democrats control eight states and Republicans fourteen. Moreover, if we focus on governors, who in the vast majority of states exercise critical veto power over congressional redistricting plans, Republicans have also turned things around: in 1991 Democrats controlled twenty-eight governorships and Republicans twenty; today Democrats control seventeen and Republicans thirty-one.[61] In sum, Republicans have dramatically reversed the field during the 1990s and now dominate the legislative and executive branches in more states than Democrats do.

Redistricting battles are typically anticipated in states that lose or gain congressional seats on account of apportionment. Table 5-4 lists nineteen such states that might be in this category (based on the projections cited here) after apportionment with unadjusted 2000 census data. Under this scenario, Republicans will again be in a strong position, assuming that partisan alignments do not change radically after the 2000 elections. Republicans currently control both legislative chambers and the governor's mansion in eight of these nineteen states: Arizona, Colorado, Florida, Michigan, Montana, Ohio, Pennsylvania, and Utah. Democrats exercise comparable control in only two: Georgia and California. In the nine states under divided government, Republicans hold the governorships in eight of them. And in all of these except one (Connecticut), Republican governors have veto power over congressional redistricting plans. Moreover, in only three of these eight states do Republican governors face Democratic dominance in both legislative chambers. In other words, Republicans are in complete or substantial control in the overwhelming majority of states where redistricting might be contentious.

One problem with this perspective is that it relies on population projections that are frequently unreliable. An alternative line of inquiry is therefore to look at states that have had high undercounts and partisan redistricting battles and are now dominated by one party. Four states clearly fall into this category: Georgia, California, Arizona, and Colorado.[62]

Arizona and Colorado, projected to gain a combined total of three new congressional seats, are currently under Republican control, which should make the Democrats nervous even without an adjustment. But California and Georgia, also projected to gain a combined total of three new seats, are under Democratic control. Of these four, California has been the biggest battleground in terms of seats at stake and intensity of partisan maneuvering. So it is useful to consider California's prospects after the 2000 census.

Focus on California

Even without an adjustment of the 2000 census, California has the Republicans worried. Recalling the beating they took with a Democrat-controlled redistricting in 1980, Republicans look apprehensively at current Democratic dominance of both legislative chambers as well as the executive. In

Table 5-4. *Partisan Dynamics in States Potentially Gaining or Losing Congressional Seats after the 2000 Census*

State	Projected gain in House seats[a]	Party control[b] Leg	Party control[b] Gov	Gubernatorial veto over congressional redistricting plans[c]	High undercount in 1990[d]	History of partisan redistricting battles[e]
Arizona	2	R	R	Y	Y	Y
California	1	D	D	Y	Y	Y
Colorado	1	R	R	Y	Y	N
Connecticut	-1	D	R	N	N	N
Florida	1	R	R	Y	Y	Y
Georgia	2	D	D	Y	Y	Y
Illinois	-1	Split	R	Y	N	Y
Indiana	-1	Split	D	Y	N	Y
Michigan	-1	R	R	Y	Y	Y
Mississippi	-1	D	R	Y	Y	N
Montana	1	R	R	N	Y	N
Nevada	1	Split	R	Y	Y	N
New York	-2	Split	R	Y	N	N
Ohio	-1	R	R	Y	N	Y
Oklahoma	-1	D	R	Y	Y	Y
Pennsylvania	-2	R	R	Y	N	Y
Texas	2	Split	R	Y	Y	N
Utah	1	R	R	Y	Y	Y
Wisconsin	-1	Split	R	Y	N	Y

a. David C. Huckabee, *House Apportionment Following the 2000 Census: Preliminary Projections*, 97-94 GOV (Washington, DC: Congressional Research Service; January 10, 1997). One projection was issued by Election Data Services on December 29, 1999 (see their website: www.electiondataservices.com). A second was done by Polidata, also released on December 29, 1999 (see www.polidata.org).

b. National Conference of State Legislatures, "1999 Partisan Composition of State Legislatures," updated January 6, 2000.

c. National Conference of State Legislatures, "Redistricting Provisions 2000: 50 State Profiles," available at (http://lije.commissions.leg.state.mn.us/scripts/esrimap.dll?Name=redistprof&Cmd=Map).

d. States that had an undercount above the national undercount (1.58 percent). Committee on Adjustment of Postcensal Estimates, *Assessment of Accuracy of Adjusted versus Unadjusted 1990 Census Base for Use in Intercensal Estimates* (Census Bureau, August 7, 1992).

e. David Butler and Bruce Cain, eds., *Congressional Redistricting: Comparative and Theoretical Perspectives* (New York: Macmillan, 1992), pp. 96–99.

1990, again without an adjustment, the state was awarded seven new seats and the Republicans did much better, albeit after a tough redistricting battle. Current projections have California gaining one new seat in 2000. Even if these projections are low, the number of new seats available to the Democrats in charge of redistricting will be nowhere near seven. But the Republicans remain anxious, and the prospect of adjustment only adds to their anxiety. The question is, how anxious should they be about adjustment?

On its face, the size of the California undercount seems sufficient cause for concern. In 1990 California had the third highest undercount rate of any state, which translated into an absolute figure of 837,557 individuals, the highest such number for all the states (with Texas a distant second with 486,028 uncounted individuals).[63] Had there been an adjustment, this figure would have been large enough to generate yet another congressional district (the average size of a California district being 572,308). Despite Jeffrey Passel's warning that "because all states are being adjusted, merely adding enough people to account for an average congressional district does not guarantee an additional seat," California would in fact have gained an extra seat from adjustment in both 1980 and in 1990.[64]

The 2000 apportionment is not likely to use adjusted census data, as stated earlier. But if it did, then the undercount figure in California might once again be high enough to generate an additional new seat (beyond the one projected from an unadjusted apportionment).[65] If this should occur, then how worried should the Republicans be?

Here again, Republican concern should be less with adjustment per se than with how the Democrats (who will almost certainly still be in control of both the executive and legislative branches) choose to deal with the new seat. The outcome depends on who is in charge of the redistricting process.

Moreover, as Passel reminds us, "because congressional districts are so large . . . adjustment has only a marginal impact."[66] Look again at the 1990 California figures. Those 837,557 uncounted individuals represented only 2.81 percent of the state's total population. In the state's congressional districts the mean undercount was 16,107—a mere drop in the bucket in districts averaging 572,308 residents. Moreover, this undercount was to a surprising degree evenly distributed across both Republican and Democratic districts. In the former the mean undercount was 2.2 percent of the district population; in the latter 3.3 percent.[67]

To be sure, these average figures obscure the fact that several congressional districts had strikingly high undercounts in 1990. Indeed, there were eleven out of fifty-two congressional districts with undercounts in excess of 20,000, mostly Democratic districts in the greater Los Angeles area. These high undercounts ranged from 35,604 in the 35th congressional district, held by Representative Maxine Waters (Democrat), to 20,420 in the 46th district, currently held by Representative Loretta Sanchez (Democrat).

But even with such relatively large undercounts, adjustment would not have had much impact. Consider the extreme case of the 35th congressional district. Adjustment in 1990 would have increased the average size of all California's congressional districts from 572,000 to 588,000. This means that the 35th district would have retained only that portion of those 35,604 previously uncounted individuals (about 16,000) that would have brought its population up to the new district average. The remaining 19,600 or so individuals would have then been distributed across several contiguous districts, whose lines would have been redrawn to bring up their populations to the new state average as well. But even if all 19,600 had been packed into a single neighboring district, the population of the average district would have been increased by only 3.4 percent.

Equally if not more important, even the most skillful such redrawing of lines would have eventually collided with the obdurate fact that these high-undercount districts have extremely low voter turnouts. This should come as no surprise. Many of those who go uncounted in the census—minority individuals, immigrants, noncitizens—either do not or simply cannot vote. And when they fail to vote, their numbers do not contribute to the partisan outcomes sought by those redrawing district lines.

None of this is meant to dismiss Republican concerns. Were a clever redistricting scheme to squeeze a Democratic seat out of such numbers, then congressional Republicans struggling to maintain control of the House with an eleven-seat margin would have reason to worry. But to repeat, the main reason for Republican jitters in California is Democratic control of redistricting, not any potential Democratic windfall from adjustment. Adjustment would add to those jitters, but only marginally.

Meanwhile, in other states Republicans have far less to fear from redistricting than they have in the recent past. That California is not the whole story is suggested by the fact that in 1990 national Republicans opposed adjustment, even though they held the California governorship and the occupant of that office, Pete Wilson, supported it. At the time, the Republicans' opposition reflected concerns about other states, where they were not well situated. Today, by contrast, Republicans are in very good shape across the nation—except in California. In sum, the advantages that Republicans enjoy in other states have been overlooked, while the risks they run from adjustment (as opposed to redistricting) in California have been exaggerated.

It is understandable that Republicans holding down a slim majority in Congress are not reassured by the news that there is no sure way to forecast the marginal partisan consequences of census adjustment. But their reluctance to gamble on those consequences hardly justifies the utter certainty with which virtually all commentators assert that adjustment would help Democrats and hurt Republicans.

Minority Concerns and Census Muddles

Of all the groups discussed here, minorities have the clearest stakes in an accurate census. Yet even here there are ambiguities as to the interests of various groups in the undercount and adjustment.

It is important to distinguish between a group's anxiety about the undercount and its support for a particular solution. Indeed, it is possible for a group to be intensely concerned about the harm done to it by the undercount while at the same time being quite uneasy with, perhaps even opposed to, proposed remedies.

Moreover, the interests of different minority groups with respect to these issues are hardly identical. As table 4-2 highlights, undercount rates vary considerably across minority groups. As suggested by the ethnographic studies discussed in chapter 4, groups with different socioeconomic and demographic characteristics are undercounted for different reasons. Such differences have implications for the remedies favored by various groups. As noted earlier, Hispanic organizations have been particularly concerned to get the INS to curtail its presence in immigrant neighborhoods at census time. African American organizations have been less enthusiastic than others about greater reliance on administrative records to reduce the undercount, apparently out of concern that such efforts would lead to intrusive inquiries about reliance on welfare programs.[68]

Similarly with adjustment, there is no reason to assume that it would benefit all undercounted minorities equally. Indeed, a pattern of unequal impacts surfaced in the 1990 postenumeration survey. Attempting to explain why, contrary to all expectations, the postenumeration survey revealed higher undercount rates for jurisdictions in the Southwest and South than in the Northeast and Midwest, Wachter argues that this methodology may have fared worse in the high-rise housing projects of New York City than in the dispersed housing of Los Angeles. The PES "may have had a harder task locating uncounted black men in old urban areas than in locating

Table 5-5. *Estimates of the Net Undercount by Race, 1990*

Percent

	1990 DA[a]	1991 PES[b]	1992 CAPE[c]
Total population	1.8	2.1	1.6
Blacks	5.7	4.8	4.4
Nonblacks	1.3	1.7	1.2
Black-nonblack differential	4.4	3.1	3.2

Sources: Howard Hogan and Gregg Robinson, "What the Census Bureau's Coverage Evaluation Tells Us about Differential Undercount," *1993 Research Conference on Undercounted Ethnic Populations* (Government Printing Office, October 1993), p. 13. Committee on the Adjustment of Postcensal Estimates, *Assessment of Accuracy of Adjusted versus Unadjusted 1990 Census Base for Use in Intercensal Estimates* (Census Bureau, August 7, 1991).

a. Estimates are based on demographic analysis (DA).

b. Estimates are from postenumeration survey (PES) data released by the Census Bureau in 1991.

c. Estimates are from *revised* PES data, generated by the Committee on Adjustment of Postcensal Estimates (CAPE) in 1992.

uncounted Hispanic men in the mixed minority areas of the Southwest."[69] Wachter also emphasizes, as have I, that for any group or jurisdiction the outcome of adjustment depends not on absolute population gains but on gains in relation to other groups or jurisdictions. Thus the PES did find uncounted black men, but apparently found proportionately more uncounted Hispanic men.

The same dynamic could play out among minorities in relation to non-minorities. Indeed, adjustment might actually improve the relative population shares of nonminorities, leaving minorities worse off. This is what happened with the revised adjusted data issued by the bureau in 1992. As indicated in table 5-5, the 1992 revisions reduced the black undercount from 4.8 to 4.4 percent. But because the nonblack undercount was reduced even more (from 1.7 to 1.2 percent), the black-nonblack differential increased from 3.1 to 3.2 percent. Though slight (and almost certainly not statistically significant), this change underscores the highly contingent and often counterintuitive nature of adjustment outcomes.

In a nutshell, adjustment could be a gamble for minority groups just as for the jurisdictions discussed above. Merely being undercounted offers no assurance that adjustment will provide relief. In fact, adjustment could leave a minority group, city, or state with lower population shares than before.

Minority leaders have not addressed these specific dilemmas of adjustment. But they have raised other concerns about proposals to rectify the differential racial undercount and to improve census accuracy more generally. Taken together, these concerns suggest that minorities are not as unqualifiedly enthusiastic about "modernizing the census" as it may appear.[70]

Indeed, among minorities there has been a discernible strain of suspicion and distrust toward adjustment and other census reform efforts.

Back in 1968, for example, when black leaders met with census officials to discuss the undercount, they were not particularly concerned about a more accurate census. They were certainly not impressed by the increased federal funds or greater representation presumably attendant on higher black population counts. On the contrary, one leader remarked to Dr. Herman Miller, chief of the bureau's Population Division: "If the count of young Negro males on a given city block increased suddenly, the Welfare Department would soon send investigators around to see if they were violating the welfare laws and the draft board would send investigators to try to find draft dodgers."[71] A few black leaders subsequently expressed skepticism about preoccupation with the undercount, pointing out that political power comes not from census data but from organization. As Leon Finney, former head of the Saul Alinsky-inspired Woodlawn Organization, remarked in 1979:

> I would not delude anybody . . . by saying that because we have an accurate count, Black people and brown people and poor people are going to get to share those resources that are allocated for them . . . we have to continue to think about organizing ourselves, developing the political muscle . . . sufficient to make sure that when those resources are allocated . . . they just don't go to those same old guys to run the same old games on us.[72]

During the 1980s misgivings about proposals to adjust the upcoming 1990 census emerged in the bureau's minority advisory committees. Ira Lowry, who combed through five volumes of their minutes and recommendations, reports: "Curiously, the committees did not support the Bureau in its plan to compensate for underenumeration of minorities by adjusting the census count."[73] One member of the Committee on the Black Population expressed concern that any preoccupation with adjustment would undercut the bureau's efforts to do the best possible job on the actual enumeration.[74]

Of course, during the 1980s skepticism about adjustment was more widespread than now. Still, it is worth emphasizing that black leaders were not adjustment's first or most enthusiastic advocates. And by the early 1990s, when black leaders did settle on adjustment as the remedy for the undercount problem they had come to regard as serious, misgivings continued to surface, this time over the Census Bureau's plan to rely on sampling for nonresponse follow-up (SNRFU) in the 2000 census.

Even before the bureau formally proposed SNRFU, members of its minority advisory committees expressed concern that such a plan could exacerbate the undercount problem. Robert Hill of Morgan State University noted at a December 1995 session, "Sampling [for non-response] poses a bigger problem of missing minority populations than enumeration does."[75] Other committee members voiced similar reservations.

Then in May 1996 Representative Carrie Meek (Democrat of Florida), joined by colleagues in the Black Congressional Caucus, sponsored legislation requiring an alternative plan. Recall that, as originally formulated by the bureau, SNRFU was to be implemented once traditional follow-up methods had obtained responses from 90 percent of the households *in each county*. H.R. 3558 would have instead mandated that traditional follow-up continue until responses were obtained from 90 percent of households *in each census tract*—at which point sampling could be used to estimate data for nonresponding households *within each tract*.[76]

Meek's legislation was inspired by the concern that in densely populated, heterogeneous metropolitan regions the 90 percent countywide goal could be met by focusing on traditionally easy-to-count areas, once again leaving minority neighborhoods with low response rates.[77] This potential problem would be resolved, argued Meek and her colleagues, by focusing on smaller census tracts. After some foot-dragging the Census Bureau agreed, and in 1997 it issued a revised SNRFU plan that used sampling to reach a 90 percent response rate in each tract. H.R. 3558 was quickly dropped.

A more general minority distrust of the Census Bureau was aroused by its persistent inability to articulate a clear and convincing rationale for SNRFU. The agency proved unable to provide an overall explanation for either SNRFU or Integrated Coverage Measurement (ICM), or for how these would figure into efforts to improve the census.

To be sure, SNRFU and ICM were complicated methodologies difficult to explain to elite audiences, never mind to the general public. But the bureau has failed to clarify even more straightforward, nontechnical matters. For example, it has been ambiguous about whether sampling is a revolutionary innovation that would transform the census or whether it is one of the bureau's traditional tools.[78] Given its well-established reliance on the long form, distributed to about one-sixth of all households, the Census Bureau can legitimately lay claim to a tradition of sampling. But as already noted, postcensus sampling for adjustment is quite different from conventional sampling. To allay concerns about adjustment, the bureau has obviously tried to wrap the new in the old. But in trying to have it both ways, the bureau has put out a muddled message.

Similarly, the bureau blurred the basic distinction between the two sampling programs that it was planning to use for the 2000 census. In technical reports and before expert audiences, it would explain the differences between SNRFU and ICM, but in other venues the bureau, as well as the various NAS panels, tended to talk more generally in terms of "sampling."[79] Doubtless this was in part an understandable effort to simplify a complicated set of methodologies for broad public consumption. But it was also an effort to avoid details that would provide opportunities for troublesome questions.

Blurring the distinction between the two sampling programs allowed the bureau to assert that it was addressing both of Congress's key concerns—improving accuracy and reducing costs—while deflecting scrutiny of the separate parts of the package it was proposing. As the bureau asserted in one of its publications, "Sampling and statistical estimation are already an integral part of every Census Bureau process. . . . [I]ncorporating widely-accepted scientific statistical methods into Census 2000 will produce a better census at less cost."[80]

Now let us look at those separate parts. As already noted, ICM was a massive postcensus survey that would be a quality check on the original enumeration and that would also generate adjusted census numbers. When asked, bureau experts would readily explain that ICM's primary goal was improved census accuracy. When pressed, they would add that "improved accuracy" referred to reduced minority undercounts. Indeed, ICM was basically an updated version of the PES, the postcensus survey around which the controversy over adjusting the 1990 census had churned. While no one at the Census Bureau sought to hide these details, the label ICM and the broad category of "sampling" helped somewhat to obscure them.

But only somewhat. More helpful was the fact that, as part of a sampling package for the 2000 census, ICM could be put forward as an exercise in "scientific sampling," when in truth it had little in common with traditional sampling and perhaps even less with science. As part of this package, ICM was also less likely to stand out as what it obviously was: an add-on to the actual enumeration that would not only increase total costs but do so for the controversial goal of adjusting the census to make up for minority undercounts.

Enter SNRFU. Unlike ICM, SNRFU *was* a conventional sampling program. Even more important, it addressed the issue of census costs, which had skyrocketed from $231 million in 1970 to $2.6 billion in 1990 (in constant dollars).[81] By eliminating the need for coverage improvement programs designed to seek out those who do not send in their forms, SNRFU was to reduce the cost of the 2000 census by $500 million.[82]

Yet SNRFU also had liabilities that stood out less visibly when it was paired with ICM. Cost reduction was obviously a plus, but census costs remained a potentially embarrassing topic for the bureau. After all, three-fourths of the increase from 1970 to 1990 could not be accounted for. Most knowledgeable observers felt that a critical component of the increase was the effort to reduce minority undercounts.[83] This was not something the bureau wanted to advertise.

SNRFU also risked fostering the perception that participation in the census was not essential. If it were, the average respondent might ask, why was the bureau no longer trying to count everyone?[84] For such reasons the bureau avoided letting SNRFU stand alone and whenever possible described it as part of a sampling package that would begin modernizing the census.

There was also a more substantive reason for treating SNRFU and ICM as a package. Among some knowledgeable insiders the two programs were seen as working in tandem. For example, SNRFU would contribute to accuracy by ensuring the timely completion of the original enumeration. This would mean, in turn, that the ICM could be launched soon enough to minimize the matching problems described in chapter 4 and to produce results in time for apportionment deadlines.[85] Indeed, this was depicted as SNRFU's primary purpose at a session of the 2000 Census Advisory Committee by a bureau official, who referred to cost reduction as a mere "side benefit."[86] In the same vein, ICM was elsewhere depicted as improving accuracy *and* reducing costs by leading the way for a "reengineered census" that would be redesigned from the bottom up.[87] To be sure, these more sophisticated rationales for ICM and SNRFU were not articulated frequently. But they were definitely part of the confusion and controversy.

Perhaps the Census Bureau had this more sophisticated scenario in mind when it described SNRFU as contributing to both accuracy and cost reduction. Or perhaps it simply got caught up telling different constituencies what each wanted to hear. In any event, announcing its plan for the millennial census early in 1996, the bureau claimed that SNRFU would "ensure that Census 2000 is built around a solid core of field results, while reducing the cost and improving the accuracy of the data on the final increment of the population."[88] Interpreting this as a claim that SNRFU would improve accuracy *and* reduce costs, congressional Republicans critical of adjustment pounced on it as evidence of the bureau's confusion.[89] On several subsequent occasions bureau officials were at pains to emphasize that SNRFU was meant only to reduce costs and that there was no evidence it would reduce the minority undercount.[90]

Yet such disavowals served mainly to antagonize minority critics of SNRFU such as Representative Meek. At one contentious hearing, she said of SNRFU: "I am very concerned that one of the motives here . . . may be to save money. I don't think this is the place we can save money."[91] Whatever the noises being made to reassure minority leaders about plans for the 2000 count, those who, like Meek, were familiar with the issue had sat through countless meetings and public sessions where bureau officials had identified their objectives as the apple-pie virtues of improving accuracy and reducing costs. Minority leaders had also heard Census Bureau officials strain to avoid mentioning why accuracy and cost were on the agenda in the first place: the minority undercount. As the report of the NAS Schultze panel stated baldly (if not prominently), "Data on race and ethnicity are involved, directly and indirectly, in most of the concern and contention about costs and quality of the 2000 census."[92]

Of these two apple-pie goals, reducing costs was by far the safer, which is why the bureau emphasized it more than improving accuracy. Even though cost reduction antagonized minority leaders like Meek, it stood the bureau in good stead among the general public and certainly in Congress. While reducing costs came across as an apolitical, good-government objective, accuracy was much more likely to be linked to the troublesome issue of the minority undercount, a connection well understood by bureau officials. A former administrator of statistical programs at the Office of Management and Budget (OMB) points out that government officials in general are unlikely to feel comfortable defending a massive, risky, and controversial policy change in terms of minority needs, particularly when the public tends to regard the undercount as largely the result of choices made by minorities themselves (a view to which the ethnographic evidence cited earlier lends support).

Minority leaders understand these dynamics, of course, and understandably fear that their interests will get short shrift in the larger political equation. So despite occasional references to racial justice by officials, minorities remain suspicious of the bureau. And their suspicion and distrust extend not only to SNRFU but to adjustment efforts more generally, as well as to the bureau's conventional coverage improvement programs.[93]

To be sure, Meek and her colleagues have also been suspicious of Republican critics of sampling and adjustment. While sharing their skepticism of the bureau's specific plans, minority legislators have expressed concern that Republicans have too readily discounted the importance of the undercount to minorities.[94] Minority leaders have also publicly doubted that opponents of sampling and adjustment would "put their money where their mouths were" and adequately fund a conventional enumeration. Another fear expressed at various times has been that a new Republican administration (either in 1996 or 2000) would pull the plug on sampling and adjustment programs and leave the bureau in even worse shape to enumerate difficult-to-count populations.

Such minority concerns have sometimes been interpreted as outright opposition to sampling and adjustment. This is not what I am arguing here. Minority leaders have never been categorically opposed to either one.[95] They have been concerned about specific proposals advanced by the bureau and have, more generally, been suspicious of the bureau's intentions.

My point is that minority support for statistical adjustment has evolved along a path neither straight nor smooth. As noted, black leaders were initially quite suspicious of census officials attempting to draw their attention to the undercount. The path ahead does not look much different. Given the unpredictability of adjustment results, minority support for such programs could weaken and even turn to opposition. Concern about the undercount does not translate into automatic support for all proposed remedies. And distrust of the government dampens minority enthusiasm for efforts to deal with the undercount. After all, if the government failed to count correctly the first time, why should it be trusted to correct its mistakes?

Do Numbers Really Matter?

Pervading the perspectives of all participants in this controversy is the assumption that population numbers matter in and of themselves: that greater census counts for a group are critical to its well-being and political fortunes. Yet a moment's thought should put this proposition in doubt. Just as with the fiscal and redistricting implications of the census, the importance of greater numbers is far from self-evident and, indeed, highly ambiguous.

This should not be surprising. There is considerable ambiguity as to what constitutes "a minority group." Is a minority defined in terms of numbers? Of its relative power in society? Or of both?[96] The last option is appealing, since demographic size and power obviously seem related. Yet one can readily think of "minorities" that have clearly been in the numerical majority but without power: blacks in apartheid South Africa, for example, or blacks in parts of the segregated American South.[97] Conversely, one can think of minorities whose small numbers have not prevented them from wielding significant power and influence: for example, Jews in contemporary America.

The point is that numbers by themselves mean little. In the formulation of redistricting experts Peter Morrison and William Clark, "A particular minority's sheer numbers—its demographic presence—may translate into a greater or lesser political presence according to how those numbers are empowered."[98] Census counts are mediated by any number of other factors that determine the implications of the raw numbers. For any given group, its age-structure, wealth, spatial concentration, level of political mobilization and organization—not to mention the political structures within which it must operate—are all critical variables affecting how the group's population numbers translate into political power.[99]

All groups, especially disadvantaged groups, want to maximize their population totals, other things being equal. But because of such mediating factors, other things are seldom equal. Recall the recent efforts of American Indian leaders to persuade the Census Bureau and OMB to move away from racial self-identification and to rely, for Indians at least, on actual enrollments of individuals recognized as tribal members. In this way, of course, Indian leaders seek to control access to federal funds and, in the case of some tribes, to the gains from various economic ventures such as casino gambling.[100] This is a special case. But the point remains that it is not always in the interest of groups to maximize their numbers.

The ambiguity of population numbers is also illustrated in the case of Jewish Americans. Nathan Glazer and Daniel Patrick Moynihan began their chapter on Jews in *Beyond the Melting Pot* with the observation: "A leading figure in Jewish community affairs relates that a Jew always eagerly asks, in any situation, 'How many are Jews?' And when he gets an answer, he asks suspiciously, 'How do you know?'"[101]

Almost four decades later, Jews are still asking such questions. Indeed, they are more concerned than ever, since declining birth rates, intermarriage, and historically high levels of non-Jewish immigration have reduced the percentage of the population that is Jewish. The desire to know "how many are Jews" is sufficiently strong that various private enumerations have been sponsored by Jewish organizations. Such a census of Jews in metropolitan Los Angeles was released in late 1998, occasioning this observation by a rabbi affiliated with the American Jewish Committee: "My sense is that we conduct these surveys as much out of fear as curiosity. We worry whether our numbers are declining or if we're assimilating away."[102] As if to drive home the rabbi's point, the results of the 1998 Los Angeles census were then challenged by Orthodox Jews arguing that the census incorrectly registered a decline in their numbers.[103]

Yet not all Jewish leaders are preoccupied with numbers. As scholar and rabbi Jacob Neusner puts it, "We're not in competition with the Chinese."[104] More to the point, Jewish concern about numbers has never weakened Jewish opposition to any change in the Census Bureau's policy against asking about religious affiliation.[105] Clearly this is a group for whom numbers have not been the sine qua non of group advancement, a possibility never acknowledged in the current debate.

Such ambiguities are even more pronounced among homosexuals. In recent years social scientists have done surveys to determine the number of gay people in the United States. The most authoritative of these was published in 1994 by a team of researchers at the University of Chicago. This study reported that 2.8 percent of men and 1.4 percent of women identified themselves either as homosexual or bisexual.[106] Much lower than previous estimates, these provoked strong reactions from gay activists as well as from their adversaries.

But as *New York Times* reporter David Dunlap observed: "How much political effect the new survey will have is open to debate." Dunlap went on to cite one politician's perspective:

> For Representative Barney Frank, a Massachusetts Democrat who is gay, the answer is, "None whatever." "How many members of the N.R.A. are there?" Mr. Frank added. "I don't know. I don't think my colleagues know. What's important politically is not how many there are, but what you do about it. The extent to which you mobilize enormously outweighs the numbers."[107]

Admittedly, Frank was being too clever by half. But any astute leader of a minority group would have said the same thing when faced with such disappointing numbers. Frank has a point, not only about the importance of political mobilization but also about the salience of group numbers more generally.

The point is refined by Randall Sell, a doctoral candidate at the Harvard School of Public Health who has studied the demographics of homosexuality. Asked by Dunlap about the controversy, Sell responded: "Why should we care? Most of the reasons people tend to be talking about are civil rights, where it just doesn't matter."[108] Sell is clearly correct. Minorities claim rights precisely because they cannot otherwise hope to attain their objectives under majoritarian rules.

Yet even on this seemingly self-evident point there is another view. As a gay activist with the Campaign for Military Service told the *Washington Post*: "Politics is very much a matter of numbers, whether money or humans. An apparent diminution [of the percentage of homosexuals] may mislead politicians into taking a particular issue less seriously. Civil rights shouldn't be a matter of numbers, but . . . they are."[109] Clearly, minority leaders have a juggling act to perform. In practical political terms, they understand that rights claims inevitably benefit from maximized group totals; but relying too much on numbers can prove a dangerous game in which their vulnerability—either in terms of numbers of in terms of power—can be exposed.

These matters are sufficiently ambiguous that minority groups and their leaders do not automatically "play the numbers game." We have seen that when black leaders were originally approached by the Census Bureau about the undercount, they were skeptical of both the problem and of the proposed remedies. At the time of the 1980 census, American Indian leaders, preoccupied with population figures for the reservations, had to be persuaded by bureau officials of the importance of maximizing Indian totals in the cities.[110] In New York the physically handicapped at first resisted being counted, out of concern that this would further stigmatize them. It was only after some deliberation that they shifted their position and realized how beneficial the political visibility of numbers can be.[111]

The pattern seems to be that most groups (Jews being the most consistent exception) tend, over time, to opt for being counted and for using government statistics to advance their visibility and influence the public agenda. Moynihan sums up this commonsense view: "At one point in the course of the 1950's John Kenneth Galbraith observed that it is the statisticians, as much as any single group, who shape public policy, for the simple reason that societies never really become effectively concerned with social problems until they learn to measure them."[112] Yet Moynihan also exaggerates. During the depression, for example, the absence of accurate national data on the number and characteristics of the unemployed did not prevent Congress from enacting massive work relief and unemployment insurance programs.[113] More recently, advocates for the homeless resisted efforts by the Census Bureau to count the homeless in 1990, arguing that no official data would be better than the flawed and misleadingly low numbers the census would and (in their opinion) did yield.[114]

So Why All the Fuss?

If the interests at stake in the census are so unpredictable and ambiguous, then why has the debate over adjustment become so intense? Where has the pressure for—and against—adjustment been coming from?

The best way to begin is to note that for more than thirty years the undercount has been scrutinized without any clearly articulated standards by which to evaluate it. More precisely, the implicit standards that have been used have been unrealistically high.

Consider how the Census Bureau evaluates its own evidence on the consistency of responses to its questions. Chapter 3 pointed out that 88.6 percent of persons identifying as "Hispanic" on the 1990 Content Reinterview Survey (CRS) answered the same way on the census.[115] For some specific Hispanic subgroups, response consistencies were even lower. Yet a team of bureau professionals concludes: "Our analysis showed overall good consistency in reporting for the Hispanic origin item as a whole."[116] The point is not to take issue with this particular evaluation but to ask why an 11.4 percent slippage of Hispanics between the census and the CRS is regarded with equanimity, while a 4.96 percent undercount of Hispanics in the census is deemed a problem requiring an unprecedented and controversial remedy.

To be sure, coverage error (individuals being completely missed by the census) is a problem distinct from classification error (counting individuals but assigning them to the wrong census categories). Arguably, it is more troubling if the census completely misses individuals than if it "merely" misclassifies them. Yet in either case, minority population counts can be adversely affected. So why all the fuss over one and not the other?

Senator Moynihan made a similar point when, amid the national debate over the Clinton administration's ill-fated proposal for universal health insurance coverage, he remarked:

> And we talk about universal care. Well, universal doesn't mean 100 percent universal coverage, I mean, because you never get 100 percent. A hundred percent of the people don't pay their taxes. . . . A hundred percent of the people aren't counted by the census. . . . But, you know, you get up toward 95 percent and you're getting to about—given the normal confusions of life—that's, that's just about everybody. In a country like this there's always going to be some guy living in a cabin out in the Klondike who did not get the word that he's supposed to have health insurance. Or if he cared, he wouldn't be living in a cabin out in the Klondike anyway, you know.[117]

It is precisely this note of realism that is missing from the arguments of those who feel that the differential racial undercount calls for statistical adjustment. Because we cannot reasonably expect *any* census data to be without error, it would be particularly helpful for adjustment advocates to specify what they would consider an acceptable level of undercount. No such standards have thus far been articulated.

Contrary to Moynihan's example, the paradigmatic case for the census is not "some guy in the Klondike" unconcerned about health care but a young black man dividing his time between his mother's and his girlfriend's households. As in most other policy realms, race greatly complicates the application of standards to the census undercount. Indeed, race seems to lead to the adoption of especially high standards. Yet no matter how rigorous, if these standards are not made explicit and the reasons for them clearly stated, we will continue to wrangle over the undercount in frustration and failure.

Now let us consider where the pressure for adjustment has been coming from. For some time now a leading proponent of adjustment has been the Census Bureau itself. It is striking that this weak and embattled federal agency has supported such a bold and controversial notion, once again countering the view that the bureau is "institutionally conservative."[118] Moreover, the bureau's support for adjustment has been evident in both Republican and Democratic administrations. The question is: Why?

To begin, it is important to acknowledge that the bureau has come to adjustment gradually, in the course of years of trials and tests. Around the time of the 1980 census it experimented with a rudimentary version of what in 1990 came to be called the postenumeration survey. The consensus among census professionals was that any such means of adjustment was not technically feasible.

Nonetheless, work on the problem continued throughout the 1980s. There were definite incentives to do so: for statisticians long constrained by the norms of an agency dominated by demographers committed to traditional methods of counting, adjustment represented a professional challenge. Toward the end of the 1980s many statisticians at the bureau were convinced that it was technically feasible to adjust the census with a postenumeration survey. Barbara Bailar, associate director for standards and methodology, who had been outspoken against adjustment at the beginning of the decade, was by then just as outspoken in favor of it.[119] There remained throughout this period sharp disagreements among census professionals over adjustment—particularly between those from the bureau's Statistical Research Division, who tended to support it, and those with planning and operational responsibilities, who tended to oppose it.[120] Nevertheless, in July 1987 Census Director John Keane decided to proceed with plans that would at least make it possible to adjust the 1990 census.

It was at this point that Keane was abruptly and heavy-handedly overruled by his superiors at the Department of Commerce. On October 30, 1987, Under Secretary of Commerce Robert Ortner issued a press release announcing: "The department does not intend to adjust the 1990 census because such an adjustment may create more problems than it solves and would impair the accuracy of the 1990 census."[121] Thus, without any warning and without much more explanation than quoted here, a political appointee of the Commerce Department, widely regarded as one of the most politicized parts of the executive branch, preempted the head of what had been long viewed as an "independent agency."[122] Indeed, Ortner's intervention contravened the precedent set in 1980, when then commerce secretary Philip Klutznick conceded that the decision to adjust the census was a technical one to be made by the director of the census.[123]

Whatever the motives of Ortner and his colleagues at the Department of Commerce, the results were disastrous. Bailar resigned and became a vocal proponent of adjustment and critic of the administration. Those who had been working on adjustment scenarios at the bureau were outraged—although, ironically, their position within the bureau was probably enhanced, while even the mildest skeptics of adjustment suddenly looked like lackeys of the Republican administration. The inevitable ill feelings were aggravated by the fact that Ortner had actually made his decision several months earlier and had sworn Director Keane to secrecy, which forced Keane on several occasions to misrepresent to his colleagues what was going on.[124]

The ensuing controversy has only exacerbated the long-term problems facing the Census Bureau. As in 1980, legal challenges to the 1990 census were a distraction that made it harder to mount a successful enumeration.[125] Perhaps more to the point, litigation has heightened the inevitable tensions between the bureau and the Department of Commerce. Specifically, it has caused political appointees and lawyers at Commerce to exert more control over the bureau. This increased scrutiny of the activities of bureau professionals has gone against the grain of an agency that prided itself on openness, collegiality, and independence.

None of this has helped the bureau's morale. Controversy and turmoil have not aided the recruitment of executive talent, as seen in the frequent vacancies in the director's position at critical periods in the planning of the decennial census.[126] Each year there have been fewer old hands able to combine technical know-how with political savvy. And after the 1990 census, some of those who had resisted the adjustment juggernaut either retired or were encouraged to transfer out of the bureau.

Yet in spite of Under Secretary Ortner's decision, the research and testing of the adjustment methodology proceeded.[127] Technical improvements eventually made adjustment look like the solution to many of the bureau's continuing problems, including declining response rates, increasing social diversity (especially of non-English-speaking immigrants), growing costs, and of course the differential racial undercount. Even though the 1990 census was never actually adjusted, the idea of adjustment continued to thrive within the bureau.

By the early 1990s, however, census professionals were not simply advocating "adjustment." Their response to these problems was a detailed strategy to produce what they called a "one-number census." In January 1993, just days after her departure as director, Bryant offered this explanation:

> What I do think now, going into 2000, is first of all, we can never do it this way again; having two numbers out there is just impossible. States became pitted against States, mayors became pitted against their own Governors—that sort of thing. We've got to find some way to build adjustment into the census-taking process, and I think we can improve accuracy by doing it.[128]

In 1996 the official bureau document laying out plans for the 2000 census stated that a key goal would be "to produce a 'one-number census' that is right the first time and allows statisticians and demographers to determine census totals, not lawyers and judges."[129] In the wake of the controversy over the 1990 enumeration, the bureau decided that the next census would have to be done so that no one could distinguish adjusted from unadjusted results. By making adjustment so integral to the census that it would not be possible to derive more than one set of numbers from it, the bureau sought to wrest control back from "lawyers and judges" and to obviate the conflicts that had arisen after 1990 over which set of numbers to use.

This bold strategy was not without a plausible rationale. To many at the bureau, integrating statistical procedures into the enumeration was the only operationally feasible way to produce improved data that met legally established deadlines. The one-number census also made sense as a way of locking in technical decisions before their effects on census outcomes could be known and consequently subjected to political pressures.[130]

Yet from outside the bureau, the one-number census looked far less reasonable. To many in Congress, "building" adjustment into the census looked more like burying it there. Such skepticism was fueled early in the debate when even sympathetic statisticians noted that the bureau was writing about the one-number census without ever actually using the word "adjustment."[131] When the bureau did use the "A-word," it would make unhelpful assertions such as: "This quality check procedure will lead to a 'one-number census' and eliminate the need for subsequent 'adjustment' of the decennial count."[132]

Insisting that the results of a one-number census could not be disaggregated, the bureau risked patronizing skeptical members of Congress and at the same time seemed to be violating its own well-established commitment to opennness.[133] Similarly unpersuasive, even counterproductive, was the agency's effort to neutralize the large number in Congress who were opposed to adjustment in any form by insisting that "the procedures have won virtually unanimous endorsement from the statistical community."[134]

In essence, the one-number census reflected the professional aspirations of bureau personnel who were attempting to respond to pressing societal needs but had in fact become excessively insulated from the political environment in which their agency operates. It was technically sophisticated but politically naive.

Doing the Right Thing

There is one more factor critical to understanding the push for adjustment from the Census Bureau as well as from other agencies and organizations: the pervasive desire to "do the right thing." The persistent and growing differential racial undercount is not just a professional challenge to Census Bureau officials. For many it represents yet another injustice inflicted on racial minorities who have long suffered mistreatment and discrimination. Bryant articulates this perspective when she explains her support for adjustment of the 1990 census: "I think the one thing overriding in my pro-adjustment position was the feeling that for 50 years, for five censuses, the Census Bureau had measured an undercount of certain segments of our population, and that it's time to right this."[135] It would be difficult to exaggerate the number of times this view gets expressed, not only by census officials and staffers but also by congressional aides, academic experts, and of course adjustment advocates. Some go further, to the point of asserting that the undercount is one more manifestation of the racism permeating American society. As should by now be evident, this is hardly the only, or the strongest, motive animating bureau officials on this issue. But it affects just about every discussion of what to do about the undercount.

Some observers have noted such sentiments at the bureau and concluded that it is dominated by partisan Democrats.[136] Given the bureau's history and the political orientation of social scientists generally, it is plausible that many of its personnel are Democrats. But there is no evidence on this point, much less on how partisan such individuals might be. What we do know is that the bureau has an unblemished reputation for being nonpartisan.[137] We also know that Bryant is no Democrat. On the contrary, she describes herself as "a Republican philosophically" and credits her appointment as census director to pollster Robert Teeter, her longtime business associate and codirector of George Bush's 1988 transition team.[138]

Of course, there are Republicans and there are *Republicans*, and one suspects that Bryant is not one of the latter. But this is all quite beside the point. To adjustment advocates both inside and outside the bureau, the undercount of minorities constitutes a fundamental denial of benefits, the correction of which must transcend politics as usual. From this perspective, census adjustment is a matter of basic fairness and justice that, rather than involving any ordinary clash of interests, would restore order to the polity so that the pursuit of mundane interests might then proceed. As discussed later in this chapter, this understanding of adjustment is one reason why its advocates rely so heavily on the rhetoric of rights.

Undeniably, the desire to "do the right thing" coexists at the bureau with the aforementioned effort to avoid highlighting the racial underpinnings of the adjustment issue. This paradox can be explained by the fact that the former perspective is almost never articulated for broad public consumption. When it is voiced publicly, as in the case of Bryant, it is invariably by an individual who has relinquished her official responsibilities.

Republican "Paranoia"

Precisely because they are loath to come out against minority rights, Republicans have focused their antiadjustment arguments on statistical and legal technicalities, particularly on the constitutional requirement of an "actual enumeration." Yet such tactical trimming belies the intensity of Republican opposition to adjustment—an intensity that, in light of the uncertainty of Republican interests at stake, needs to be explained.

Any such explanation must begin by noting the instinctive distrust of many Republicans toward social scientists and their research. As Moynihan observes: "Individuals and groups that have been most resistant to liberal social change have quite accurately perceived that social statistics are all too readily transformed into political dynamite."[139] To this one must add Republican opposition to affirmative action. For while racial and ethnic data gathered by the census do not directly benefit individual members of minority groups, the collection of such data is inevitably linked in the minds of many Republicans with policies they strongly criticize.

Still more compelling, though, are Republican memories of having been bested by aggressive Democratic gerrymandering in 1980 and to a lesser extent in 1990. Tales of Democratic chicanery in Indiana and California are now part of the lore passed on to new members of the House Republican caucus. As John Pitney, an academic specialist on congressional Republicans and a former Republican National Committee staffer, remarks, Republicans are "paranoid" on the subject of Democrats and redistricting.[140] Despite their much stronger position in the nation's statehouses today than in 1990, Republicans are clearly shaken by the fact that Democrats have regained control of the key battleground state of California, where Democrats were in control during the debacle of the Burton gerrymander after 1980. Nor were these Republican worries allayed when President Bill Clinton named to the bipartisan Census Monitoring Board Tony Coelho, the former Democratic congressman and majority whip who during the 1980s played a key role in ensuring Republican defeat in a disputed congressional election in Indiana.[141]

Given such bad memories, it seems paradoxical that Republican members of Congress (not unlike their Democratic colleagues, as we saw in chapter 2) have paid so little attention to census issues. Yet in light of the highly contingent nature of adjustment's impact on apportionment and redistricting outcomes, as well as the inability of members of Congress (unlike other legislators) to redraw their own districts, it is understandable that members have invested scant time or energy in a highly technical undertaking that occurs once every ten years. Even though their political survival might hinge on the results, it is difficult to conclude that they are behaving irrationally.

But under such conditions it is also highly unlikely that thoughtful analyses of the undercount and adjustment would emerge from Congress. Far more likely are what we have seen: instinctive reactions based on quick studies and fearsome memories. To most Republican members of Congress, adjustment appears at best a gamble whose uncertain outcome they would just as soon avoid. This was true before the Republican majority slipped to a margin of eleven seats; it is all the more true now.

Democratic Opportunism and Minority Symbolism

Census adjustment is fraught with risks for Democrats as well. As discussed earlier, adjustment could weaken nonminority Democratic incumbents and might even strengthen Republicans. Still, Democrats do not want to say no to minorities on this one: for party leaders especially, adjustment is a gamble that they cannot afford *not* to take.

Why is this? First, the risks involved are merely risks, not certainties. Indeed, from the perspective of the mid-1990s, when the Democratic position crystallized, these were risks that would not have to be addressed for several years, if ever. Second and more important, the census is highly symbolic to minorities, especially to African Americans. Moreover, compared with other demands that minorities are likely to make on Democrats—such as affirmative action, increased minimum wages, or greater educational expenditures—census adjustment seems *relatively* costless. Like redistricting, adjustment is a highly technical issue not likely to arouse much opposition among the general public.[142] And given the seemingly intractable nature of many minority and urban problems, the differential racial undercount is one malady for which there appears to be a clear remedy. For these reasons, therefore, adjustment has been an inexpensive concession for Democrats; they might prefer to say no, but feel that it is not worth doing so.

Despite their distrust of adjustment methodologies, minority leaders have found adjustment appealing for the same reasons Democrats have: it appears to be a low cost, straightforward solution to an apparently pressing social problem. Certainly three decades of affirmative action have attuned minority leaders to the importance of maximizing their group numbers. Of Hispanics, political scientist and current census director Kenneth Prewitt has noted, "More than any group in American political history, Hispanic Americans have turned to the national statistical system as an instrument for advancing their political and economic interests."[143] Blacks have felt compelled to follow suit, if only because their declining numbers in relation to Hispanics have pushed them into a defensive preoccupation with population totals.

But minority support for adjustment involves much more than narrow calculations of concrete interests. For black Americans in particular, the census is redolent with the hurtful symbolism of the Three Fifths Compromise, by which the Constitution originally required that each slave be counted as three-fifths of a person. Minority leaders often interpret the undercount in this light, as did Representative Cynthia McKinney (Democrat of Georgia) when she declared on the House floor: "If the Republican Party has their way [in opposing adjustment], they will return us to the days of Dred Scott, where poor people and people of color count as three-fifths of a person."[144] In the same vein, Representative Carrie Meek has referred to the Three Fifths Compromise as a "constitutionally mandated undercount of African-Americans" and declared that "we continue to see its legacy in the taking of the census."[145]

The Plaintiffs' Incentives

Nonetheless, the most visible and sustained impetus for adjustment has come less from minority groups than from cities and other jurisdictions. Certainly in the numerous legal battles that have transpired, minorities have not been in the front ranks; rather these battles have typically been fought by surrogates invoking minority interests. This little-noted fact might be attributed to limited organizational and political resources. But one suspects that if minority leaders and organizations regarded the undercount as a priority issue, then they would have invested more heavily in it.

As for officials in undercounted jurisdictions, adjustment would be a gamble for them just as for the other political actors discussed. Yet the incentives facing such officials are such that there has been little downside to participating in the battle for adjustment, while standing pat would have had a potentially high price. As demonstrated earlier, adjustment could leave a city demographically or fiscally worse off in relation to other jurisdictions. But no individual jurisdiction would have any control over such an outcome. So, faced with the alternatives of staying on the sidelines and being accused of inaction or of joining in the fray, public officials in undercounted jurisdictions have had good reasons to get involved—in addition, of course, to their own beliefs that adjustment would result in real benefits.

It helps that such officials have been able to get local law firms to litigate on the community's behalf on a pro bono basis. This reflects the fact that cities partake of a natural boosterism that focuses on population growth as a measure of vitality. Census adjustment has consequently been one issue where beleaguered mayors and city administrators can prove themselves responsive *both* to business and to minority interests. The Census Bureau's lack of political savvy has also made it a relatively easy target. Such political dynamics have encouraged local officials to indulge in rhetoric articulating whatever principled objections they may have to the undercount, as did one official with the city of Los Angeles who referred to the undercount as "the last vestige of racism."

Different dynamics have similarly prompted public officials generally to make exaggerated claims about the costs of the undercount to their jurisdictions. Such claims have in part been fueled by the fact that legal standing in adjustment suits is typically based not on demonstration of the actual or total costs of the undercount, but merely of *some* negative impact. This lax standard reinforces a more basic bureaucratic dynamic: because it is extremely difficult and time-consuming to determine the actual fiscal impacts of the undercount for specific jurisdictions, the bureaucrats to whom local officials turn for estimates invariably have insufficient time and resources for any thorough investigation. Understandably unwilling to displease their superiors, these public servants generate numbers that are gross approximations erring generously on the side of their jurisdictions.

This explains how, as highlighted above, the New York City planning department could come up with an estimated loss per uncounted resident— $200 per year—about ten times what researchers found. More recently, the city of Los Angeles has projected that without an adjustment of the 2000 census, it will lose $18 million per year in federal and state funds over the decade 2000–10.[146] Even without scrutinizing the assumptions on which it is based, this figure represents less than 1 percent of the city's annual expenditures.[147] Yet when picked up by the media, such numbers are taken out of context and bandied about uncritically. They take on a life of their own, as does the notion that huge fiscal stakes are at issue.[148] As Maurice and Nathan observe: "Representatives of cities have issued exaggerated and unsubstantiated statements, some of which have been repeated so often that they are sometimes mistaken for facts."[149] In the words of the assistant director of the GAO, "Common wisdom drives you to think that these numbers control a lot more dollars than they do. . . . They aren't the huge factor these mayors think they are. A lot of these mayors are more worried than they need to be."[150]

The Risk of Participation Meltdown

If the interests at stake in adjustment are cloudy, some of the risks are clear. Prominent among these is "participation meltdown": a dramatic decline in cooperation with the census due to the perception that adjustment would obviate the need to fill out census forms. Asks the NAS panel chaired by Keith Rust: "Will people assume that they do not need to respond by mail because the use of sampling means that their participation makes no difference to the results?"[151] Or as Charles Schultze, chair of another NAS panel, said in response to a skeptical member of Congress: "You put your finger on what is a real problem that has to be surmounted, which is keeping people interested in doing it right when you say you're going to do statistical sampling."[152]

Experts believe that census participation is threatened more by SNRFU-type programs than by postcensus sampling. While postcensus sampling occurs some months after the census is completed, SNRFU is designed to be in the field at the same time as the actual enumeration and might therefore create an immediate disincentive to filling out questionnaires. Although SNRFU is no longer a component of the 2000 census, these concerns are still worth examining.

Specifically addressing SNRFU, the NAS Schultze panel has warned

> that an excessively early truncation of census follow-up activities may be perceived by the public as not trying to count the entire population. This, in turn, could lower mail response rates, raise costs, and lower the quality of the census for small areas. The panel believes that it is important to maintain both the actuality and the public perception that the census is mandatory and that the census makes the attempt to count every person.[153]

At a recent 2000 Census Advisory Committee meeting, a county commissioner was quoted inquiring about SNRFU: "Does that mean you're not going to count all my people?" The short answer would have to be yes. There is a fundamental tension between the mandatory nature of participation in the census and the message inevitably conveyed by SNRFU (or postcensus sampling, for that matter): that nonparticipation is an acceptable response, for which contingency plans have been drawn up. In operational terms, it is difficult to fathom how the Census Bureau could simultaneously emphasize the obligatory nature of census cooperation *and* its own reliance on sampling.

Worries about the negative impact of SNRFU on census participation are necessarily conjectural, since there is virtually no empirical research on the topic.[154] But as the policy process unfolds, methodologies such as SNRFU are likely to resurface, and with them many unanswered questions. Would local jurisdictions bother with their own promotional and outreach efforts, on which the bureau has in the past depended? How would elected officials muster support for local expenditures on outreach and promotion if the public believed that (to repeat the words of the NAS Rust panel) "participation makes no difference to the results"?

If SNRFU did cause participation to decline, the cost of the census would increase. For example, each additional percentage point of mail-out nonresponse will add $25 million to the cost of the 2000 census.[155] So increased expenditures would likely generate pressure for greater reliance on SNRFU, whose primary appeal is, after all, cost reduction. And since, from a technical standpoint, SNRFU could be implemented when many fewer than 90 percent of households in a given geographic area have responded, such pressure would be intense.[156]

Given the distrust that SNRFU has fueled among minority leaders, as well as heightened distrust toward government among Americans generally, there is reason to be concerned about increasing public confusion about even relatively straightforward aspects of the census. Again, systematic evidence is hard to come by. But my own experiences are telling. I recall, for example, trying to explain SNRFU to a colleague at Harvard Law School, whose immediate response was, "This stuff's too complicated." On another occasion, at a 2000 Census Advisory Committee meeting, a demographer sheepishly asked a question, adding that he might have missed the answer while dozing off. Then there is the distinguished demographer Nathan Keyfitz, who calmly reports: "I tried explaining sampling to my highly literate but not numerate wife, and after a few minutes, by mutual consent, we changed the subject."[157] If the trained expert or the highly educated consumer of public policy research finds these issues slow going, one can hardly expect that they will engage the average American.

This is not news to those conducting the census. One of the bureau's four "fundamental strategies" for Census 2000 is "keep it simple." As it explains, "The simpler and easier Census 2000 is, the more accurate and less expensive it will be. Simplicity is a goal for every part of the process."[158] Yet the bureau neglects to explain how it plans to reconcile this fundamental strategy with another: "use statistical methods."[159]

Similarly, the NAS Rust panel acknowledges the concerns discussed here but then brushes them aside. The panel's report specifically cites "increasing cynicism toward government"[160] and "public perception of the use of sampling"[161] as concerns worthy of attention. Yet the panel's analysis of these issues, which was a component of the bureau's planning for the 2000 census, is unhelpfully constricted. Having cited the problem of cynicism toward government, the panel then assumes that the only source of cynicism about the census is the differential racial undercount. Not considered is the possibility that cynicism might also be fueled by difficult-to-explain sampling and adjustment methodologies. With regard to public perceptions of sampling, the panel limits its analysis to a consideration of alternative sampling methodologies and says nothing at all about what impact sampling might have on public confidence in the census.

Without systematic evidence, any judgment is perforce speculative. Yet there are a handful of episodes, regrettably not mentioned in the bureau's or the NAS panels' analyses, that provide some clues for policymakers. None of these involve SNRFU, which is not surprising since it has never actually been implemented. And while SNRFU, postcensus sampling, and adjustment are distinct endeavors that should not be confused, it seems prudent to examine whatever evidence is available, especially since the differences among these programs are not understood by the public, who (encouraged by the bureau) tend to think simply in terms of "sampling and adjustment"— and whose perceptions are, after all, the focus of our concern.

What can we glean from these episodes? The first occurred during the debate over adjustment of the 1990 census. After working hard to attain the highest voluntary mail response rate in the nation, Wisconsin elected officials (of both parties) expressed dismay when they realized that adjustment would penalize their state with the loss of a congressional seat. Representative Thomas Petri (Republican of Wisconsin) asked rhetorically, "If the adjustment is going to be done in any event, why should they [the states] spend any money at the local level to encourage compliance with the census procedures?"[162]

The second episode was highlighted at the beginning of this chapter: the error in the 1991 adjusted census data. If Secretary of Commerce Mosbacher had decided to use those unrevised numbers, a congressional seat would have shifted from Pennsylvania to Arizona because of a computer program error.[163] The next step, surely, would have been charges that the adjustment had been politically driven, and public confidence in the integrity of the census would have been compromised.

A third episode is related by Bryant. In her memoir of her tenure as census director, she presents indirect but persuasive evidence that the bureau would have found this 1991 error exceedingly difficult to explain. Recounting the public relations disaster that the bureau had in 1990 when local governments challenged preliminary (unadjusted) census counts as too low, she argues that local politicians grossly exaggerated the number of missed housing units. Acknowledging that the bureau did make mistakes, Bryant also maintains that it was fighting a losing battle because "technical errors were impossible to explain to the public."[164]

Would not technical errors associated with an unprecedented adjustment methodology be equally impossible to explain? Having attended numerous meetings at the Census Bureau where knowledgeable professionals have confused one another about statistical sampling and adjustment, I cannot believe that they would be any more adept at explaining their efforts, erroneous or otherwise, to lay people. Nor can I believe that such explanations would be well received by those on whose behalf census adjustment is advocated: the least advantaged and often most alienated.

On this very point there is a striking piece of evidence from the one study that has attempted to examine the impact of adjustment on census participation. In 1991 the Census Bureau commissioned the National Opinion Research Center (NORC) to conduct a survey on the effects that adjustment of the 1990 census would have on participation in the 2000 census. The findings were inconsistent and inconclusive, in large part because Americans were ill-informed and confused about the census. Indeed, in the middle of a prolonged public controversy over adjustment, only 5 percent of those surveyed displayed any understanding of the issue.[165]

Nevertheless, the survey did find that it was not so much the decision to adjust or not to adjust that affected intentions to participate in the next census. Rather, the more respondents heard about census adjustment and the controversy surrounding it, the less inclined they were to cooperate next time. And among respondents, minorities were as put off as nonminorities, if not more so.[166]

Clearly we should not put too much weight on a single study, especially one probing intentions to do or not to do something nine years hence. Yet it is highly suggestive that the controversy over adjustment alienated respondents, particularly minority respondents. This is reminiscent of what Hugh Heclo calls the "everything causes cancer" syndrome. Concerned with the challenge technical expertise poses to our democratic values, Heclo identified the perverse dynamic whereby debate among experts results less in enlightenment than in disaffection among nonspecialists, who become "inclined to concede everything and believe nothing."[167]

A Right to Be Counted?

Beyond such practical concerns lie more fundamental issues raised by the arguments of adjustment advocates. Of particular interest are efforts to extricate the census from politics, either by invocation of a "right to be counted" or by appeals to scientific authority. I address first the right to be counted.

The claiming of rights is one path around—or, more accurately, above—politics. Such claims resonate widely in a regime such as ours that is based on natural rights. As various commentators have recently noted, we Americans are all too prone to "rights talk."[168] For adjustment advocates, the right to be counted is arguably an even more tempting means of transcending politics than science.

Rights claims have often been advanced in the various legal battles that have sought to compel the bureau to adjust its data.[169] Yet such claims have been even more frequent in the broader public debate over census adjustment, on which I focus here.

Senator Charles Schumer (Democrat of New York) has made the case as directly as anyone: "The Constitution, of course, guarantees the right of every person residing in the United States to be counted."[170] Moynihan similarly cast the undercount in terms of rights back in 1968: "Inasmuch as Negroes and other 'minorities' are concentrated in specific urban locations, to undercount significantly the population in those areas is to deny residents their rights under Article I, Section 3 of the Constitution."[171] Today, the right to be counted is so widely accepted that even opponents of adjustment assert it, albeit on behalf of those who participate in the conventional enumeration but might have their numbers reduced by adjustment. As Representative John Boehner (Republican of Ohio) has argued: "Sampling corrupts a basic sense of fairness by treating people as numbers that can be estimated, rather than individuals who have a right to be counted."[172]

Yet adjustment advocates do not regard this as any ordinary right. The clear racial dimension to the undercount has led them to frame this in classic civil rights terms. Attorney Peter Zimroth, who litigated for adjustment on behalf on New York City during the late 1980s and early 1990s, emphasizes:

> I always viewed this case primarily as a civil rights case, and I think in fact it is one of the most important civil rights cases in the country

today. . . . I think you'll see that the undercount is directly correlated to the incidence of poverty, which is correlated to race.[173]

In the same vein, Jeffrey Wice, who monitored the decennial census for the New York State Assembly for many years, has described his work "as a continuation of what Al Lowenstein believed in and worked for: civil rights and voter empowerment."[174] Or as a spokesman for the Mexican American Legal Defense and Educational Fund (MALDEF) put it: "This is a civil rights issue because the majority of the people missed were Latinos, African-Americans, Asians, and Native Americans."[175]

Because of the obvious connection between the census and redistricting, the right to be counted has been linked to the right to vote.[176] Declares Jessica Heinz of the Los Angeles City Attorney's Office: "An accurate census is the cornerstone of our democratic government—without it, the promise of one person, one vote is an illusive [sic] dream."[177] Some have pushed the argument even further. Journalist Miguel Perez has written: "For racial and ethnic groups, it is perhaps more important than the right to vote, an even more basic human right: the right to be counted."[178]

More typical is the view that going uncounted in the census is equivalent to being denied representation, even to being disenfranchised. In 1991 Democratic National Committee chairman Ron Brown offered this characterization of the Bush administration's decision against adjustment: "President Bush has accomplished in one step what it took the Reagan administration a decade to achieve—to disenfranchise millions of Americans, working Americans, and in effect say they don't matter."[179]

To be sure, census data on race and ethnicity are critical to the implementation of laws and programs intended to foster and protect various rights. But this fact hardly translates into a right to be counted. The illogic of such a leap is quickly demonstrated by means of a brief thought experiment. Virtually all parties to the adjustment controversy concede that if the undercount rates for minorities were equivalent to those for nonminorities, then there would be no controversy.[180] But if being counted is a right, how can this be so? This is like arguing that it would be permissible to deny the right of free speech as long as it were done evenly across all sectors of society.

It might perhaps be argued that the right to be counted inheres not in individuals but in groups, and that such a right would be satisfied if all groups were equally undercounted. But the right to be counted has been advanced as an individual, not a group right. If the differential racial undercount were eliminated, large numbers of individuals would still go uncounted, and their putative rights would be violated. That most of us would tolerate such an outcome suggests that we are not dealing here with anything as fundamental as rights.

Another problem with the right to be counted is that participation in the census has been construed historically not as a right but as an obligation mandated by law.[181] To be sure, this obligation has seldom been enforced.[182] The relatively relaxed posture typically taken by the federal government is evident in Franklin Roosevelt's 1940 presidential proclamation announcing the sixteenth decennial census: "The prompt, complete, and accurate answering of all official inquiries addressed to each person by Census officials should be regarded by him as one of the requirements of good citizenship."[183] Today, even this has been weakened by our political culture's emphasis on self-interest and individual rights over civic obligation.

The Framers certainly entertained no notion of a right to be counted. As discussed in chapter 2, their conception of the census drew on classical antecedents, infused with notions of virtue and civic duty. In the modern regime they established, the census was understood to balance the opposing incentives of representation and taxation. The results of such a process were understood as approximations, which were hardly consistent with the precise and demanding requirements of rights.

The right to be counted has been further undermined by the arguments of adjustment advocates themselves. While urging the importance of this right, these advocates also point out that adjustment would help reduce the burgeoning cost of the decennial census. The NAS Schultze panel argues that "it is critical to challenge the attitude that the census needs to be improved without regard to costs and cost-effectiveness."[184] But if disadvantaged minorities were truly being denied a right, then costs would not be a consideration.[185]

Equally problematic is the presumed equivalence of being counted in the census and voting. Curiously, this equivalence is made on both sides of the adjustment controversy.

Adjustment advocates argue that because the uncounted are not included in the one-person/one-vote calculations on which legislative district lines are based, then being uncounted is tantamount to being disenfranchised. Opponents of adjustment adopt a similar logic. Also asserting a right to be counted, they argue that where adjustment would result in decreased counts, the enumerated individuals thereby eliminated (what statistician David Freedman calls "negative persons")[186] would be deprived of the franchise.

Thus opponents conclude that adjusting the census is tantamount to rigging an election.

These arguments may work rhetorically, but the underlying assumption is, I am suggesting, highly problematic. By equating a presumed right to be counted with the right to vote, both sides are advancing an extraordinarily formalistic conception of the political process. Can individuals or groups be regarded as represented regardless of their efforts in the political arena—merely by being counted in the census, for example? I do not believe so. Conversely, can individuals or groups who are not counted in the census vote, engage in political action, and organize others to do so? Most definitely. To equate the undercount with disenfranchisement, or the elimination of enumerated individuals with election fraud, is to assume away any notion of a self-reliant, proactive citizenry.

Furthermore, if the right to be counted is premised on an equivalence with the franchise, then what about those who are supposed to be counted but who cannot vote? Children accounted for more than half of the total net undercount in 1990.[187] Noncitizens, either legal or illegal aliens, represented another substantial, albeit unknown, segment of the undercount. The claims of these two broad groups on American society are quite different. After all, it is plausible to argue that minors who are American citizens have a presumed right to representation that, in the view of adjustment advocates, then implies a right to be counted. But any such case made on behalf of noncitizens is much less plausible. In any event, it surely makes little sense to speak of uncounted children and noncitizens as being disenfranchised.

Despite such defects, the right to be counted has strong appeal to adjustment advocates because it holds out the promise of concrete benefits without getting mired in the usual give-and-take of politics. Shep Melnick has observed: "The language of rights serves to emphasize the benefits conferred on rights-holders while obscuring the nature, extent, and distribution of the program's costs."[188] We Americans are particularly prone to overlooking the fact that rights claims, especially in behalf of racial minorities, necessitate the power and hence the politics to enforce those claims.

Science or Politics?

I now turn to the persistent but wrongheaded view of the census as a properly apolitical, scientific undertaking. This understanding extends to census adjustment, usually advocated as a scientific procedure that transcends partisan or political interests. While there is no scientific consensus on statistical adjustment, it does enjoy support from many scientists. Indeed, adjustment has been endorsed by the Population Association of America, the Association of American Geographers, and the American Statistical Association.[189]

The scientists who favor adjustment show signs of impatience with non-scientists who disagree. One prominent demographer, exasperated with the resistance to adjustment on Capitol Hill, remarked at a Census Bureau advisory committee meeting, "There is agreement in the professional community—so what's the problem?"[190] At times this impatience verges on condescension, interpreting all opposition to adjustment as the result of ignorance, at best. In the words of the American Statistical Association: "We believe the critics may have misunderstood the scientific basis of the Census Bureau's sampling plans."[191] When the NAS Schultze panel entitles its report in favor of adjustment *Modernizing the U.S. Census*, the implication is that to oppose adjustment is to resist the forward thrust of history.[192]

One pores over the statements and reports of these scientists without finding any acknowledgment of the limits of scientific expertise in a democratic society. Nor do these scientists recognize much, if any, role for politics in a process that was, after all, embedded in the Constitution by the Framers to deal with the inherently political tasks of apportioning representation and taxes. Scientists advocating adjustment do not necessarily make explicit or extravagant claims for science, but neither do they typically leave much room for the prerogatives of politics.

By contrast, a very different tone was struck by a NAS panel that considered census adjustment back in 1985: "Granting that a data set can never be completely accurate, one must decide what constitutes sufficient accuracy for particular uses and whether adjustments that can be made represent sufficiently significant improvements. . . . *Ultimately, these are political judgments*" (emphasis added).[193] In the current controversy it is precisely this perspective that is absent from the pronouncements of scientists.

The notion that scientists are uniquely capable of resolving intractable political wrangles is itself curiously out of date. It is reminiscent of Progressive-era bromides about there being "no Republican or Democratic way to pick up the garbage or repair the streets." Progressive reformers looked expectantly to science for authoritative answers to otherwise unresolvable political conflicts, a view rooted in the nineteenth-century understanding of science as providing definitive answers to all questions. One need not subscribe to the fashionable Kuhnian view of science as merely a social and political construct to be struck by the irony that those who advocate updating the census with the latest tools of statistical science are themselves relying on a conception of science so outmoded as to be almost quaint.[194]

Contemporary understandings of science are attuned to the myriad ways that it is influenced by value choices and broad social and political forces. The science of statistics cannot tell us which phenomena to observe and to measure, nor how to categorize data once they are gathered. Writes statistical policy analyst Judith Innes:

> Even the most straightforward of measures depends on some assumptions and on how one defines a problem. . . . Imagine, for example, a classroom full of chairs and tables. The professor would count the number of places to sit, the janitor would count the pieces of furniture in categories demanded for his inventory, perhaps the number of each type of chair or table according to which department owns it, and a junk dealer might simply want the weight of scrap metals and wood.[195]

Or as Paul Starr comments: "The structuring of information allows room for discretionary choice and, therefore, necessarily receives direction from broader social and political values and frames of reference."[196] Science is simply not the source of transcendent answers to the profoundly political dilemmas faced by the census.

The scientific basis of statistical sampling is undeniable. But as we have seen, adjustment is a massive logistical undertaking that involves much more than any conventional sample survey. Quite aside from operational considerations, politics permeates even the most technical aspects of sampling and adjustment. Recall how black leaders objected to the original plan to use counties as the geographic unit for SNRFU and successfully lobbied for the use of census tracts instead.[197] The bureau's initial formulation of SNRFU was driven not by science but by the need to reduce the cost of the 2000 census, and for that reason its initial resistance to changes was on fiscal grounds. When the bureau finally did alter SNRFU, it was responding at least in part to the threat of Representative Meek's legislation. Such decisions were clearly guided by political, not scientific considerations.

The same point can be made about the Census Bureau's original decision to truncate traditional follow-up once 90 percent of households in a given geographic unit had responded. As noted earlier, from a scientific perspective the truncation point could have been much lower than 90 percent. The bureau has made no effort to hide the fact that this figure was chosen on the basis of focus group results indicating that anything lower would undermine public confidence in the census.[198]

We have already seen how politics seeps into adjustment when (as in 1991) statisticians produce multiple alternatives to unadjusted census data. Faced with such alternative "goods," any one of which would be "better" than unadjusted numbers, how shall we decide among them, especially when each set of numbers produces different winners and losers? In the making of such necessarily political choices, statistical science has no guidance to offer.

Even when statisticians are careful to focus on technical questions and avoid politics, they do not succeed. Take, for example, the Undercount Steering Committee, the nine-person body set up within the Census Bureau to advise the director on adjusting the 1990 census. By a 7–2 vote, the committee concluded that "adjusted counts are more accurate than census counts."[199] Endeavoring to base its analysis on exclusively "technical" grounds, the committee not only entitled its June 1991 report *Technical Assessment of the Accuracy of Unadjusted versus Adjusted 1990 Census Counts,* but also emphasized that it had self-consciously avoided the explicitly political ramifications of its deliberations.[200] Yet when the committee reported that "the majority judges that the improvement in counts on the average for the Nation, States, and places over 100,000 population outweighs the risk that the accuracy of adjusted counts might be less for small areas," it was clearly on political, not technical terrain.[201] Such assessment of risks, like the weighing of costs and benefits, may be aided by expertise and science but rests ultimately on political values. The committee intimated as much when it offered this defense of its decision: "The majority noted that the 39 states gaining accuracy through adjustment include those with disproportionate numbers of hard-to-enumerate populations. The 11 States whose loss function analysis suggests lower accuracy with adjusted population shares still would gain in absolute numbers and incur only small relative losses."[202] In other words, the relative losses to those eleven states are justified by the gains to undercounted minorities. This is a defensible position. But again, it is political, not technical in nature.

Where politics and science collide most dramatically is in the "prespecification" process. One outcome of the litigation over the 1990 census was the agreement among the various parties that the procedures to produce a set of adjusted numbers would be specified in advance, or "prespecified."[203] In this way the discretion of the statisticians would be limited, and their deliberations insulated from political influence. The theory was clear: if all the procedures to adjust were agreed on by the various parties in advance, then politics would be, and would be perceived to be, excluded from the process.

But prespecification did not quite work out as planned. One critical pre-specified step was the smoothing of the raw adjustment factors. As discussed in chapter 4, these were subject to considerable sampling error. Yet even before the statisticians got to that anticipated step, the standard errors of those raw adjustment factors were also found to be subject to substantial variation. This troubling result had *not* been anticipated in the prespecification agreement. Nevertheless, after careful consultation, Census Bureau statisticians decided that something had to be done. And it was: before the raw adjustment factors were smoothed, the extreme outlying standard errors were removed by means of a regression model. This unanticipated step has come to be known as "presmoothing."[204]

In the adjustment litigation, there was considerable dispute about pre-smoothing. Critics charged that it had not been part of the agreement. They also argued that presmoothing was based on circular reasoning: that it had been used because it produced the desired adjustments in the minority undercounts, thereby violating the letter and spirit of prespecification.[205] Other statisticians disagreed, arguing that presmoothing was a detail implicit in the prespecification agreement.[206]

Such disagreements obviously cannot be resolved here. But the larger point stands: it is inherently problematic to seek prior agreement on procedures that are not only complex but likely to result in unpredictable outcomes. The effort to stave off uncertainty and to avoid perceptions of political manipulation through prespecification failed in this instance, as did the effort to limit the discretion of the statisticians performing the adjustment (in the eyes of some statisticians, at least).

It is difficult to see how it could have been otherwise. On the one hand, census adjustment is such a complicated process that anticipating even the most important scenarios seems unlikely. On the other hand, because adjustment outcomes are so difficult to predict and often counterintuitive (which is one reason why the parties agree to prespecification), once those outcomes are in view, there will be pressure to resort to techniques that will change those results which have a negative impact on some group's interests. Said the Census Bureau's Undercount Steering Committee in jus-tification of presmoothing: "It would have been a mistake not to have cor-rected a major problem simply because the solution had not been fully prespecified."[207]

Another factor in the controversy over the 1990 census involved the two sets of numbers: the unadjusted data and the adjusted totals. John Rolph, a statistician particularly attentive to political dynamics, observes:

> Two sets of counts were produced and the decisionmaker, the Secretary of Commerce, was required to choose one or the other *after the consequences of his decision were apparent. He knew which states would be the winners and which would be the losers as well as the general pattern of shifting within states.* It is unavoidable that any decision under these circumstances will be criticized as being politically motivated.[208]

Rolph's point is well taken: under these conditions, Mosbacher's decision was inevitably going to be perceived as politically driven.

But Rolph's solution to the problem he identifies has similar shortcomings. Decrying the admittedly "fishbowl aspect" of the 1990 adjustment process, Rolph and others advocate a "one-number census" that would remove the process from public view by building adjustment into the very core of the census process, thereby obviating the bind that Secretary Mosbacher encountered in 1990. Yet as the presmoothing episode shows, even a one-number census would not escape political challenge. Once the results were in view, those who perceived their interests to be harmed would attack the process, which would be susceptible to such challenge because of its reliance on modeling assumptions. Furthermore, the attempt to keep the details "out of the fishbowl" would itself be denounced by disgruntled parties as unwarranted secrecy, not to mention violated by whistle-blowers and leakers. One way or another, the process would become highly politicized.

Prespecification and the one-number census are both "doomsday machines" intended to prevent political manipulation of census adjustment. But they are themselves doomed to fail. The complexity and contingency of adjustment mean that at some point the unanticipated will occur, and that someone will require the discretion to deal with it. Perhaps not surprisingly, Rolph would like to see statisticians invested with considerably more discretion than they enjoyed under the prespecification agreement guiding the 1990 process. Others understandably feel uneasy about affording scientists too much influence over what inevitably involves political interests. The latter would limit the discretion of statisticians, or at least make them subject to oversight by officials answerable to the political process. I can offer no resolution of this dilemma here. But I will say that I remain unpersuaded by those, like Rolph, who would increase the discretion of statisticians on the grounds that their work would be less subject to political challenge.

Rolph offers a variant of such proposals when he and Thomas Belin urge their fellow statisticians to arrive at a "negotiated settlement" of the adjustment controversy and then to urge Congress to assume appropriate responsibility over the census: "Congress should state what it needs from the Census Bureau and should support the best professional judgment of the Census Bureau on how to get there."[209]

Things seldom work out this neatly. Congress rarely makes clear and definitive statements of "what it needs," particularly to agencies to whom it is delegating authority. One reason for this is the recent decentralization of Congress's structure, which makes it hard to reach agreement on legislative goals and purposes. But perhaps a more fundamental reason is Congress's disinclination to commit itself to an uncertain future. In essence, Congress is unwilling to tie its hands by delegating clearly articulated goals to subordinate agencies. This is especially true in the case of the census, whose outcomes (with or without adjustment) are extremely unpredictable. Congress has neither the desire nor the ability to declare "what it needs" and turn the statisticians loose. Instinctively, politicians understand that any undertaking as complicated as census adjustment has implicit and explicit political choices built into it. More bluntly, they know that someone is going to win and someone else is going to lose, and they do not wish to relinquish the power to determine those results to statisticians professing to be neutral.

Statisticians of course pride themselves on being able to deal with uncertainty. "One of our great callings in life," remarks one, "is to continually remind people that they're making decisions under uncertainty."[210] Yet do most people, especially politicians, really need such reminders? Is not the constant presence of uncertainty a chief reason why most people, especially politicians, avoid making decisions whenever possible?

In fairness, what statisticians are trying to say is that tough decisions must be faced and not avoided in the expectation that better information will be available. Such advice is hard to fault in the abstract. But in practice, things are more complicated. The critical issues before decisionmakers involve uncertainty, to be sure. But they also involve consequences. And as we have seen, statisticians disagree over the consequences of adjustment. It is not evident that they have any particular expertise on such matters.

One revealing episode underscores the limits of what statisticians and other experts have to teach public officials. Indeed, this incident suggests that when they trade places with policymakers, some statisticians are likely to change their views. The issue at hand concerns the intercensal population estimates. Published between censuses every two years, these estimates are used for many of the same purposes as the decennial results. In December 1992 Director Bryant had the opportunity to adjust the census numbers used as the base for these intercensal estimates. Eighteen months earlier, Bryant had argued in favor of adjusting the decennial census numbers but was overruled by Secretary Mosbacher. By the end of 1992, however, Mosbacher was no longer in government, and his successor had delegated to Bryant full authority to make this subsequent decision. As with the 1991 adjustment decision, this process was guided by an in-house group of bureau experts, the Committee on Adjustment of Postcensal Estimates (CAPE). As noted earlier, the August 1992 CAPE report identified errors in the 1991 PES data such that the undercount estimate was reduced from 2.08 to 1.58 percent. In that same report, CAPE supported adjustment of the intercensal data on grounds very similar to what the Undercount Steering Committee had offered in support of adjusting the 1990 census data one year earlier: "On average, an adjustment to the 1990 base at the national and state levels for use in intercensal estimates would lead to an improvement in the accuracy of the intercensal estimates."[211] However, the committee could not come to any firm conclusions about accuracy below the state level, which again resembled the findings of the Undercount Steering Committee in 1991.

The public response to the CAPE report was swift and negative. States that stood to lose population shares and federal grants with an adjustment of the intercensal numbers lobbied vigorously against the proposal. Director Bryant delayed her decision to allow for maximum input, but on December 29, 1992, she finally announced her finding: she "reluctantly" opted not to adjust.[212] As Bryant subsequently explained, government lawyers warned her that if the intercensal population estimates had been adjusted, then the bureau would likely have faced legal challenges from many of the nation's 44,000 jurisdictions whose numbers might be negatively affected, even though the bureau's 1992 numbers were better overall than the 1991 numbers (1.58 percent versus 2.08 percent undercount). Bryant recalls that the bureau "could not prove that by improving a state's estimate, we had made no errors at the local level."[213]

Thus, with the decision in her hands, faced with the real possibility "that key Census Bureau personnel could be tied up for years defending unprovable results,"[214] Bryant came to a decision not unlike Mosbacher's. She overruled her own experts—the CAPE committee of which she had been a member—and decided on political grounds that adjustment was just too fraught with peril for her agency.[215]

Interests, rights, and science—sooner or later all three rationales get invoked by adjustment advocates. Each reinforces the others in what John Kingdon calls "the policy primeval soup."[216] More to the point, they depend on one another because each by itself is not very persuasive. A pertinent example is this statement by Mervyn Dymally, former chair of the House Subcommittee on Census and Population: "When we are talking about a guarantee of constitutional rights, we should settle for nothing less than the most accurate figures modern science will allow us to produce."[217] Such an assertion of rights does not cohabit easily with appeals to science, especially when the science in question is statistics, which deals with probabilities and degrees of uncertainty. In this spirit one member of the Census Bureau's Undercount Steering Committee wore emblazoned on his T-shirt: "Being a statistician means never having to say I'm certain."[218]

The difficulty comes in reconciling this lack of certainty with the more demanding standard of rights. As noted, statisticians who favor adjustment acknowledge that the outcome would be estimates that, subject to sampling error, would be closer to the truth *on average*—which is to say, not in every case. Adjusted numbers might well be closer to the truth than unadjusted numbers in the majority of cases.[219] But to argue for adjustment on such grounds is to defend the rights of racial minorities by means of an incongruous utilitarian logic: that the interests of the greatest number outweigh those of the numerical minority negatively affected by adjustment.

CHAPTER SIX

The Census in the New American Political System

The appeals to scientific expertise and rights heard in the debate over census adjustment may be familiar themes in American politics. But in the contemporary context they have particular resonance. Over the past thirty years our institutions have undergone a transformation so extensive that political scientists now refer to "the new American political system."[1] Expertise and rights figure prominently in this regime, whose implications for the census and census adjustment will be explored in this chapter.

This new system has its origins in the upheavals of the 1960s. Yet in a rarely acknowledged irony, what began as a movement to secure the political participation of previously excluded segments of American society has eventuated in a regime in which participation has been exchanged for representation of an extremely formalistic nature. Having relied heavily on the courts and administrative bureaucracies, erstwhile reformers and even radicals are now insiders with weak ties and little accountability to those whom they represent. In this context, census numbers and other such data are important, but more as instruments of bureaucratic administration than as levers of political mobilization.

In this new American political system, politics is undeniably more open than ever before, but it is also more contentious, which would not be so bad except that issues never seem to get resolved. This is in part because the problems addressed by public policy are so intractable, but also because the combatants have few incentives to settle their differences. As a result, cynicism about politics is widespread and profound. The risks of a process as technically complicated and difficult to predict as census adjustment are consequently even greater than indicated in chapter 5.

From Participation to Representation

It has been acknowledged throughout this volume that statistics in general and census data in particular have frequently played an important role in helping marginal groups mobilize or at least make themselves politically visible. Political scientist and current census director Kenneth Prewitt cites the classic example of the book that helped to spark the War on Poverty, Michael Harrington's *The Other America*, and points out how statistics helped black Americans launch and sustain the civil rights movement: "Statistical description can bring social conditions to public attention, mobilize disadvantaged groups, and broaden the political agenda in ways that lessen the bias inherent in an electoral-representation system based largely on the resources of wealth and political organization."[2] Hispanics are perhaps the preeminent example of this dynamic. For it was the creation of the "Hispanic" category on the census that helped give public policy definition to the concerns of disparate groups that had hitherto been ignored by national policymakers and that had not even seen themselves as a politically coherent entity.[3]

Yet if statistics once helped resource-poor groups mobilize for greater visibility, they do not necessarily serve this same purpose in today's very different regime. Our political system has come to emphasize the representation of the interests of the disadvantaged over their actual participation in the political process.[4] Hispanics, for example, are today better represented than they are mobilized or organized. Caught up in this representation-participation trade-off, we have come to emphasize group numbers over what groups actually do with their numbers. In a rights-oriented regime where entitlements from the welfare state are based at least as much on numbers as on political clout, statistics are a political resource. They do represent a kind of political power. Accurate statistics are clearly a critical tool for policymakers and important to the interests of the disadvantaged. Yet this is not to say that statistics are vital to the political mobilization of minorities. Indeed, it may well be that in the context of the contemporary administrative state, statistics may obviate the need for mobilization and organization.

Moreover, during this same period of transformation our notions of representation have also changed. I am not referring here to the controversial shift away from the representation of individuals toward the representation of racial and ethnic groups. I have in mind the equally if not more important shift, widely overlooked, toward more formalistic notions of representation. In our eagerness to ensure that diverse groups are represented, we have grown accustomed to paying little or no attention to the nature of that representation. More specifically, we seldom look at its organizational basis. Were we to do so, we would realize that its entities representing minority interests are quite unlike traditional political organizations.

The phenomenon has been highlighted by demographer William Petersen. He observes that the various racial and ethnic groups targeted by the Census Bureau are often "categories" more than they are "groups." His point is that the ubiquitous term "group" implies a level of self-conscious cohesion and solidarity that is typically lacking in what are sometimes merely demographic aggregates. Petersen draws an analogy between his differentiation of a "category" from a "group" and Marx's differentiation of a "class in itself" from a "class for itself." Petersen then distinguishes a "group" from a "community": in his view, a "community" is based not only on a self-conscious awareness of its differences from other groups but also on the possession of its own organizational structure.[5] In Petersen's typology, many of the racial and ethnic groups mentioned on the census questionnaire are categories; some are groups; few are communities.

To be sure, one would not prudently characterize black Americans as a "category" lacking self-conscious cohesion and solidarity. Yet the term does seem more appropriate when applied to designations such as "Asian or Pacific Islander" or "Hispanic." When we look at the organizational life underlying these various "groups," we find a significant and revealing void.

Hispanics, as already noted, have benefited greatly from this new regime. Yet it is also the case that neither Hispanic identity nor Hispanic organizations are particularly strong. The former is still emergent, fuzzy at the edges, and much less salient than subcategories such as Mexican, Puerto Rican, or Cuban. But of greater interest is the organizational expression of Hispanic identity and interests. If we look at the organizations that the Census Bureau turned to for help with the 1990 census—the League of United Latin American Citizens (LULAC) and the Mexican American Legal Defense and Educational Fund (MALDEF)—neither has a strong membership base.[6] LULAC has an extremely weak membership, while MALDEF does not even claim to be a membership organization. Even among black Americans, who constitute a much more self-conscious group (in Petersen's rigorous sense), an organization such as the National Association for the Advancement of Colored People has suffered from a declining membership base. But more to the point, each of these organizations is basically dominated by headquarters staff who are as dependent on support from third-party funders as from dues-paying members.[7] So the membership becomes only one, and arguably not the most important, among several constituencies to satisfy.

Hispanic organizations are particularly prone to this organizational dynamic in part because immigrants, especially illegal aliens and noncitizens, are difficult to organize for political ends. Yet such organizations also reflect the emergence of a new type of politics: public interest politics.

Public Interest Politics

Public interest politics came to fruition during the 1960s, when it became apparent that various unorganized or hard-to-organize interests were not being heard in the usual din of pluralist politics. These interests might have involved campaign finance, the environment, or racial justice. They were also regarded, correctly or incorrectly, as transcending the ordinary self-interested basis of day-to-day politics in a way that spoke to the needs of the broader community: that is, to the public interest. The formalism that Petersen identifies reflects the impatience of activists and lawyers moving in a crisis atmosphere in which the need for spokesmen representing the aggrieved and the excluded was felt to be urgent. As a result, scrutiny of the nature of that representation was minimal.

Efforts to organize and represent such broad, diffuse interests share certain characteristics. For one thing, public interest organizations rely heavily on third-party funding from wealthy patrons, corporations, and especially foundations, and depend comparatively little on dues from members. Making a virtue out of the free rider problem, public interest organizations have greatly reduced the costs of membership. A few like MALDEF have reduced those costs to zero and have no members at all.

When public interest organizations do have members, they make weak demands on them. Members tend to be widely dispersed, with direct but not very strong ties to the organization and extremely weak or nonexistent ties to one another. Political scientist Jeffrey Berry characterizes this as "cheap" membership requiring limited commitments of time and energy, often no more than writing a check for annual membership dues.[8] Such "checkbook organizations" are described by Robert Putnam as low on "social connectedness." Their members typically do not attend meetings and "most are unlikely ever (knowingly) to encounter any other member."[9] Members are bound to one another and to the organization by abstract appeals and symbols rather than by active participation. In Albert Hirschman's terms, such members are not likely to exercise "voice" or "loyalty." Rather, if dissatisfied with the direction of the organization, they are likely simply to "exit."[10] Explains political scientist Jack Walker, "The activities of the groups are marginal to the daily needs and responsibilities of the members."[11] This is particularly true when compared with the activities of more narrowly defined and explicitly self-interested groups such as unions and professional or business organizations.

These characteristics present various opportunities and challenges to those who lead public interest organizations. On the one hand, leaders and staff have considerable discretion with regard to such an organization's overall direction and day-to-day operations. On the other hand, leaders and staff must continually seek to maintain the interest and support of third-party patrons as well as weakly connected individual members. This is a critical reason why public interest organizations tend to adopt "outside strategies" that result in public—especially media—attention. One major study of public interest law firms concludes that such organizations are best understood as maximizing not profit but publicity. Their publicity-maximizing behavior may be due in part to the fact that favorable media attention attracts funding, particularly in a nonmarket environment where the effectiveness of public interest work is otherwise difficult for supporters to assess.[12] Walker reaches similar conclusions about public interest organizations generally. He further traces the tendency toward outside strategies to the need to satisfy private patrons who "often show a pronounced affinity toward broad efforts to reshape public attitudes or values."[13]

Walker also points to the membership base. Precisely because public interest organizations are not rooted in the face-to-face interactions of individuals living or working together on a daily basis, they must rely on the media to inform their widely dispersed members (and patrons) of organizational developments. To be sure, members are kept informed through newsletters and other internal media. But as Walker emphasizes, those drawn to *public* interest efforts expect to see results in the *public* arena.

Although Walker does not put it this way, his analysis suggests that public interest organizations become drawn into a kind of revivalism that requires continual—and public—rededication to stated goals.[14] Because their membership ties are, in Putnam's words, "to common symbols, common leaders, and perhaps common ideals, but not to one another,"[15] such rededication is essential in holding these organizations together. This process can also be contentious and conflictual, both internally and externally, when conducted in the public glare of the media.

The ongoing controversy over the census undercount and adjustment illustrates both facets of public interest politics: the need to gratify heavily invested elite patrons and supporters; and the need to maintain the involvement of tenuously connected rank-and-file members or would-be members. The elite-oriented effort is evident in the high-visibility, mediagenic litigation that has been pursued on various fronts for about twenty years, first by pro-adjustment advocates and more recently by their anti-adjustment adversaries.

But the more intriguing facet of public interest politics here is the effort to involve the rank and file. Those concerned about the differential racial undercount understand that until adjustment becomes Census Bureau policy, it is critical that members of minority groups be urged to cooperate with the census in order to maximize group totals. Much of this urging is carried out by means of the same high-visibility, media-oriented methods that the litigators use. Census litigation itself serves this purpose.

Black, Hispanic, and other minority leaders and organizations pursue every possible means to encourage individuals to get themselves counted. But it is definitely a struggle. As the ethnographic research reviewed in chapter 4 dramatically reveals, when it comes to filling out (or not filling out) census questionnaires, individual minority group members perceive their interests very differently from minority leaders. In many instances individuals and group leaders have quite opposed interests.

More noteworthy than this difference of perception is that minority leaders today have so few means of persuading their rank and file that it is in their interest to cooperate with the census. No wonder leaders publicize the undercount, litigate against the Census Bureau, and direct all possible attention to potential remedies. Such efforts are not only the tactics of a policy battle; they are also, to recall a theme from earlier chapters, one of the few ways that minority leaders have of exerting authority over the individuals in their "groups."

Because minority leaders today lack the organizational ties to their rank and file that earlier generations of machine politicians or union chiefs enjoyed, they must "go public" with media campaigns. They do not sit atop large membership organizations with the kind of resources or incentives that could motivate large numbers of minority individuals to cooperate with the census. Nor do minority leaders today have an organizational presence at the grass-roots level that would enable them to allay the anxieties and fears of individuals by intervening on their behalf when cooperation with the census did result in the loss of benefits or other sanctions.

An apparent exception to this dynamic illustrates the point. We have seen that American Indians experience one of the highest undercounts of all minority groups. Yet Indians have been relatively quiescent in the controversy over the undercount and adjustment. Why?

One factor is undoubtedly the organizational fragmentation of Indians into myriad tribes, which has long hindered their ability to coalesce for concerted political action. Another, more relevant to this analysis, may be that Indian tribes are formally organized political entities, in which membership and the material benefits accruing therefrom are secured through official designation based upon legally recognized rules and procedures. Thus individuals *do* stand to benefit directly and materially when they claim formal status (as opposed to mere self-identification on the census) as "American Indian." Tribal leaders are consequently in a very different situation from other minority leaders. Their concern must be to enforce group boundaries and to limit membership to eligible individuals; otherwise they risk depleting tribal resources. Moreover, as duly constituted tribal leaders, they have the legal and organizational means to accomplish these goals.[16]

By contrast, non-Indian minority leaders have no such means at their disposal. What black and Hispanic leaders do have is the instrumentalities of public interest politics, which they rely on to convince individual members of their more loosely defined and weakly organized groups that it is in their self-interest—first, to fill out the census questionnaire and, second, to identify themselves as blacks, Hispanics, or other minorities.[17] In pursuit of these goals, minority leaders appeal to their rank and file not in terms of civic duty but of group identity and loyalty. Such appeals invariably offend nonminorities and can therefore be divisive.

This dynamic is central to the politics of the undercount. Nevertheless, it is important not to miss the irony here. The highly visible and sometimes strident appeals to group identity that advocates make in connection with the census stem directly from the fact that (with the exception of Indian tribes) minority groups are so weakly constituted. If these leaders had stronger organizational bonds to their members, then they would have more reliable means of mobilizing them and would depend less on appeals to group identity.[18]

The New American Political System

Public interest politics is one facet of the new American political system. Under this rubric the current generation of political scientists has sought to make sense of the enormous changes in our political life since the 1960s. To begin, these analysts dispute the conventional interpretation of the American regime that, strongly influenced by Madison's exegesis in *The Federalist*, depicts it as constrained by narrowly self-interested actors who, in a highly fragmented polity, have myriad means of stymieing broadly based coalitions for change. The result has been characterized by some as deadlock; by others as the genius of American politics.[19]

This new generation sees a different reality. While political scientists today do not all agree on the fine points, they tend to concur that, for better or worse, we now have a political system that is frequently capable of overcoming the deadlock that the Framers built into our government. This is not to say that this new system has displaced the Framers' enduring work, but rather to describe a regime that overlies the Madisonian system against whose constraints reformers have long struggled.

Many analyses of these changes focus on the turbulent politics of the past three decades. Yet others expand the focus to include the changes wrought by the New Deal.[20] Much of this reconsideration can be traced intellectually to Theodore Lowi's scathing critique of the New Deal origins of what he disdainfully referred to as "interest group liberalism."[21]

What precisely are the lineaments of this new American political system? First is a transformed Congress that is not only more activist than ever before, but also more willing to delegate important decisions to the courts and to administrative agencies directly and indirectly linked to the executive branch. With greatly augmented staffs, including highly educated professionals and specialized policy experts, individual members of Congress have the resources and freedom to become policy entrepreneurs. Yet this congressional activism results in vaguely worded statutes that paper over important technical matters or policy differences and then leave critical details for federal agencies and the courts to interpret and implement.[22] At the same time, those same staff resources afford Congress the capacity to engage in intensive legislative oversight. In other words, Congress gets to pass vague statutes and then to criticize those whose task it is to make sense of them.[23]

In this new regime, the "iron triangles" in which power and influence were once wielded, largely out of public view, by pressure groups, agency bureaucrats, and members of Congress (or their agents) have been broken up and exposed to the light of day. Power now is dispersed among continually shifting and formless "issue networks" of policy experts, whose ties to concrete interests are more tenuous than those binding lobbyists to interest groups. Critical to these developments are the media, which since the 1960s have become not only a more important source of information but also a more aggressively reformist player.

Another critical element, as we have seen, is the representation of interests that used to be absent from the political fray. Today, any number of constituencies that are either hard to organize (illegal immigrants, taxpayers, airline passengers) or impossible to organize (snail darters, redwoods, the unborn) are represented in political and legal contests. Public interest organizations have already been examined. Similarly revealing are class action lawsuits, which have also come into vogue in recent decades. Facilitated in part by third-party funding and by media-savvy entrepreneurs, such efforts are in essence legal fictions, in which the formalities of actual group membership, never mind self-conscious identification with the group, are relaxed. The result is what James Q. Wilson has called "vicarious representation."[24] Yet such lawsuits have exerted considerable influence, even pressure, on politicians and government bureaucrats. They also reveal that in addition to high-visibility campaigning on the "outside," this new regime also relies on "inside" maneuvering among technocrats and lawyers.

Undergirding this new American political system is an intellectual revolution in the meaning and scope of rights. Whether recognized by the courts or granted by Congress, rights have become the means by which all variety of interests make their claims on the wider polity. Shep Melnick puts it well:

> The "rights revolution" refers to the tendency to define nearly every public issue in terms of legally protected rights of individuals. Rights of the handicapped, rights of workers, rights of students, rights of racial, linguistic, and religious minorities, rights of women, rights of consumers, the right to a hearing, the right to know—these have become the stock and trade of American political discourse.[25]

Even more to the point, the assertion of such rights is meant to thwart the political opposition by suggesting that what is being claimed transcends the normally self-interested basis of politics. Thus to oppose rights claims is to risk appearing churlish and mean-spirited.

The consequences of these developments are manifold. In this new regime it is easier than ever before to overcome the inertia—or alternatively, depending on one's perspective, the stability—of the Madisonian system. It is easier to undertake rapid policy change in the absence of widespread public concern, much less outrage, about a given issue. And it is easier to undertake change that goes against public opinion.[26] Yet the system's newly developed capacity for change also carries with it a certain volatility and faddishness, especially among elites.[27]

Underlying these dynamics is a politics not only more and more moved by symbols and ideas, but also increasingly untethered from material interests. This is not to say that conventional interest politics has disappeared or is no longer dominant. That would be an outlandish exaggeration. But the cutting edge of American politics today, particularly with regard to social policy, is characterized by vaguely defined interests, interpreted by elites whose ties to the constituencies they seek to represent are often weaker than to third-party funding sources.[28]

The virtue here, as has been said, is that previously excluded interests and groups are now represented in the political process. The vice is that the process is generally more contentious and less civil. Partly this is because it is difficult to bargain and compromise in a politics of ideas and symbols. As one journalist recently quipped, "Symbols cannot be split in two."[29] But more important, public interest politics relies heavily on the media, with their well-known tendency to seek out and encourage the dramatic and the outrageous.

The fact that contemporary American politics revels in contention and conflict is directly traceable to its structural underpinnings. In order to sustain the interest and contributions of tenuously connected members and would-be members, public interest organizations need to point to the threats posed by their adversaries. The same "the-sky-is-falling" techniques help to convince third-party benefactors that their funds are being used to fight the good fight.[30] Donald Brand observes: "It is highly likely . . . that public-interest groups will always be more combative than their interest-based counterparts because conflict generates publicity and allows public-interest groups to mobilize their constituents."[31]

Catalyst for Cynicism

When looked at as a whole, the new American political system presents a striking paradox. On the one hand, the workings of government are more transparent and open than ever before. On the other, politics itself is more insular and removed from the lives of ordinary Americans. Hugh Heclo aptly notes: "Despite the forms of greater democratic openness in the system (in fact often because of them), policy-making in the postmodern era revolves around contending bodies of activists who are largely detached from the bulk of ordinary citizens."[32] In another context Heclo elaborates:

> The reformers of the 1960s and 1970s were institution challengers, not builders. With the major exception of the civil rights movement, their work remained generally detached from the political lives and affiliations of ordinary Americans. . . . Procedural rights of participation were a reality for only small circles of activists. Their efforts penetrated the arcane world of administrative law and legal maneuverings but not street-level politics. The reformers could capture media attention, but they were much less interested in the mundane work of grass-roots organizing and precinct politicking.[33]

Contrary to the participatory ethos of the 1960s, political participation and voting levels are now at historically low levels. Ordinary Americans are bewildered by the array of issues and disputes that arise when their government concerns itself with virtually all aspects of contemporary life. And while some of this confusion may arise from the technical or scientific nature of many issues, an equally important factor is the nature of the governmental venues where policies are now made and implemented: courts and bureaucratic agencies that were never intended to promote democratic participation and deliberation. Not unreasonably, Americans have come to feel that they do not have much control over institutions making important decisions about their lives, families, and communities.[34] Milkis concludes:

> Neither the current Democrats nor the Republicans respect principles that might provide the foundation for a revival of those political institutions, such as political parties and local governments, that nurture an active and competent citizenry. Rather, the current political debates tend to take place within bureaucratic agencies and courts in such a way that enervates representative democracy.[35]

According to Wilson Carey McWilliams, we now have "two-tier politics," with one tier for the activists and insiders and the other for the mass electorate, which is very much on the outside.[36] It is a system, in Heclo's summary, "of the activists, by the activists, and for the activists."[37]

Among the voters, the effect of this transformation is more than just confusion; it is also cynicism and distrust. Americans are not all off at the beach, happily relinquishing their civic responsibilities. They are suspicious of government and of the political process generally. To some degree this is simply because they are Americans. But it also reflects the enduring legacy—on the political right and of course on the left—of 1960s antinomianism, in which various claims of individual rights were used simultaneously to make demands on government and to express distrust of it.[38] McWilliams explains: "For thirty years or so, liberalism has promoted government responsibility for economic and social life; at the same time, it has defended a panoply of liberties, rights, and entitlements, especially for favored constituencies, that create immunities from politics, reducing government authority."[39]

Fueling the traditional American distrust of government is the enhanced role of experts in the new political system. These influential actors not only lack democratic legitimacy but also tend to disagree in policy debates, causing the general public to believe that those running the government do not know what they are doing. One result among ordinary citizens is, as noted in chapter 5, the cynical response that "everything causes cancer."[40]

Then there is the difficulty of assigning responsibility and monitoring accountability. To be sure, this has long been a problem in our fragmented, decentralized regime. But here, too, traditional distrust has been exacerbated by the increased dispersion of power and influence—specifically, by the growing delegation of authority to courts and to administrative bureaucracies. Critics such as Lowi argue that this is hardly an accident, since in his view the essence of the post–New Deal state is evasion of the authority and coercion that are inherent in governing.[41]

Cynicism is also fostered by a hyperactive government that inevitably and repeatedly promises more than it can deliver. Government can and does build bridges and send astronauts into space. But it is not so successful at promoting racial harmony or curtailing child abuse. When government attempts such ambitious goals, it raises expectations whose disappointment undermines faith in its ability to do anything.

Finally, cynicism is fueled by the fact that public policy disputes never seem to get settled. As Heclo has observed about the 1960s, "in one field of public affairs after another, policy-making became a permanent campaign of competing activists warring over the carcass of legitimate government power."[42] He elaborates: "In the end, it appears that a great deal of postmodern policy-making is not really concerned with 'policy-making' in the sense of finding a settled course of public action that people can live with. It is aimed at crusading for a cause by confronting power with power."[43]

When the number of political actors proliferates and governmental authority is dispersed, no one is able or willing to make the tough decisions. Ultimately, this continual roiling of the political waters reflects the vagueness of interests loosely attached to ambiguously defined groups, as well as the vagueness of standards by which to judge progress or its lack. The only test of whether individuals or governments are "doing the right thing" is the strength and sincerity of their intentions. Yet because intentions can be so opaque, such an ethic of intentions is simultaneously the catalyst and the antidote for cynicism.[44]

Whom Would Adjustment Empower?

At first glance, the census might appear to have nothing to do with such features of the new American political system. After all, this is not some newfangled program trying to do what government has not previously attempted. As we have seen, census-taking is one of the most fundamental and enduring state functions, whether ancient or modern.

Yet in many respects the ongoing controversy over the census undercount and adjustment *does* reflect the complicated cross-currents of this new regime: the extraordinarily high expectations placed on the census; the lack of clear standards by which to evaluate results; the shift of power away from political actors representing concrete interests and toward issue networks and public interest advocates articulating the vaguely defined interests of hard-to-organize constituencies; the expansive conception of rights; a politics of symbols and ideas that is contentious, media-driven, and seemingly never-ending; the reliance on experts and the appeals to science; and finally, the paradox of governmental openness and citizen distrust.

Understood in the context of the new American political system, census adjustment looks to be yet another step toward "two-tier politics." The disincentives to citizen cooperation posed by adjustment have already been emphasized. The politics that has been swirling about the census may be messy and imperfect, but it has not been without democratic vitality. But if statistical adjustment were implemented, then the political action would shift away from local jurisdictions and minority groups pressuring the Census Bureau to reach out to their constituents (and pressuring their constituents to stand up and be counted), and toward experts and bureaucrats haggling over complex technical issues such as truncation points, correlation bias, and smoothing of variances. Even local leaders and officials would be enveloped by a much tidier but more restricted insider politics.

One of many ironies in this controversy is the Census Bureau's declared emphasis on building partnerships with state and local governments as well as community groups. In the plans for the 2000 census, such partnerships were listed as one of "four fundamental strategies."[45] Testifying before Congress, Under Secretary of Commerce Everett Ehrlich stated that one problem with the 1990 census was that the bureau "tried to do everything itself."[46] Echoing this same theme in her remarks at the preview of the 2000 census, Census Director Martha Riche declared: "For states and localities, the 2000 census will be something done *with* you, not *to* you or *for* you."[47] Neither of these officials ever explained how this strategy of building community-based partnerships would be reconciled with another goal that they both affirmed in the next breath: the statistically adjusted "one-number census."

To put the matter differently, adjustment would not (despite the rhetoric of rights and science) eliminate politics from the census.[48] The resulting politics would just be of a different order: arcane and technocratic. The process would be as open to view as a glass-partitioned, climate controlled computer center. But the vast majority of us, especially the most disadvantaged and least sophisticated among us, would be on the outside looking in.

Yet what if, in spite of all such objections, adjustment still afforded some benefits to hard-pressed minority groups? I have argued that those potential benefits have been greatly exaggerated. Moreover, adjustment could help some minorities while actually hurting others. In fact, adjustment outcomes—whether demographic, fiscal, or political—would be almost impossible to predict. Still, it is likely that census adjustment would confer some of the promised benefits on some minorities. What then?

My response is that such benefits would come at too high a price. At best, adjustment would be a palliative. More likely, it would leave minorities worse off. Instead of fostering the empowerment and organization of minorities, adjustment would undermine them. By reducing the incentives for minority groups to mobilize around cooperating with the census to maximize their totals, adjustment would render them less able to challenge critical technical decisions affecting their communities. Once the capacity to mobilize people around the actual count was lost, it would not likely be regained around the arcane issues that would ensue. Again, adjustment would not obviate the need for political clout but rather would shift census politics into a rarefied arena where the relative political strengths of the disadvantaged—community networks and grass-roots relationships—would be of little use.

I have no illusions that such arguments will dissuade minority leaders and their allies from pressing for census adjustment. These leaders may even be correct that certain short-term benefits would ensue. But their championing of adjustment as enfranchisement or empowerment of the disadvantaged is perversely wide of the mark.

However problematic it may be to discern the benefits of adjustment to the undercounted, its advantages for various elites are numerous. In a period when the electorate is substantially demobilized, elected officials, party leaders, journalists, and foundation executives find it easier to advocate census adjustment than to address the more fundamental problems facing the disadvantaged. Whether one focuses on their social and economic problems or the obstacles to their political mobilization, remedies are far from clear. Even when a proposal surfaces, the political will to implement it is not easily summoned. Whether it be increased taxes for some new social program or the threat to established political forces posed by the mobilization of new and demanding constituencies, these are not issues that even the most enlightened political leaders face willingly. How much safer to focus on a seemingly more tractable issue like the census undercount, whose remedy—adjustment—is couched in terms of enfranchisement and empowerment! Even for opponents of adjustment, this debate is a more comfortable one than many likely alternatives.

Contemporary political actors are so enmeshed in the logic of the administrative state that few are capable of challenging the pervasive assumption that minority advancement depends critically on sheer numbers. Still less do they consider the possibility that adjustment would further disadvantage its intended beneficiaries by shifting decisions that are inescapably political into an arcane administrative realm dominated by technically sophisticated professionals.

One analyst who has transcended this administrative logic is Harvard law professor Lani Guinier. Unfortunately, Guinier's insightful critique of the Voting Rights Act (VRA) was obscured by the controversy over her 1993 nomination as assistant attorney general for civil rights. Yet in various law review articles Guinier had argued that the VRA reduced assessments of minority empowerment to the mere counting of officeholders, in lieu of broader inquiries into minority political mobilization and community-level organization between elections.[49] Future Lani Guiniers might well write similar critiques of census adjustment as a suspiciously technocratic proposal that crowded out more thoroughgoing discussions of minority empowerment.

One final perspective on adjustment's place in this new American political system: In his essay on "the sociology of official statistics," Paul Starr likens modern statistical systems to laws and constitutions, sets of agreed upon impersonal rules that restrain power and enlarge liberty. As he writes, "statistical systems . . . may also contribute to our freedom."[50] Starr's analogy is suggestive and his conclusion undoubtedly correct. But listening to adjustment advocates cite the benefits flowing from accurate census totals, one gets the impression that Americans today do not need to be taught that the census can "enlarge their liberty."[51] However mundanely we construe that elegant phrase, we have absorbed its meaning. At the same time, I would argue that Americans today *do* need to be reminded that the census—and, by extension, modern government—is not simply about expanded benefits and enlarged liberties. It is also about things we find less appealing: authority, power, and ultimately coercion.

At various points in this analysis I have been at pains to emphasize this other side of the census, most notably in the inevitable but unacknowledged limits on the regime principle of self-identification. However powerfully embedded the idea of choosing one's own race and ethnicity may be in our individualistic culture, the realities of public policy eventually intrude and require that the government impose order on the congeries of individual responses to such questions.

But as I have also emphasized, this is not something readily acknowledged by politicians or public officials who must explain themselves to an aggressively democratic people. Nor are such officials especially willing to acknowledge the coercion implicit more generally in the various benefits bestowed by the modern state. This aversion to be seen wielding, or even acknowledging the existence of, modern government's power is doubtless a preeminent reason why the administrative state has flourished.

Yet this is not some libertarian lament about state coercion. Rather it is a reminder that a more balanced view of the census, and of the contemporary state, would address not only the passing out of benefits but also the powering necessary to do so.[52] The census is an important tool in the administration of the welfare state. But it is also an instrument of state power and authority. Surely this more balanced view has been absent from much of the debate over census adjustment, which remains enshrouded in the administrative fog that now pervades the new American political system.

CHAPTER SEVEN

Conclusion

"I welcome the thought that the undercount may not plague the future as it has the past." So wrote Daniel Patrick Moynihan nearly twenty years ago.[1] Clearly, his hopes have been dashed. In part, this is on account of the demographic transformation the nation has been experiencing, which is an ongoing challenge to the Census Bureau. But the controversy over the undercount and adjustment is also sustained by the forces of the new American political system. Despite the Supreme Court's January 1999 ruling against the use of sampling for apportionment, the Census Bureau will produce two sets of numbers (unadjusted and adjusted) from the 2000 census. This will ensure continued controversy over which set to use, a repeat of the 1990 experience that the bureau sought to avoid with a one-number census. Thus recent setbacks for adjustment advocates will hardly resolve the matter, and the issue will continue to simmer on the crowded back burners of American politics and public policy.

Meanwhile, a new issue promises to vex the 2000 census. It concerns the bureau's tabulation of responses to its racial and ethnic questions. Recall that in 2000 respondents will for the first time be allowed to check off more than one such category. What remains to be seen is how the bureau will tabulate the many combinations—"black/white," "Chinese/American Indian," "American Indian/black/white," and the like—that it will receive. As of this writing, the bureau apparently intends to publish lower and upper limits for each racial and ethnic category. For example, it will report the number of blacks as ranging from a low, say, of 32 million (those who identified as exclusively "black") to a high, say, of 60 million (those who identified as partly "black"). Whatever the bureau decides to do, the result will almost certainly be considerable confusion and turmoil. Eventually the bureau, or more precisely the Office of Management and Budget (OMB), will have to issue more restrictive criteria for the tabulation of these data. Once again, the regime principle of self-identification will collide with the imperatives of administration and public policy, affording ample opportunity to observe how the bureau and OMB wield authority in this sensitive realm.

Nevertheless, the undercount and adjustment will continue to be the major issues bedeviling the Census Bureau, despite the fact that the stakes involved are greatly exaggerated. Impelled by the dynamics of public interest politics, adjustment advocates will continue to talk as though the undercount were a major obstacle to the representation of minority interests—when its consequences are in fact dwarfed by low voter mobilization among minorities.

I have argued here that while the benefits of adjustment are elusive, even illusory, the risks are tangible and substantial. Putting aside the real possibility of serious technical error of the sort that has already surfaced, a fair reading of the American character and of our recent political history argues that public confidence would not be enhanced by reliance on such arcane technical procedures. Furthermore, because adjustment might not produce the benefits anticipated by minorities, and could result in worse outcomes for some of them, the risks include increased distrust and alienation among adjustment's presumed beneficiaries.

Of course, one could interpret the ethnographic studies reviewed in chapter 4 as a brief *for* adjustment: because of the many cognitive and motivational factors in play, it is futile to attempt to reduce the minority undercount by means of traditional, nonstatistical methods. To be sure, this perspective is not typically voiced by adjustment advocates, since it risks shifting the onus for the undercount away from the Census Bureau and toward the undercounted themselves. Nonetheless, it is possible to draw such a conclusion from this research.

Yet again, I am not persuaded. Rather than encourage us to incur the risks of adjustment, this research ought to lead us toward a more realistic appreciation of the limits of what the census can reasonably be expected to do. Moreover, there are various alternatives to adjustment that should be considered.

First it might be useful to highlight some options that are technically feasible but politically unacceptable. For example, Turkey requires all inhabitants to remain in their residences on census day until the enumeration is complete.[2] Alternatively, various European countries maintain national registers, requiring all residents to notify the government of their status and whereabouts. Given the high levels of immigration and geographic mobility in the United States, such a policy would be something of a technical challenge. But more to the point, it would cut so directly against the grain of our individualistic, libertarian values as to be political anathema. Nevertheless, it is instructive to sketch the outer limits of what Americans would find acceptable.

Within those limits, several alternatives have been mentioned, though each has evident shortcomings. One notion is the official designation of "Census Day" as a national holiday, a day off during which all forms would be completed. Although enjoying self-evident mass appeal, this proposal has really gone nowhere.[3] An idea particularly popular among members of Congress is the introduction of a shortened census questionnaire. Some have even floated the idea of a "post-card census."[4] Yet experts believe such efforts would bring limited results.[5] In any event, the short form questionnaire for the 2000 census has substantially fewer questions than did the 1990 short form.

Another idea that is hardly an alternative to adjustment but that immigrant advocates nevertheless urge is the curtailment of interior enforcement by the Immigration and Naturalization Service (INS) during census enumeration. Yet as noted, the bureau's ethnographic research offers little reason to believe that such a policy would significantly improve the undercount of Hispanic and other immigrant populations. To be sure, this research does not specifically argue against an INS pullback, but it should temper our expectations.

Similarly attractive to immigrant and minority leaders are efforts to ingratiate the Census Bureau with local communities by hiring enumerators who speak the appropriate language, reside in the vicinity, or possess firsthand knowledge of otherwise difficult-to-know neighborhoods. This is obviously a complicated business, with many factors in play. And while it is difficult to believe that, other things being equal, it would not help to have enumerators who speak the language and share some of the background of hard-to-count populations, once again the ethnographic evidence is not encouraging. Demonstrating that noncooperation with the census is significantly caused by pervasive fear and distrust of one's own neighbors, this research suggests that enumerators sharing local neighborhood characteristics would be only marginally helpful and might even be a hindrance to improving results.

More promising perhaps, but again hardly full-fledged alternatives to adjustment, are some of the Census Bureau's proposed innovations for the 2000 count. These include less controlled distribution of census questionnaires, which means making them readily available like tax forms in public places, instead of, as in the past, only mailing questionnaires to households.[6] In 2000 there will also be expanded distribution of questionnaires in various foreign languages.[7] And the 2000 census will be the first to use paid (as opposed to pro bono) advertising.[8]

Another proposal calls for greater reliance on administrative records to obtain critical data on difficult-to-count populations.[9] More promising still is the Census Bureau's "continuous measurement" program. Eventually this could involve a dramatic shift away from the focus on the decennial census and toward the provision of more frequent social and economic data to local jurisdictions. The American Community Survey, basically a large monthly household sample, will publish its findings on a yearly basis, thereby moving the Census Bureau in the direction of the Bureau of Labor Statistics, which provides unemployment data on a monthly basis.[10] One anticipated result of such frequent, periodic data would be to greatly reduce the perceived stakes in once-a-decade results and therefore to possibly weaken the political pressure for adjustment.

A few statisticians have proposed an alternative to the complex and controversial adjustment method examined here. The procedure, known as "scaling" or "raking," would also adjust census numbers, but on the basis of data from demographic analysis (DA). DA, it will be recalled, relies on birth and death certificates as well as other administrative records to derive population estimates for the nation as a whole. Raking would rely on DA to add individuals to undercounted groups at the national, state, and even block levels. Though not without problems, raking is advocated as being much less complicated and more "transparent" than sampling and dual-system estimation, and as being much less dependent on assumption-driven statistical models.[11]

A number of other possible alternatives to adjustment come under the purview not of demographers and statisticians but of politicians. For example, Congress could increase the size of the House of Representatives to decrease the zero-sum nature of apportionment and redistricting—basically the solution relied upon for much of our history.[12] In addition, there is no reason why individual states could not conduct their own censuses, or modify the federal government's census data, for their own redistricting and fiscal purposes.[13] In the same vein, Congress is not obligated to use census numbers for the allocation of federal funds; it could use any numbers it chooses, or simply alter grant formulas to produce the desired outcomes. And although adjusted numbers have been determined by the Supreme Court to be invalid for purposes of apportionment, there is nothing preventing Congress from using them for fiscal purposes.[14]

To be sure, any one of these proposals is much easier said than done. Renegotiating established grant formulas for hundreds of federal programs is presumably not a task that Congress would approach with enthusiasm. Having someone else undertake the effort—whether judges in the courts or statisticians at the Census Bureau—would almost certainly be preferable. But that is precisely the point. Scrutinized in light of such alternatives, census adjustment is revealed for what it truly is: a way for elected officials to avoid difficult political decisions.

I now return to the larger questions lurking in the background of the adjustment controversy. Far more important than any specific technique for enumerating the population is how we conceive of the census as a public policy endeavor. What does this controversy tell us about contemporary American politics, especially racial and ethnic politics?

Consider chapter 5's discussion of the lack of standards by which to evaluate the severity of the undercount and to gauge whatever progress might be made overcoming it. This lack reflects a fundamental problem of our era—namely, the inability or unwillingness of those in government or other positions of authority to make tough judgment calls. I offer no remedy for this problem. But I do believe that an awareness of it must inform how we approach difficult public policy challenges, whether evaluating the North Atlantic Treaty Organization's military action in the Balkans or dealing with the census undercount here in the United States.

Or look at the widespread assumption that improved accuracy necessarily results in greater public confidence in the census process. In many areas of public life, it is widely assumed that more accurate information is an antidote to public cynicism. Yet recall the computer coding error in the postenumeration survey (PES) conducted after the 1990 census. On the basis of that PES, the undercount was originally estimated at 2.08 percent. After the coding error and some other problems were addressed, the undercount was reduced to 1.58 percent. Had the first set of figures been used to adjust the census in 1991, only to be deemed incorrect a year later, the result would have been greater accuracy (at least as defined by adjustment advocates) on both occasions, but clearly at the expense of decreased public confidence. In other words, although seldom acknowledged in the adjustment debate, there is a trade-off between accuracy and public confidence.

Another such trade-off looming here is between census accuracy and social or cultural diversity. The nature of this dilemma is stated straightforwardly by Census Bureau professionals:

> The level of inconsistent reporting in the Other API, Other race, and Other Hispanic categories is of importance, because it seems to reflect reporting problems among immigrant populations that have grown rapidly during the last two decades. They are projected to represent ever increasing percentages of the American population.[15]

In addition to the cognitive and language issues discussed in chapter 4, immigrants pose an array of attitudinal and motivational challenges to an accurate census. On a more basic level, the complex, informal, and sometimes hidden networks in which immigrants often function do not partake of the neat and ordered society on which the bureau necessarily bases its massive logistical operations.

This is why many turn-of-the-century Progressives—state builders concerned about moving American society "away from drift and toward mastery" (to paraphrase Walter Lippman)—saw immigration as a major obstacle and turned toward restriction. Today many Americans value diversity as well as the change and spontaneity that accompany it. But while prizing these developments, we must also acknowledge that they impose limits on our expectations for accuracy in endeavors such as the census— and, more generally, on our aspirations for rigorous standards of equality. The historian John Higham identifies this trade-off in his analysis of "pluralistic integration," the curious amalgam of assimilationism and pluralism in contemporary America that results in loosely bounded racial and ethnic groups into and out of which individuals move relatively freely. Higham observes: "Obviously pluralistic integration depends on a lack of precision in social categories, and a general acceptance of complexity and ambiguity."[16]

These challenges to an orderly, accurate census arise not only when immigrants are newly arrived. To the contrary, as immigrants and their children assimilate, the census faces ever newer challenges. Assimilation is accompanied by economic and social mobility, including intermarriage, all of which weaken the ties of individuals to their communities and groups of origin. It is against the backdrop of such powerful trends that group leaders and advocates seek to maximize their census totals—an effort rather like trying to fill a leaky bucket.

Thus, while it would be an exaggeration to say that assimilation drives immigrant leaders to do whatever they can to augment their numbers, it is fair to suggest that assimilation heightens their incentives to do so. The results, as noted, include lobbying the Census Bureau for just the right question wording, for the best placement of the question on the census form, and for the appropriate racial or ethnic categorization—each intended to maximize the number of people who self-identify as members of a given group. As assimilation continues to erode group attachments, leaders are increasingly reluctant to leave it to chance whether an individual fills out his census form, in particular whether he checks off the item that identifies him as, say, "Hispanic." Hence the reliance on litigation, high-visibility outreach efforts, and media campaigns.

Some critics dismiss all such efforts as rearguard maneuvers by interest groups desperate to fend off inevitable changes. But this view is much too simplistic. Among other shortcomings, it fails to acknowledge the persistence, however attenuated, of genuine racial and ethnic group attachments across a wide swath of American society. Such critics also overlook the possibility that the irresistible currents of assimilation lead many individuals to identify with their groups of origin. Such identification arises not simply or necessarily out of crass material interest but also out of deeply felt psychological and social needs.[17]

In response to the intense group lobbying that surrounds the census, some recoil in fear that America is "balkanizing" into a nation of mutually hostile groups. Such critics typically point to affirmative action as the culprit. Yet as discussed earlier, the fact that affirmative action programs rely on racial and ethnic data collected by the Census Bureau does not afford minority individuals any incentives to cooperate with the census. No one has ever received any affirmative action benefit from self-identifying as a member of a specific minority group on the census questionnaire; the system simply does not work that way. If it did, then minority leaders would not have to struggle so hard to persuade their rank and file to be counted.

Furthermore, there is no compelling evidence that the United States is "balkanizing."[18] On the contrary, individualism in America is so robust that it weakens the bonds that in more communally based societies hold racial and ethnic groups together. To be sure, the demands of various racial and ethnic groups for recognition and benefits are proving disturbingly rancorous and divisive. But it is precisely because such groups are so weak that their leaders are so shrill and, in this instance, preoccupied with maximizing their group totals.

These arguments do not appease alarmists who are convinced that the census is one cause of our fragmentation and therefore call for an end to the collection of all racial and ethnic data. These critics will no doubt interpret the evidence in chapter 3 on the limited accuracy of racial and ethnic numbers as further support for their argument that it is imprudent of the census to be "counting by race."

Yet the same body of research leads me to a quite different conclusion. Race and ethnicity continue to be real forces in American social, economic, and political life and cannot be cavalierly dismissed as, to use Newt Gingrich's term, "artificial."[19] The stubborn persistence of racial and ethnic categories is underscored by the fact that even those who would criticize them cannot do without them. Dinesh D'Souza, for example, buttresses his argument that race categories are being obviated by powerful assimilative forces by citing the rising rates of intermarriage among groups—an argument that he would not be able to make if the census did not collect racial and ethnic data![20]

My own view parallels that of demographer William Petersen. A staunch critic of much that the Census Bureau has done in the past thirty years in the realm of race and ethnicity, Petersen nonetheless allows that, for all their flaws, such data serve genuine needs that in the absence of such information would otherwise be filled by rumor, innuendo, folk wisdom, and of course, prejudice.[21]

Yet to accept the need for these data should also be to accept as inevitable both their limitations and the constant political maneuvering that goes into their collection, interpretation, and publication. With regard to the limitations, it must be said that while the Census Bureau's ethnic and racial data provide critical information about broad social trends, our reliance on such numbers must be informed by a sturdy realism about their imperfections. At the same time, we must not forget that the census is an inherently political undertaking, and that trying to cleanse this "national ceremony" of politics would be like trying to cure horse racing of competition. After all, the untidy politics in which the census is now enmeshed is surely what the Framers had in mind. Statistical adjustment might well reduce some of the visible and divisive lobbying around the census. But it would also steer us in the wrong direction: away from the contentiousness of a vigorous politics and toward the false harmony of an administered democracy.[22]

1990 U.S. Census Questionnaire (abridged)

Appendix A presents a facsimile of a page from the short form of the 1990 census questionnaire. This page includes most of the questions on race and ethnicity discussed in the text. The 1990 short form questionnaire was sent to approximately 83 percent of all households. The 1990 long form, which was sent to a 17 percent sample of all households, includes the short form questions as well as many others, a few of which also pertain to the racial and ethnic issues examined in the text. Facsimiles of the latter questions are also presented in this appendix.

*Selected Census
1990 Short
Form Questions*

	PERSON 1
Please fill one column ➡ for each person listed in Question 1a on page 1.	Last name First name Middle initial

2. How is this person related to PERSON 1?

Fill ONE circle for each person.

If **Other relative** of person in column 1, fill circle and print exact relationship, such as mother-in-law, grandparent, son-in-law, niece, cousin, and so on.

> START in this column with the household member (or one of the members) in whose name the home is owned, being bought, or rented.
>
> If there is no such person, start in this column with any adult household member.
>
> ■

3. Sex
Fill ONE circle for each person.

   ○ Male   ○ Female

4. Race
Fill ONE circle for the race that the person considers himself/herself to be.

     If **Indian (Amer.)**, print the name of the enrolled or principal tribe. ⟶

If **Other Asian or Pacific Islander (API)**, print one group, for example: Hmong, Fijian, Laotian, Thai, Tongan, Pakistani, Cambodian, and so on. ⟶

If **Other race**, print race. ⟶

   ○ White
   ○ Black or Negro
   ○ Indian (Amer.) (Print the name of the enrolled or principal tribe.) ⌐
       [_____]
   ○ Eskimo
   ○ Aleut   Asian or Pacific Islander (API)
   ○ Chinese   ○ Japanese
   ○ Filipino   ■   ○ Asian Indian
   ○ Hawaiian   ○ Samoan
   ○ Korean   ○ Guamanian
   ○ Vietnamese   ○ Other API ⌐
       [_____]
   ○ Other race (Print race) ⌐

5. Age and year of birth

   a. Print each person's age at last birthday. Fill in the matching circle below each box.

   b. Print each person's year of birth and fill the matching circle below each box.

a. Age	b. Year of birth
	1
0 0 0 0	1 ● 8 ○ 0 ○ 0 ○
1 ○ 1 ○ 1	9 ○ 1 ○ 1 ○
2 ○ 2	2 ○ 2 ○
3 ○ 3	3 ○ 3 ○
4 ○ 4	■ 4 ○ 4 ○
5 ○ 5	5 ○ 5 ○
6 ○ 6	6 ○ 6 ○
7 ○ 7	7 ○ 7 ○
8 ○ 8	8 ○ 8 ○
9 ○ 9	9 ○ 9 ○

6. Marital status

Fill ONE circle for each person.

   ○ Now married   ○ Separated
   ○ Widowed   ○ Never married
   ○ Divorced

7. Is this person of Spanish/Hispanic origin?

Fill ONE circle for each person.

If **Yes, other Spanish/Hispanic**, print one group. ⟶

   ○ No (not Spanish/Hispanic)
   ○ Yes, Mexican, Mexican-Am., Chicano
   ○ Yes, Puerto Rican
   ○ Yes, Cuban   ■
   ○ Yes, other Spanish/Hispanic
     (Print one group, for example: Argentinean, Colombian, Dominican, Nicaraguan, Salvadoran, Spaniard, and so on.) ⌐
     [_____]

FOR CENSUS USE ⟶

   ○
   ○

8. In what U.S. State or foreign country was this person born?

(Name of State or foreign country; or Puerto Rico, Guam, etc.)

13. What is this person's ancestry or ethnic origin?
(See instruction guide for further information.)

(For example: German, Italian, Afro-Amer., Croatian,
Cape Verdean, Dominican, Ecuadoran, Haitian, Cajun,
French Canadian, Jamaican, Korean, Lebanese, Mexican,
Nigerian, Irish, Polish, Slovak, Taiwanese, Thai,
Ukrainian, etc.)

15a. Does this person speak a language other than English at home?

○ Yes   ○ No — *Skip to 16*

b. What is this language?

(For example: Chinese, Italian, Spanish, Vietnamese)

c. How well does this person speak English?

○ Very well   ○ Not well
○ Well   ○ Not at all

1990 U.S. Census Questionnaire Instructions (abridged)

Appendix B presents instructions accompanying questions pertaining to race and ethnicity selected from the 1990 census questionnaire (both short and long forms).

Selected Instructions

2. Fill one circle to show how each person is related to the person in column 1.

If **Other relative** of the person in coumn 1, print the exact relationship such as son-in-law, daughter-in-law, grandparent, nephew, niece, mother-in-law, father-in-law, cousin, and so on.

If the **Stepson/stepdaughter** of the person in column 1 also has been legally adopted by the person in column 1, mark **Stepson/stepdaughter** but do not mark **Natural-born or adopted son/daughter**. In other words, **Stepson/stepdaughter** takes precedence over **Adopted son/daughter**.

4. Fill ONE circle for the race each person considers himself/herself to be.

If you fill the **Indian (Amer.)** circle, print the name of the tribe or tribes in which the person is enrolled. If the person is not enrolled in a tribe, print the name of the principal tribe(s)

If you fill the **Other API** circle [under **Asian or Pacific Islander (API)**], **only** print the name of the group to which the person belongs. For example, the **Other API** category includes persons who identify as Burmese, Fijian, Hmong, Indonesian, Laotian, Bangladeshi, Pakistani, Tongan, Thai, Cambodian, Sri Lankan, and so on.

If you fill the **Other Race** circle, be sure to print the name of the race.

If the person considers himself/herself to be **White, Black or Negro, Eskimo or Aleut, fill one circle only. Please do not print the race in the boxes**.

The **Black or Negro** category also includes persons who identify as African-American, Afro-American, Haitian, Jamaican, West Indian, Nigerian, and so on.

All persons, regardless of citizenship status, should answer the question.

5. Print age at last birthday in the space provided (print "00" for babies less than 1 year old). Fill in the matching circle below each box. Also, print year of birth in the space provided. Then fill in the matching circle below each box. For an illustration of how to complete question 5, see the **Example** on page 2 of this guide.

6. If the person's only marriage was annulled, mark **Never Married**.

7. A person is of Spanish/Hispanic origin if the person's origin (ancestry) is Mexican, Mexican-Am., Chicano, Puerto Rican, Cuban, Argentinean, Colombian, Costa Rican, Dominican, Ecuadoran, Guatemalan, Honduran, Nicaraguan, Peruvian, Salvadoran, from other Spanish-speaking countries of the Caribbean or Central or South America, or from Spain.

If you fill the **Yes, other Spanish/Hispanic** circle, print one group.

A person who is not of Spanish/Hispanic origin should answer this question by filling the **No (not Spanish/Hispanic)** circle. Note that the term **"Mexican-Am."** refers only to persons of Mexican origin or ancestry.

All persons, regardless of citizenship status, should answer this question.

8. *For persons born in the United States:*

Print the name of the State in which this person was born. If the person was born in Washington, D.C., print District of Columbia. If the person was born in a U.S. territory or commonwealth, print Puerto Rico, U.S. Virgin Islands, Guam, American Samoa, or Northern Marianas.

For persons born outside the United States:

Print the name of the foreign country or area where the person was born. Use current boundaries, not boundaries at the time of the person's birth. Specify whether Northern Ireland or Republic of Ireland (Eire); East or West Germany; North or South Korea; England, Scotland, or Wales (not Great Britain or United Kingdom). Specify the particular country or island in the Caribbean (not, for example, West Indies).

13. Print the ancestry group. Ancestry refers to the person's ethnic origin or descent, "roots," or heritage. Ancestry also may refer to the country of birth of the person or the person's parents or ancestors before their arrival in the United States. *All* persons, regardless of citizenship status, should answer this question.

Persons who have more than one origin and cannot identify with a single ancestry group may report two ancestry groups (for example, German-Irish).

Be specific. For example, print whether West Indian, Asian Indian, or American Indian. West Indian includes persons whose ancestors came from Jamaica, Trinidad, Haiti, etc. Distinguish Cape Verdean from Portuguese; French Canadian from Canadian; and Dominican Republic from Dominica Island.

A religious group should not be reported as a person's ancestry.

15. Mark **Yes** if the person sometimes or always speaks a language other than English at home.

Do not mark **Yes** for a language spoken only at school or if speaking is limited to a few expressions or slang.

Print the name of the language spoken at home. If this person speaks more than one non-English language and cannot determine which is spoken more often, report the first language the person learned to speak.

2000 U.S. Census Questionnaire (abridged)

Appendix C presents a facsimile of the first page of the short form of the 2000 census questionnaire. This page includes most of the questions on race and ethnicity discussed in the text. The 2000 short form questionnaire is sent to approximately 83 percent of all households. The 2000 long form, which is sent to a 17 percent sample of all households, includes the short form questions as well as many others, a few of which also pertain to the racial and ethnic issues examined in the text. Facsimiles of the latter questions are also presented in this appendix.

Census 2000 Short Form Questions

United States Census 2000

U.S. Department of Commerce • Bureau of the Census

This is the official form for all the people at this address. It is quick and easy, and your answers are protected by law. Complete the Census and help your community get what it needs — today and in the future!

Start Here

Please use a black or blue pen.

1. How many people were living or staying in this house, apartment, or mobile home on April 1, 2000?

☐☐ Number of people

INCLUDE in this number:
- foster children, roomers, or housemates
- people staying here on April 1, 2000 who have no other permanent place to stay
- people living here most of the time while working, even if they have another place to live

DO NOT INCLUDE in this number:
- college students living away while attending college
- people in a correctional facility, nursing home, or mental hospital on April 1, 2000
- Armed Forces personnel living somewhere else
- people who live or stay at another place most of the time

2. Is this house, apartment, or mobile home — Mark ☒ ONE box.

☐ Owned by you or someone in this household with a mortgage or loan?
☐ Owned by you or someone in this household free and clear (without a mortgage or loan)?
☐ Rented for cash rent?
☐ Occupied without payment of cash rent?

3. Please answer the following questions for each person living in this house, apartment, or mobile home. Start with the name of one of the people living here who owns, is buying, or rents this house, apartment, or mobile home. If there is no such person, start with any adult living or staying here. We will refer to this person as Person 1.

What is this person's name? Print name below.

Last Name
☐☐☐☐☐☐☐☐☐☐☐☐☐☐☐
First Name   MI
☐☐☐☐☐☐☐☐☐☐☐☐ ☐

4. What is Person 1's telephone number? We may call this person if we don't understand an answer.

Area Code + Number

5. What is Person 1's sex? Mark ☒ ONE box.
☐ Male ☐ Female

6. What is Person 1's age and what is Person 1's date of birth?
Age on April 1, 2000

☐☐☐

Print numbers in boxes.
Month   Day   Year of birth
☐☐   ☐☐   ☐☐☐☐

→ **NOTE: Please answer BOTH Questions 7 and 8.**

7. Is Person 1 Spanish/Hispanic/Latino? Mark ☒ the **"No"** box if **not** Spanish/Hispanic/Latino.

☐ No, not Spanish/Hispanic/Latino ☐ Yes, Puerto Rican
☐ Yes, Mexican, Mexican Am., Chicano ☐ Yes, Cuban
☐ Yes, other Spanish/Hispanic/Latino — Print group ↙

☐☐☐☐☐☐☐☐☐☐☐☐☐☐☐☐☐☐

8. What is Person 1's race? Mark ☒ one or more races to indicate what this person considers himself/herself to be.

☐ White
☐ Black, African Am., or Negro
☐ American Indian or Alaska Native — Print name of enrolled or principal tribe. ↙

☐☐☐☐☐☐☐☐☐☐☐☐☐☐☐☐☐☐

☐ Asian Indian ☐ Japanese ☐ Native Hawaiian
☐ Chinese ☐ Korean ☐ Guamanian or Chamorro
☐ Filipino ☐ Vietnamese ☐ Samoan
☐ Other Asian — Print race. ↙ ☐ Other Pacific Islander — Print race. ↙

☐☐☐☐☐☐☐☐☐☐☐☐☐☐☐☐☐☐

☐ Some other race — Print race ↙

☐☐☐☐☐☐☐☐☐☐☐☐☐☐☐☐☐☐

→ **If more people live here, continue with Person 2.**

Selected Census 2000 Long Form Questions

What is this person's ancestry or ethnic origin?

(For example: Italian, Jamaican, African Am., Cambodian, Cape Verdean, Norwegian, Dominican, French Canadian, Haitian, Korean, Lebanese, Polish, Nigerian, Mexican, Taiwanese, Ukrainian, and so on.)

11 a. Does this person speak a language other than English at home?

☐ Yes
☐ No → Skip to 12

b. What is this language?

(For example: Korean, Italian, Spanish, Vietnamese)

c. How well does this person speak English?

☐ Very well
☐ Well
☐ Not well
☐ Not at all

12 Where was this person born?

☐ In the United States — Print name of state.

☐ Outside the United States — Print name of foreign country, or Puerto Rico, Guam, etc.

Notes

Chapter One

1. The term is from Barry Edmonston and Charles Schultze, eds., *Modernizing the U.S. Census* (Washington, D.C.: National Academy Press, 1995).

2. For example, this view is put forth in John J. Miller, *The Unmaking of Americans: How Multiculturalism Has Undermined the Assimilation Ethic* (New York: Free Press, 1998), p. 241.

3. *Oversight Hearing to Review the Progress of Coverage Evaluation Procedures*, Hearing before the Subcommittee on Census and Population of the House Committee on Post Office and Civil Service, 102 Cong. 1 sess. (Government Printing Office, 1991), p. 66.

4. See Bureau of the Census, *Factfinder for the Nation*, CFF 18 (May 1990).

5. See, for example, "For Political Justice, Adjust the Census," *New York Times*, June 15, 1991, sec. 1, p. 1: "The latest census figures measure national injustice, the record-setting undercount of millions of Americans and its glaringly uneven distribution." See also "Not the Best Census Ever," *New York Times*, April 15, 1991, p. A24.

6. William Kruskal, testimony in *Federal Statistics and National Needs*, Committee Print Prepared for the Subcommittee on Energy, Nuclear Proliferation, and Government Processes of the Senate Committee on Governmental Affairs, 98 Cong. 1 sess. (GPO, 1984), p. 49.

7. This is not literally true, since in most cases one member of a household answers the census questions for the others. But as will be seen, individual self-identification in the census is the operative assumption.

8. See Anthony King, ed., *The New American Political System*, 2d ed. (Washington, D.C.: AEI Press, 1990).

Chapter Two

1. Steven A. Holmes, "Political Interests Arouse Raging Debate on Census," *New York Times*, April 12, 1998, sec. 1, pp. 1, 16.

2. Nathan Keyfitz, "Statistics, Law, and Census Reporting," *Society*, vol. 18 (January/February 1981), p. 5

3. Herman Habermann, "The Census—A Cornerstone in the Construction of a Nation," speech delivered at the Central Statistical Service in Pretoria, South Africa, November 17, 1995.

4. Arlene W. Saxonhouse, *Fear of Diversity: The Birth of Political Science in Ancient Greek Thought* (University of Chicago Press, 1992), p. 227.

5. For a contrary, skeptical view of the need for governments to gather statistics, see Nicholas Eberstadt, *The Tyranny of Numbers: Mismeasurement and Misrule* (Washington, D.C.: AEI Press, 1995).

6. Dan Halacy, *Census: 190 Years of Counting America* (New York: Elsevier/Nelson, 1980), p. 16.

7. On King David's census, see *The New Oxford Annotated Bible*, 2 Sam. 24:1–25. On the perceived biblical injunction against census-taking in the early American republic, see Halacy, *Census*, pp. 33–37.

8. *The New Oxford Annotated Bible*, Luke 2:1–5.

9. *Columbia Desk Encyclopedia*, 5th ed. (Columbia University Press, 1993), p. 781.

10. Halacy, *Census*, p. 27.

11. Aristotle, *The Athenian Constitution*, translated by P. J. Rhodes (Penguin Books, 1984), p. 63; see also Victor Ehrenberg, *From Solon to Socrates: Greek History and Civilization during the Sixth and Fifth Centuries B.C.*, 2d ed. (London: Methuen, 1973), pp. 90–103.

12. Robert Nisbet, *The Social Philosophers: Community and Conflict in Western Thought* (New York: Thomas Y. Crowell, 1973), p. 32.

13. Nisbet, *The Social Philosophers*, p. 33.

14. See Meyer Zitter, "Enumerating Americans Living Abroad," *Society*, vol. 25 (March/April 1988), pp. 56–60. See also Walter P. Hollmann, "Applying Residence Rules to the Military," *Society*, vol. 25 (March/April 1988), pp. 54–55. Less controversial has been the designation for counting purposes of the residences of college students. See Margo J. Anderson, "Planning the Future in the Context of the Past," *Society*, vol. 25 (March/April 1988).

15. *Federation for American Immigration Reform v. Klutznick*, 486 F. Supp. 564 (D. D.C. 1980). See also Thomas M. Durbin, "The 1990 Decennial Census and the Counting of Illegal Aliens," Congressional Research Service Report for Congress (January 13, 1988).

16. Blocks are the smallest geographic units for which the Census Bureau collects and publishes data. With an average population of 70, census blocks are, as the term suggests, often rectangular areas bounded by four streets. Census tracts are made up of scores of blocks and average about 4,000 people. Tracts generally have stable boundaries from one census to the next.

17. Anderson, "Planning the Future in the Context of the Past," p. 44.

18. See Martin Dale Montoya, "Ethnographic Evaluation of the Behavioral Causes of Undercount: Woodburn, Oregon," U.S. Bureau of the Census, Ethnographic Evaluation of the 1990 Decennial Census, Report 25 (November 1992), p. 10.

19. William Petersen, "Politics and the Measurement of Ethnicity," in William Alonso and Paul Starr, eds., *The Politics of Numbers* (New York: Russell Sage Foundation, 1987), pp. 214–15.

20. Stephan Thernstrom, "American Ethnic Statistics," in Donald L. Horowitz and Ger-

ard Noiriel, eds., *Immigrants in Two Democracies: French and American Experience* (New York University Press, 1992); Hyman Alterman, *Counting People: The Census in History* (New York: Harcourt Brace & World, 1969), p. 276.

21. For an example of this cynical view, see William Petersen, "The Classification of Subnations in Hawaii: An Essay in the Sociology of Knowledge," *American Sociological Review*, vol. 34 (December 1969), pp. 863–77. For a concurring view, see Charles Hirschman, "How to Measure Ethnicity: An Immodest Proposal," in Statistics Canada and U.S. Bureau of the Census, *Challenges of Measuring An Ethnic World: Science, Politics, and Reality* (GPO, 1993), pp. 547–60, esp. pp. 552–53.

22. Petersen, "Politics and the Measurement of Ethnicity," pp. 232–33. See also Ira S. Lowry, "Counting Ethnic Minorities in the 1990 Census," unpublished paper, Pacific Palisades, Calif., September 1989, pp. 21–22: "The ethnic advisory committees each consisted of nine to twelve persons manifestly chosen more for their ethnic political connections than for their knowledge of survey research." A similar point, is made by former Census Bureau official Morris Hansen in "Morris Hansen: Oral History" (Washington, D.C.: Bureau of the Census, History Staff, n.d.), p. 24.

23. "Vincent P. Barabba: Oral History" (Washington, D.C.: Bureau of the Census, History Staff, n.d.), p. 46.

24. Alexander Hamilton, James Madison, and John Jay, eds., *The Federalist* (New York: Modern Library, 1937), pp. 358–59.

25. See Hamilton and others, *The Federalist*, Federalist No. 54, pp. 353–54.

26. John P. Diggins, *The Lost Soul of American Politics: Virtue, Self-Interest, and the Foundations of Liberalism* (New York: Basic Books, 1984), p. 197.

27. Winston Churchill, quoted in the President's Reorganization Project for the Federal Statistical System, "Improving the Federal Statistics System: Issues and Options," *Statistical Reporter*, February 1981, p. 178.

28. James T. Bonnen, "Coordination Today: A Disaster or Disgrace?" *American Statistician*, vol. 37 (August 1983), p. 188. See also Paul Starr, "The Sociology of Official Statistics," in William Alonso and Paul Starr, eds., *The Politics of Numbers* (New York: Russell Sage Foundation, 1987).

29. "Morris Hansen: Oral History," pp. 40–41.

30. "C. Louis Kincannon: Oral History" (Washington, D.C.: Bureau of the Census, History Staff, n.d.), p. 32.

31. See Frederick C. Calhoun, "Agents of Federalism: U.S. Marshalls, 1789–1797," *Quarterly of the National Archives*, vol. 21, no. 4 (1989), p. 351.

32. Alterman, *Counting People*, p. 241.

33. See U.S. Constitution, art. 1, sec. 2: "The actual Enumeration shall be made within three Years after the first Meeting of the Congress of the United States, and within every subsequent Term of ten Years, *in such Manner as they shall by Law direct*" (emphasis added).

34. Alterman, *Counting People*, p. 222.

35. Anderson, *The American Census*, pp. 77–78, 99–100, 201.

36. Alterman, *Counting People*, p. 287. See also Halacy, *Census*, p. 169.

37. See the comments of Congressman Charles Schumer in *The Decennial Census Improvement Act*, Hearing before the Subcommittee on Census and Population of the House Committee on Post Office and Civil Service, 100 Cong. 2 sess. (GPO, 1988), pp. 66–67.

38. See Maggie Mahar, "Numbers Game: A Census Bureau Wage Report Takes Five Months to Surface," *Barron's*, May 18, 1992, p. 17.

39. "Barabba: Oral History," p. 41.

40. Edwin Goldfield, former assistant director for program development at the Census Bureau, has offered a qualified defense of the referral system. See "Edwin D. Goldfield: Oral

History" (Washington, D.C.: Bureau of the Census, History Staff, n.d.), pp. 63–65. More critical of it has been Morris Hansen, former associate director for research and development. See "Hansen: Oral History," pp. 41–42. See also Harvey M. Choldin, *Looking for the Last Percent: The Controversy over Census Undercounts* (Rutgers University Press, 1994).

41. See Mahar, "Numbers Game," pp. 16–17. Also Jason DeParle, "Report, Delayed Months, Says Lowest Income Group Grew Sharply," *New York Times*, May 12, 1992, p. A15.

42. *Investigation of Possible Politicization of Federal Statistical Programs*, House Committee on Post Office and Civil Service, 92 Cong. 2 Sess., Report 92-1536 (October 5, 1972), pp. 6–9. See also Joseph W. Duncan and William C. Shelton, *Revolution in United States Government Statistics, 1926–1976* (GPO, 1978), p. 167; Philip M. Hauser, "Statistics and Politics," *American Statistician*, vol. 27 (April 1973), pp. 68–71; Judith Eleanor Innes, *Knowledge and Public Policy: The Search for Meaningful Indicators*, 2d exp. ed. (New Brunswick, N.J.: Transaction Books, 1990), pp. 137–38.

43. "Conrad Taeuber: Oral History" (Washington, D.C.: Bureau of the Census, History Staff, n.d.), p. 14.

44. Quoted in Choldin, *Looking for the Last Percent*, p. 34. For more on Nixon's efforts to manipulate the bureau, see "Taeuber: Oral History," pp. 12–13; and "A. Ross Eckler: Oral History" (Washington, D.C.: Bureau of the Census, History Staff, n.d.), pp. 38–39.

45. See "Goldfield: Oral History," pp. 4–7.

46. Myron Magnet, "Behind the Bad-News Census: A Once Great Demography Agency Can't Cope with Depopulated Cities," *Fortune*, February 9, 1981, pp. 88–93.

47. "Barabba: Oral History," p. 7.

48. Raymond Vernon, "The Politics of Comparative Economic Statistics: Three Cultures and Three Cases," in William Alonso and Paul Starr, *The Politics of Numbers* (New York: Russell Sage Foundation, 1987), pp. 70–72.

49. Anderson, *The American Census*, p. 110.

50. "Richard M. Scammon: Oral History" (Washington, D.C.: Bureau of the Census, History Staff, n.d.), pp. 6–7.

51. "Scammon: Oral History," pp. 5–7.

52. "Scammon: Oral History," p. 8.

53. President's Commission on Federal Statistics, *Federal Statistics: Report of the President's Commission*, vol. 1 (GPO, 1971), p. 47.

54. Innes, *Knowledge and Public Policy*, p. 282.

55. "Barabba: Oral History," pp. 44–45; see also Choldin, *Looking for the Last Percent*.

56. "Kincannon: Oral History," p. 31; "Taeuber: Oral History," p. 15.

57. James T. Bonnen, quoting an OMB official, in testimony before Congress explaining why statistical policy had been neglected at the agency. See *Federal Government Statistics and Statistical Policy*, Hearing before a Subcommittee of the House Committee on Government Operations, 97 Cong. 2 sess. (GPO, 1983), p. 11.

58. See "Barabba: Oral History," pp. 6–8, 12. See also Stephen Barr, "Daley Pledge on Patronage Is Applauded," *Washington Post*, January 24, 1997.

59. See Al Kamen and Ann Devroy, "In Cabinet Choices, Gore Has Seat at Head Table," *Washington Post*, December 13, 1992, p. A23.

60. Holmes, "Political Interests Arouse Raging Debate," pp. 1, 16.

61. Janet L. Norwood, *Organizing to Count: Change in the Federal Statistical System* (Washington, D.C.: Urban Institute Press, 1995), p. 28.

62. Barbara Everitt Bryant and William Dunn, *Moving Power and Money: The Politics of Census Taking* (Ithaca, N.Y.: New Strategist Publications, 1995), pp. 158–59.

63. "Goldfield: Oral History," p. 86.

64. Norwood, *Organizing to Count*, pp. 30–31, 81–82. See also Rochelle L. Stanfield, "Statistics Gap," *National Journal*, April 13, 1991, pp. 844–49.

65. Norwood, *Organizing to Count*, p. 30.

66. On the responsibilities of the under secretary and the substantial overlap of responsibilities between the under secretary and the census director, see Bryant and Dunn, *Moving Power and Money*, p. 201.

67. "Kincannon: Oral History," p. 29.

68. "Goldfield: Oral History," pp. 51–53.

69. Meeting, 2000 Census Advisory Committee; Embassy Row Hotel, Washington, D.C., May 16–17, 1996.

70. "Kincannon: Oral History," p. 25.

71. "Kincannon: Oral History," p. 26.

72. Bryant and Dunn, *Moving Power and Money*, p. 175.

73. Karl Taeuber, "Census: Encyclopedia Entry," University of Wisconsin, CDE Working Paper 91-27 (1991), pp. 6–7.

74. Anderson, *The American Census*, p. 187; "Goldfield: Oral History," p. 8.

75. President's Commission, *Federal Statistics*, p. 56.

76. See, for example, "Goldfield: Oral History," p. 51.

77. "Goldfield: Oral History," p. 24.

78. On how well the Census Bureau functioned and then faltered technologically, see Joseph W. Duncan, "Technology, Costs, and the New Economics of Statistics," in William Alonso and Paul Starr, eds., *The Politics of Numbers* (New York: Russell Sage Foundation, 1987).

79. "Goldfield: Oral History," pp. 24–26.

80. Meeting, 2000 Census Advisory Committee; May 16–17, 1996.

81. "Scammon: Oral History," p. 8.

82. Bryant and Dunn, *Moving Power and Money*, pp. 193–94.

83. Choldin, *Looking for the Last Percent*, p. 20.

84. Daniel P. Moynihan, "Foreword," in David M. Heer, ed., *Social Statistics and the City* (Cambridge, Mass.: Joint Center for Urban Studies, 1968), p. iv.

85. On the public as the bureau's primary constituency, see the President's Commission, *Federal Statistics*, pp. 47–48.

86. Bryant and Dunn, *Moving Power and Money*, pp. 158–59.

87. Bryant and Dunn, *Moving Power and Money*, p. 221.

88. One feasible step would be to give the census director the same fixed term as the commissioner of labor statistics, though it is not clear how effective such a change would be by itself. See Norwood, *Organizing to Count*, pp. 81–82.

89. Stanley Lieberson, "The Enumeration of Ethnic and Racial Groups in the Census: Some Devilish Principles," in Statistics Canada and U.S. Bureau of the Census, *Challenges of Measuring the Ethnic World: Science, Politics, and Reality* (GPO, 1993), pp. 26–27.

90. Christopher Jencks, "The Politics of Income Measurement," in William Alonso and Paul Starr, eds., *The Politics of Numbers* (New York: Russell Sage Foundation, 1987), p. 131.

91. Starr, "The Sociology of Official Statistics," p. 50; this point was made previously in the President's Commission, *Federal Statistics*, pp. 47–48.

92. See James Q. Wilson, *Bureaucracy: What Government Agencies Do and Why They Do It* (New York: Basic Books, 1989), pp. 118–19, 179–85.

93. Barry Edmonston and others, eds., *Spotlight on Heterogeneity: The Federal Standards for Racial and Ethnic Classification* (Washington, D.C.: National Academy Press, 1996), p. 12.

94. Edmonston and others, *Spotlight on Heterogeneity*, p. 9.

95. See, for example, David E. Hayes-Bautista, "Identifying 'Hispanic' Populations: The Influence of Research Methodology upon Public Policy," *American Journal of Public Health*, vol. 70 (April 1980), pp. 353–56.

96. See the President's Commission, *Federal Statistics*, pp. 46–49.

97. Dennis Hevesi, "Census Count of Homeless Is Disputed," *New York Times*, April 13, 1991, sec. 1, p. 26.

98. See, for example, the series of reports issued by the Census Bureau under the title *Factfinder for the Nation*: esp. "History and Organization," CFF 4 (May 1988); "Census Bureau Programs and Products," CFF 18 (May 1990). See also Charles P. Kaplan and Thomas L. Van Valey, *Census '80: Continuing the Factfinder Tradition* (Washington, D.C.: Bureau of the Census, January 1980).

99. Starr, "The Sociology of Official Statistics," p. 41.

100. See the President's Commission, *Federal Statistics*, p. 47; see also Innes, *Knowledge and Public Policy*, p. 99.

101. See Choldin, *Looking for the Last Percent*, p. 39; "Goldfield: Oral History," p. 51.

102. Ira S. Lowry, *The Science and Politics of Ethnic Enumeration*, P-6435-1 (Santa Monica, Calif.: Rand, January 1980), p. 23.

103. Jencks, "The Politics of Income Measurement," p. 127. A similar point is made in Innes, *Knowledge and Public Policy*, pp. 99–100.

104. Innes, *Knowledge and Public Policy*, p. 99.

105. Ian I. Mitroff, Richard O. Mason, and Vincent P. Barabba, *The 1980 Census: Policymaking amid Turbulence* (Lexington, Mass.: D. C. Heath, 1983), pp. 237–38.

106. Halacy, *Census*, pp. 139–40.

107. Conrad Taeuber, "Invasion of Privacy: The Case of the United States Census," in Martin Bulmer, ed., *Censuses, Surveys and Privacy* (New York: Holmes and Meier, 1979), p. 171. Of course, the Census Bureau makes individual level data available to historians and other researchers once several generations have passed.

108. William Petersen, "The Protection of Privacy and the United States Census," in Martin Bulmer, ed., *Censuses, Surveys and Privacy* (New York: Holmes and Meier, 1979), p. 182. Intriguingly, Petersen makes the same point in William Petersen, "The Census: Constitutional Right or Neomercantilist Tool?" *American Demographics*, vol. 1 (October 1979), pp. 25–31, where he criticizes the census for being too intrusive.

109. See William Petersen, *Japanese Americans: Oppression and Success* (New York: Random House, 1971).

110. On the bureau's embarrassment, see "Goldfield: Oral History," pp. 9–10. For a critical perspective on the bureau, see Raymond Y. Okamura, "The Myth of Census Confidentiality," *Amerasia Journal*, vol. 8, no. 2 (1981), pp. 111–20.

111. For more on the Japanese internment episode, see Bryant and Dunn, *Moving Power and Money*, pp. 32–33; also Choldin, *Looking for the Last Percent*, pp. 19, 239–40. A more skeptical account of this episode is found in Anderson, *The American Census*, pp. 193–94.

112. Petersen, "The Protection of Privacy," p. 272, n. 10.

113. Bryant and Dunn, *Moving Power and Money*, p. 33.

114. 13 U.S.C. 9.

115. Wilson, *Bureaucracy*, pp. 54–65, 149–53.

116. Marc K. Landy and others, *The Environmental Protection Agency: Asking the Wrong Questions*, expanded ed. (Oxford University Press, 1994), pp. 196–99.

117. For one occasion when a bureau official invoked the authority of science, see Kenneth Prewitt, "Census 2000: Science Meets Politics," *Science*, vol. 283 (February 12, 1999), p. 935.

118. This is the first of a handful of observations and quotations obtained through not-for-attribution interviews. Accordingly, all such sources will not be cited.

119. William Alonso and Paul Starr, "Introduction," in William Alonso and Paul Starr, eds., *The Politics of Numbers* (New York: Russell Sage Foundation, 1987), p. 3.

120. Quoted in Lewis M. Killian, "The Collection of Official Data on Ethnicity and Reli-

gion: The U.S. Experience," *New Community*, Autumn/Winter 1983, pp. 77–78. See also William Petersen, "Religious Statistics in the United States," *Journal for the Scientific Study of Religion*, vol. 1 (1962), pp. 165–78.

121. Petersen, "Politics and the Measurement of Ethnicity," p. 222.

122. Killian, "The Collection of Official Data on Ethnicity and Religion," p. 79. Public Law 94-521 prohibits the Census Bureau from collecting information on religion on a mandatory basis. For more on this point, see Arthur R. Cresce and others, "Preliminary Evaluation of Data from the Race and Ethnic Origin Questions in the 1990 Census," paper presented at the Annual Meeting of the American Statistical Association, Boston, August 10–13, 1992, p. 38.

123. This is the exact wording of the question on the 1980 census long form, which was sent to a sample of U.S. households. On the 1990 census the ancestry question was slightly altered: "What is this person's ancestry or ethnic origin?"

124. Stephan Thernstrom, "Counting Heads: New Data on the Ethnic Composition of the American Population," *Journal of Interdisciplinary History*, vol. 20 (Summer 1989), pp. 107–16.

125. "Kincannon: Oral History," p. 14.

126. William Petersen, *Ethnicity Counts* (New Brunswick, N.J.: Transaction Books, 1997), pp. 120–21.

127. This episode is chronicled in Harvey M. Choldin, "Statistics and Politics: The 'Hispanic Issue' in the 1980 Census," *Demography*, vol. 23 (August 1986), pp. 403–18.

128. "Taeuber: Oral History," p. 9.

129. See Jacob S. Siegel and Jeffrey S. Passel, "Coverage of the Hispanic Population of the United States in the 1970 Census: A Methodological Analysis," *Current Population Reports*, P-23, no. 82 (GPO, 1979).

130. Public Law 94-311. See Joan Moore and Harry Pachon, *Hispanics in the United States* (Englewood Cliffs, N.J.: Prentice-Hall, 1985), p. 196; also Lowry, "Counting Ethnic Minorities," p. 25.

131. See Office of Management and Budget (OMB), "Directive No. 15: Race and Ethnic Standards for Federal Statistics and Administrative Reporting," *Federal Register*, vol. 43 (May 4, 1978), p. 19269.

132. Lowry, "Counting Ethnic Minorities," pp. 21–22. See also Petersen, "Politics and the Measurement of Ethnicity," p. 233; "Hansen: Oral History," p 24.

133. Choldin, "Statistics and Politics."

134. Thernstrom, "American Ethnic Statistics," p. 100; Cresce and others, "Preliminary Evaluation," pp. 65, 73.

135. Lowry, "Counting Ethnic Minorities," pp. 25–26.

136. Cresce and others, "Preliminary Evaluation of Data from the Race and Ethnic Origin Questions in the 1990 Census," p. 175.

137. Robert Reinhold, "Census Questions on Race Assailed as Political by Population Experts," *New York Times*, May 14, 1978, sec. 1, pp. 1, 14.

138. OMB, "Standards for the Classification of Federal Data on Race and Ethnicity," *Federal Register*, vol. 60 (August 28, 1995), p. 44675.

139. A point echoed in print by other Census Bureau officials. See Nampeo R. McKenney and Arthur R. Cresce, "Measurement of Ethnicity in the United States: Experiences of the U.S. Census Bureau," in Statistics Canada and U.S. Bureau of the Census, *Challenges of Measuring an Ethnic World: Science, Politics and Reality* (GPO, 1993), p. 181.

140. Edmonston and others, *Spotlight on Heterogeneity*, pp. 28–29.

141. See, for example, Charles K. Kamasaki, *An Hispanic Assessment of the Federal Standard for Race and Ethnicity*, National Council of La Raza Workshop on Race and Eth-

nicity Classification, sponsored by the Committee on National Statistics, National Academy of Sciences, February 17, 1994, pp. 5–6. Similarly, see testimony of Sonia Perez, representing the National Council of La Raza (NCLR) in *Review of Federal Measurements of Race and Ethnicity*, Hearing before the Subcommittee on Census, Statistics, and Postal Personnel of the House Committee on Post Office and Civil Service, 103 Cong. 1 sess. (GPO, 1994), p. 177. For evidence that after the finding "some Hispanics, including the Census Hispanic Advisory Committee and most Hispanic organizations, oppose a single, combined question," see OMB, "Recommendations from the Interagency Committee for the Review of Racial and Ethnic Standards to the Office of Management and Budget Concerning Changes to the Standards for the Classification of Federal Data on Race and Ethnicity," *Federal Register*, vol. 62 (July 9, 1997), p. 36939. The Mexican American Legal Defense and Educational Fund took a different stand from NCLR in 1993. It was cautious and urged research before merging the questions. See *Review of Federal Measurements of Race and Ethnicity*, Hearing, pp. 178–79.

142. For a detailed analysis of these CPS findings, see Peter Skerry, "Many American Dilemmas: The Statistical Politics of Counting by Race and Ethnicity," *Brookings Review*, vol. 14 (Summer 1996), pp. 36–39.

143. General Accounting Office (GAO), *Census Reform: Early Outreach and Decisions Needed on Race and Ethnic Questions*, GAO/GGD-93-36 (January 1993), p. 18.

144. McKenney and Cresce, "Measurement of Ethnicity in the United States," p. 180.

145. For the most complete account of these events, see Lowry, "Counting Ethnic Minorities," pp. 27–32. For other such accounts, see Cresce and others, "Preliminary Evaluation of Data from the Race and Ethnic Origin Questions in the 1990 Census," pp. 6–7; also *Content Determination Reports: Race and Ethnic Origin*, CDR-6 (1990); *1990 Census of Housing and Population* (GPO, February 1991), pp. 15–16.

146. On this point, see GAO, *Census Reform*, pp. 19–20. Also OMB, "Recommendations from the Interagency Committee," pp. 36924–25.

Chapter Three

1. Ira S. Lowry, *The Science and Politics of Ethnic Enumeration*, P-6435-1 (Santa Monica, Calif.: Rand, January 1980), p. 2.

2. See Office of Management and Budget (OMB), "Directive No. 15: Race and Ethnic Standards for Federal Statistics and Administrative Reporting," *Federal Register*, vol. 43 (May 4, 1978), p. 19269.

3. OMB, "Recommendations from the Interagency Committee for the Review of the Racial and Ethnic Standards to the Office of Management and Budget Concerning Changes to the Standards for the Classification of Federal Data on Race and Ethnicity," *Federal Register*, vol. 62 (July 9, 1997), p. 36881.

4. Barry Edmonston and others, eds., *Spotlight on Heterogeneity: The Federal Standards for Racial and Ethnic Classification* (Washington D.C.: National Academy Press, 1996), p. 37.

5. Edmonston and others, *Spotlight on Heterogeneity*, p. 18. See also Lowry, *The Science and Politics of Ethnic Enumeration*, p. 1. For an example of this dominant social science perspective, see John Stone, *Racial Conflict in Contemporary Society* (Harvard University Press, 1985).

6. The 1990 short and long form questionnaires, for example, were accompanied by detailed instructions that elaborated on the race and ethnic categories but did not delineate where one category ends and another begins. See appendix B.

7. See, for example, Fredrick Barth, ed., *Ethnic Groups and Boundaries: the Social Organization of Culture Differences* (Boston, Mass.: Little, Brown, 1969); Alan Wolfe, "Democ-

racy versus Sociology: Boundaries and Their Political Consequences," in Michele Lamont and Marcel Fournier, eds., *Cultivating Differences: Symbolic Boundaries and the Making of Inequality* (University of Chicago Press, 1992), pp. 309–25.

8. Michael Omi and Howard Winant, *Racial Formation in the United States: From the 1960s to the 1990s,* 2d ed. (New York: Routledge, 1994), p. 3. See also William Petersen, "Politics and the Measurement of Ethnicity," in William Alonso and Paul Starr, eds., *The Politics of Numbers* (New York: Russell Sage Foundation, 1987), p. 204.

9. For more on the development of this question, see U.S. Bureau of the Census, *Content Determination Reports: Race and Ethnic Origin,* 1990 CDR-6 (February 1991), pp. 12–13.

10. OMB, "Standards for the Classification of Federal Data on Race and Ethnicity," *Federal Register,* vol. 60 (August 28, 1995), p. 44692.

11. OMB, "Recommendations from the Interagency Committee," p. 36874; see also Edmonston and others, *Spotlight on Heterogeneity,* p. 17.

12. Edmonston and others, *Spotlight on Heterogeneity,* p. 41.

13. Margo J. Anderson, *The American Census: A Social History* (Yale University Press, 1988), pp. 201–02.

14. But even questions about parentage are not wholly objective. In Canada until 1981, individuals were asked to trace their ethnic origin through their paternal ancestor only. See Pamela M. White and others, "Measuring Ethnicity in Canadian Censuses," in Statistics Canada and U.S. Bureau of the Census, *Challenges of Measuring an Ethnic World: Science, Politics, and Reality* (GPO, 1993), p. 229.

15. Tom W. Smith, "The Subjectivity of Ethnicity," in Charles F. Turner and Elizabeth Martin, eds., *Surveying Subjective Phenomena* (New York: Russell Sage Foundation, 1984), p. 121.

16. Smith, "The Subjectivity of Ethnicity," p. 126.

17. But for precisely such an argument by a defender of affirmative action, see Christopher A. Ford, "Administering Identity: The Determination of 'Race' in Race-Conscious Law," *California Law Review,* vol. 82 (1994), pp. 1231–85.

18. Stanley Lieberson, "The Enumeration of Ethnic and Racial Groups in the Census: Some Devilish Principles," in Statistics Canada and U.S. Bureau of the Census, *Challenges of Measuring an Ethnic World* (GPO, 1993), p. 32.

19. For a thoughtful analysis of the evolving nature of this gap between our values and practices in the context of naturalization, see Arthur Mann, *The One and the Many: Reflections on the American Identity* (University of Chicago Press, 1979), pp. 86–96.

20. Michael Walzer, "Pluralism in Political Perspective," in Michael Walzer and others, eds., *The Politics of Ethnicity* (Harvard University Press, 1982), p. 21.

21. John Higham, *Send These to Me: Jews and Other Immigrants in Urban America* (New York: Atheneum, 1975), p. 242.

22. Such developments reflect what Herbert Gans refers to as "symbolic ethnicity." See Herbert J. Gans, "Symbolic Ethnicity: The Future of Ethnic Groups and Cultures in America," *Ethnic and Racial Studies,* vol. 1, no. 1 (1979), pp. 1–19.

23. David A. Hollinger, *Postethnic America: Beyond Multiculturalism* (New York: Basic Books, 1995), pp. 6–7.

24. Edmonston and others, *Spotlight on Heterogeneity,* p. 18.

25. Stephan Thernstrom, "American Ethnic Statistics," in Donald L. Horowitz and Gerard Noiriel, eds., *Immigrants in Two Democracies: French and American Experience* (New York University Press, 1992), p. 97.

26. OMB, "Recommendations from the Interagency Committee," p. 36874.

27. Felicity Barringer, "Counting the Homeless: Inexact but Not Invalid?" *New York Times,* March 4, 1990, p. 24; Barbara Vobejda, "Census-Takers Struggle to Tally the Homeless," *Washington Post,* March 21, 1990, pp. A1, A14.

28. See Ford, "Administering Identity"; Edmonston and others, *Spotlight on Heterogeneity*, p. 41.

29. Edmonston and others, *Spotlight on Heterogeneity*, pp. 12–13.

30. Arthur R. Cresce and others, "Preliminary Evaluation of Data from the Race and Ethnic Origin Questions in the 1990 Census," paper presented at the Annual Meeting of the American Statistical Association, Boston, August 10–13, 1992, p. 12; Edmonston and others, *Spotlight on Heterogeneity*, p. 23; Barry Edmonston and Charles Schultze, eds., *Modernizing the U.S. Census* (Washington, D.C.: National Academy Press, 1995), pp. 142–43, 373–74.

31. Cresce and others, "Preliminary Evaluation of Data from the Race and Ethnic Origin Questions in the 1990 Census," p. 42; Edmonston and others, *Spotlight on Heterogeneity*, p. 23.

32. General Accounting Office (GAO), *Census Reform: Early Outreach and Decisions Needed on Race and Ethnic Questions*, GAO/GGD-93-36 (January 1993), pp. 26–28; see also Cresce and others, "Preliminary Evaluation of Data from the Race and Ethnic Origin Questions," p. 12; Harry Scarr testimony in *Review of Federal Measurements of Race and Ethnicity*, Hearing before the Subcommittee on Census, Statistics, and Postal Personnel of the House Committee on Post Office and Civil Service, 103 Cong. 1 sess. (GPO, 1994), p. 32.

33. Edmonston and others, *Spotlight on Heterogeneity*, p. 39.

34. Edmonston and Schultze, *Modernizing the U.S. Census*, p. 379.

35. OMB, "Directive No. 15," p. 19269.

36. I use this term advisedly, on the basis of data gathered by the CPS. See OMB, "Recommendations from the Interagency Committee," p. 36920, which reports that more than half of the respondents in the CPS study preferred "American Indian." For general information on American Indians and the census, see Petersen, "Politics and the Measurement of Ethnicity," pp. 217–18.

37. OMB, "Directive No. 15," p. 19269.

38. OMB, "Recommendations from the Interagency Committee," p. 36920.

39. Edmonston and others, *Spotlight on Heterogeneity*, p. 30.

40. OMB, "Recommendations from the Interagency Committee," p. 36920.

41. OMB, "Standards for the Classification of Federal Data on Race and Ethnicity," p. 44679.

42. Edmonston and others, *Spotlight on Heterogeneity*, p. 30; Department of the Interior, Bureau of Indian Affairs, "Detailed Questions for Federal Agency Representatives on the Implementation of Directive No. 15," National Research Council Workshop on Race and Ethnicity Classification: An Assessment of the Federal Standard for Race and Ethnicity Classification, February 17–18, 1994.

43. In 1990, 8.7 million persons reported in the ancestry question that they were American Indians, but only 1.9 million reported American Indian race. OMB, "Standards for the Classification of Federal Data on Race and Ethnicity," p. 44679.

44. OMB, "Recommendations from the Interagency Committee," p. 36897.

45. See Susan Graham, executive director of PROJECT RACE, Inc., presentation before the National Research Council Workshop on Race and Ethnicity Classification. For an overall analysis of the multiracial issue, see Joel Perlman, *Reflecting the Changing Face of America: Multiracials, Racial Classification, and American Intermarriage*, Jerome Levy Economics Institute, Public Policy Brief 35 (1997).

46. OMB, "Recommendations from the Interagency Committee," p. 36903.

47. OMB, "Recommendations from the Interagency Committee," p. 36907.

48. Edmonston and others, *Spotlight on Heterogeneity*, p. 39.

49. See Linda Mathews, "More Than Identity Rides on a New Racial Category," *New York Times*, July 6, 1996, sec. 1, p. 1.

50. Edmonston and others, *Spotlight on Heterogeneity*, p. 38.

51. Edmonston and others, *Spotlight on Heterogeneity*, p. 13. See also National Center for Education, *Statistics, Racial and Ethnic Classifications Used by Public Schools* (GPO, 1996).

52. Edmonston and others, *Spotlight on Heterogeneity*, p. 18; see also OMB, "Standards for the Classification of Federal Data on Race and Ethnicity," pp. 44675–76.

53. Lowry, *The Science and Politics of Ethnic Enumeration*, p. 21.

54. Susan Graham presentation, National Research Council, Workshop on Race and Ethnicity Classification, p. 1.

55. Letter from Deval L. Patrick, assistant attorney general, Civil Rights Division, U.S. Department of Justice, to Katherine K. Wallman, chief of statistical policy, Office of Information and Regulatory Affairs, Office of Management and Budget, October 18, 1994, p. 4. See also OMB, "Standards for the Classification of Federal Data on Race and Ethnicity," p. 44679.

56. Ford, "Administering Identity," esp. pp. 1280–85.

57. Suzanne Oboler, *Ethnic Labels, Latino Lives: Identity and the Politics of (Re)Presentation in the United States* (University of Minnesota Press, 1995), p. 129.

58. Paul Farhi, "Living on Edge in Mount Pleasant," *Washington Post*, October 7, 1990, p. A1.

59. "True Count," *Washington Post*, July, 10, 1997, p. A18.

60. Special Census Bureau tabulations for author.

61. F. James Davis, *Who Is Black? One Nation's Definition* (Pennsylvania State University Press, 1991), p. 11.

62. Dinesh D'Souza, "My Color 'Tis of Thee," *Weekly Standard*, December 16, 1994.

63. D'Souza, "My Color 'Tis of Thee," p. 48. John Miller also believes that the "census sorts individuals by race." See John J. Miller, *The Unmaking of Americans: How Multiculturalism Has Undermined the Assimilation Ethic* (New York: Free Press, 1998), p. 241.

64. Since 1989 births in the United States have been classified by the race of the mother. See Edmonston and others, *Spotlight on Heterogeneity*, pp. 26, 66. In very specific interview circumstances, Census Bureau officials suggest that respondents use the race of their mother when unable to provide a single response. See Cresce and others, "Preliminary Evaluation of Data from the Race and Ethnic Origin Questions in the 1990 Census," p. 42.

65. The one obvious exception, as indicated earlier in this chapter, is the tribal classification of American Indians.

66. For more evidence on this, see Robert A. Hahn, "The Coding of Race and Ethnicity in Federal Health Statistics: Problems and Prospects," paper prepared for the National Academy of Sciences Meeting on Office of Management and Budget Directive 15, Washington, D.C., February 17–18, 1994, p. 14.

67. Charles Hirschman, "How to Measure Ethnicity: An Immodest Proposal," in Statistics Canada and U.S. Bureau of the Census, *Challenges of Measuring an Ethnic World: Science, Politics, and Reality* (GPO, 1993), p. 547.

68. Nampeo R. McKenney and others, "Evaluating Racial and Ethnic Reporting in the 1990 Census," in American Statistical Association, *Proceedings of the Section on Survey Research Methods* (Alexandria, Va.: ASA, 1993), p. 71.

69. McKenney, "Evaluating Racial and Ethnic Reporting in the 1990 Census," p. 71.

70. Jeffrey S. Passel and David L. Word, "Problems in Analyzing Race and Hispanic Origin Data from the 1980 Census: Solutions Based on Constructing Consistent Populations for Micro-Level Data," paper presented at the 1987 Annual Meeting of the Population Association of America, Chicago, Ill., April–May, 1987, pp. 9–10.

71. Cresce and others, "Preliminary Evaluation of Data from the Race and Ethnic Origin Questions in the 1990 Census," pp. 18–22; GAO, *Census Reform*, pp. 16–17.

72. Cresce and others, "Preliminary Evaluation of Data from the Race and Ethnic Origin Questions in the 1990 Census," p. 20.

73. Cresce and others, "Preliminary Evaluation of Data from the Race and Ethnic Origin Questions in the 1990 Census," p. 20.

74. Nampeo R. Mckenney and Arthur R. Cresce, "Measurement of Ethnicity in the United States: Experiences of the U.S. Census Bureau," in Statistics Canada and U.S. Bureau of the Census, *Challenges of Measuring an Ethnic World: Science, Politics, and Reality* (GPO, 1993), p. 182.

75. See Lowry, *The Science and Politics of Ethnic Enumeration*, p. 2; Hollinger, *Postethnic America*, pp. 34–42; John Stone, *Racial Conflict in Contemporary Society* (Harvard University Press, 1985), pp. 34–61; William Petersen, "Concepts of Ethnicity," in Stephan Thernstrom, ed., *Harvard Encyclopedia of American Ethnic Groups* (Harvard University Press, 1980), pp. 234–242; and John Higham, "From Process to Structure: Formulations of American Immigration History," in Peter Kvisto and Dag Blanck, eds., *American Immigrants and Their Generations: Studies and Commentaries on the Hansen Thesis after Fifty Years* (University of Illinois Press, 1990), pp. 19–21. Most recently and provocatively, see Orlando Patterson, *The Ordeal of Integration: Progress and Resentment in America's "Racial" Crisis* (Washington, D.C.: Civitas/Counterpoint, 1997) and "The Race Trap," *New York Times*, July 11, 1997, p. A27.

76. Edmonston and others, *Spotlight on Heterogeneity*, p. 41.

77. For types of "consistency," see Cresce and others, "Preliminary Evaluation of Data from the Race and Ethnic Origin Questions in the 1990 Census."

78. On reliability and validity, see Edmonston and others, *Spotlight on Heterogeneity*, p. 41. More generally, see Janet Buttolph Johnson and Richard A. Joslyn, *Political Science Research Methods*, 3d ed. (Washington, D.C.: CQ Press, 1995), pp. 67–77; Edward A. Suchman, "Principles and Practice of Evaluative Research," in John T. Doby, ed., *An Introduction to Social Research*, 2d ed. (New York: Appleton-Century-Crofts, 1967), pp. 344–45.

79. Tom W. Smith, "Ethnic Measurement and Identification," *Ethnicity*, vol. 7 (1980), p. 78.

80. Jeff Passel, "Discussion," in *Proceedings from the 1993 Research Conference on Undercounted Ethnic Populations* (GPO, October 1993), p. 348.

81. Edmonston and others, *Spotlight on Heterogeneity*, p. 45.

82. *Review of Federal Measurements of Race and Ethnicity*, Hearing, p. 54.

83. See OMB, "Standards for the Classification of Federal Data on Race and Ethnicity," p. 44682.

84. Cresce and others, "Preliminary Evaluation of Data from the Race and Ethnic Origin Questions in the 1990 Census," p. 34. In 1980 the ancestry question had an open-ended, write-in format for which there could be multiple responses, unlike the race and Hispanic-origin questions.

85. Cresce and others, "Preliminary Evaluation of Data from the Race and Ethnic Origin Questions in the 1990 Census," pp. 31–35; Edmonston and Schultze, *Modernizing the U.S. Census*, p. 377.

86. See Farley testimony in *Review of Federal Measurements of Race and Ethnicity*, Hearing, pp. 54–55. For similar problems with the Canadian census, see White and others, "Measuring Ethnicity in Canadian Censuses," p. 240.

87. Edmonston and others, *Spotlight on Heterogeneity*, p. 45.

88. U.S. Bureau of the Census, *Content Reinterview Survey: Accuracy of Data for Selected Population and Housing Characteristics as Measured by Reinterview*, 1990 CPH-E-1 (October 1993), pp. 27–34; McKenney and others, "Evaluating Racial and Ethnic Reporting in the 1990 Census," p. 67.

89. U.S. Bureau of the Census, *Content Reinterview Survey*, p. 22.

90. See U.S. Bureau of the Census, *Content Reinterview Survey*, p. 22.

91. McKenney and others, "Evaluating Racial and Ethnic Reporting in the 1990 Census," p. 73. Also see Nampeo R. McKenney and others, "The Quality of the Race and Spanish Origin Information Reported in the 1980 Census," paper presented at the Annual Meeting of the American Statistical Association, Las Vegas, Nev., 1985.

92. McKenney and others, "Evaluating Racial and Ethnic Reporting in the 1990 Census," p. 73.

93. Edmonston and others, *Spotlight on Heterogeneity*, p. 30.

94. Cresce and others, "Preliminary Evaluation of Data from the Race and Ethnic Origin Questions in the 1990 Census," table 1a and p. 57. See more generally, David Harris, "Meaning of the 1990 Census Count of American Indians: What Do the Numbers Really Mean?" *Social Science Quarterly*, vol. 75 (September 1994), p. 583.

95. McKenney and others, "Evaluating Racial and Ethnic Reporting in the 1990 Census," p. 73; McKenney and others, "The Quality of the Race and Spanish Origin Information Reported in the 1980 Census."

96. GAO, *Census Reform*, p. 27.

97. GAO, *Census Reform*, p. 25.

98. GAO, *Census Reform*, p. 26.

99. U.S. Bureau of the Census, *Content Reinterview Survey*, p. 21.

100. Census Bureau responses to questions posed at the National Research Council Workshop on Race and Ethnicity Classification, February 17–18, 1994, pp. 4–5.

101. Edmonston and Schultze, *Modernizing the U.S. Census*, p. 376.

102. Edmonston and Schultze, *Modernizing the U.S. Census*, p. 376.

103. Edmonston and others, *Spotlight on Heterogeneity*, p. 29. Or as census staffer Arthur Cresce puts it: "Census definitions state that persons of Hispanic origin can be of any race . . . but the data suggest that many Hispanics view their Hispanicity as synonymous with race." See Cresce and others, "Preliminary Evaluation of Data from the Race and Ethnic Origin Questions in the 1990 Census," p. 12.

104. See Martin and others, "Context Effects for Census Measures of Race and Hispanic Origin," *Public Opinion Quarterly*, vol. 54, no. 4 (Winter 1990); Cresce and others, "Preliminary Evaluation of Data from the Race and Ethnic Origin Questions in the 1990 Census," p. 41; also Edmonston and others, *Spotlight on Heterogeneity*, p. 24.

105. Jacob S. Siegel and Jeffrey S. Passel, "Coverage of the Hispanic Population on the United States in the 1970 Census: A Methodological Analysis," *Current Population Reports*, P-23, no. 82 (GPO, 1979), p. 2.

106. Passel and Word, "Problems Analyzing Race and Hispanic Origin Data from the 1980 Census," p. 9.

107. McKenney and others, "The Quality of the Race and Spanish Origin Information Reported in the 1980 Census," table 3.

108. McKenney and others, "Evaluating Racial and Ethnic Reporting in the 1990 Census," p. 73.

109. McKenney and others, "Evaluating Racial and Ethnic Reporting in the 1990 Census," p. 73.

110. Edmonston and others, *Spotlight on Heterogeneity*, p. 41.

111. Hirschman, "How to Measure Ethnicity," p. 547. The low response reliability of Hispanic data is also a major reason why survey data on Hispanic attitudes and voting behavior are notoriously volatile and unreliable. See Peter Skerry, *Mexican Americans: The Ambivalent Minority* (Harvard University Press, 1993), pp. 308–12. It also explains why, in the most visible and important Voting Rights litigation involving Hispanics, *Garza* v. *Los Angeles County Board of Supervisors*, the defendants argued (albeit unsuccessfully) that Filipinos, Cubans, and Hispanics of European ancestry should not be considered Hispanics for pur-

poses of creating Hispanic-majority electoral districts. See William O'Hare, "The Use of Demographic Data in Voting Rights Litigation," *Evaluation Review*, vol. 15 (December 1991), p. 738.

112. Explained by Cresce and others, "Preliminary Evaluation of Data from the Race and Ethnic Origin Questions in the 1990 Census," p. 13.

113. Cresce and others, "Preliminary Evaluation of Data from the Race and Ethnic Origin Questions in the 1990 Census," p. 46.

114. Edmonston and Schultze, *Modernizing the U.S. Census*, p. 384.

115. McKenney and Cresce, "Measurement of Ethnicity in the United States"; also Cresce and others, "Preliminary Evaluation of Data from the Race and Ethnic Origin Questions in the 1990 Census."

116. See Cresce and others, "Preliminary Evaluation of Data from the Race and Ethnic Origin Questions in the 1990 Census," p. 70. These data refer specifically to the short, not the long form, which had different allocation rates. See Edmonston and Schultze, *Modernizing the U.S. Census*, p. 388.

117. Cresce and others, "Preliminary Evaluation of Data from the Race and Ethnic Origin Questions in the 1990 Census," p. 24.

118. GAO, *Census Reform*, p. 24.

119. GAO, *Census Reform*, p. 25; Cresce and others, "Preliminary Evaluation of Data from the Race and Ethnic Origin Questions in the 1990 Census," p. 28. See also McKenney and others, "Evaluating Racial and Ethnic Reporting in the 1990 Census," p. 70.

120. Cresce and others, "Preliminary Evaluation of Data from the Race and Ethnic Origin Questions in the 1990 Census," p. 69.

121. It is useful here to recall that the fiction of self-identification obscures the fact that it is usually one person in each household who fills out the form for the other members. Thus many individuals "fail to respond" with no actual knowledge that they have done so.

122. Here and throughout this segment I rely on Cresce and others, "Preliminary Evaluation of Data from the Race and Ethnic Origin Questions in the 1990 Census," pp. 24–28.

123. For a brief explanation of hot-deck procedure, see Edmonston and others, *Spotlight on Heterogeneity*, p. 21.

124. The definitive research on the residential concentration of Hispanics in relation to that of blacks, for example, is Douglas S. Massey and Nancy Denton, *American Apartheid: Segregation and the Making of the Underclass* (Harvard University Press, 1993), esp. pp. 74–78.

125. Cresce and others, "Preliminary Evaluation of Data from the Race and Ethnic Origin Questions in the 1990 Census," pp. 26–28, 45–46.

126. Edmonston and Schultze, *Modernizing the U.S. Census*, p. 375. See also Cresce and others, "Preliminary Evaluation of Data from the Race and Ethnic Origin Questions in the 1990 Census," p. 46.

127. GAO, *Federal Data Collection: Agencies' Use of Consistent Race and Ethnic Definitions*, GAO/GGD-93-25 (December 1992), pp. 4–5.

128. If neither parent's race is reported on the birth certificate, the infant's race is imputed to be the race of the mother on the preceding record with known race. For an overview of this complicated issue, see Edmonston and others, *Spotlight on Heterogeneity*, pp. 26–28.

129. The study's findings were summarized in Edmonston and others, *Spotlight on Heterogeneity*, pp. 26–27.

130. Robert A. Hahn and others, "Inconsistencies in Coding of Race and Ethnicity between Birth and Death in U.S. Infants: A New Look at Infant Mortality, 1983 through 1985," *Journal of the American Medical Association*, vol. 267 (January 8, 1992), pp. 259–63. See also the discussion and review of research in OMB, "Recommendations from the Interagency Committee," p. 36910.

131. Again, for a review of such research, see OMB, "Recommendations from the Interagency Committee," p. 36910.

132. See Edmonston and others, *Spotlight on Heterogeneity*, pp. 12–13, 18.

133. Edmonston and others, *Spotlight on Heterogeneity*, p. 28.

134. Sir Josiah Charles Stamp (1880–1941), quoted in "Background Books: Statistics," *Wilson Quarterly*, vol. 9 (Summer 1985), p. 123.

135. Lieberson, "The Enumeration of Ethnic and Racial Groups in the Census," p. 32.

136. Passel, "Discussion," p. 348.

137. On Arabs pushing for their own separate category and its implications, see OMB, "Standards for the Classification of Federal Data on Race and Ethnicity," p. 44681.

138. See OMB, "Standards for the Classification of Federal Data on Race and Ethnicity," p. 44676. Also Suzann Evinger, "How Shall We Measure Our Nation's Diversity?" *Chance*, vol. 8, no. 1 (1995), p. 14.

139. William Kruskal, testimony in *Federal Statistics and National Needs*, Committee Print Prepared for the Subcommittee on Energy, Nuclear Proliferation, and Government Processes of the Senate Committee on Governmental Affairs, 98 Cong. 1 sess. (GPO, 1984), p. 49.

140. Hollinger, *Postethnic America*, p. 24.

141. Edmonston and others, *Spotlight on Heterogeneity*, p. 8.

142. OMB, "Directive No. 15," pp. 19269–70.

143. Edmonston and others, *Spotlight on Heterogeneity*, p. 9.

144. Edmonston and others, *Spotlight on Heterogeneity*, p. 8.

145. Edmonston and Schultze, *Modernizing the U.S. Census*, p. 380.

146. Edmonston and others, *Spotlight on Heterogeneity*, p. 36.

147. Suzann Evinger, "How to Record Race," *American Demographics*, vol. 18 (May 1996), p. 36.

148. Edmonston and others, *Spotlight on Heterogeneity*, p. 36.

149. OMB, "Recommendations from the Interagency Committee," p. 36874.

150. OMB, "Directive No. 15," p. 19269.

151. Evinger, "How Shall We Measure Our Nation's Diversity?" p. 14.

152. OMB, "Recommendations from the Interagency Committee," p. 36874.

153. OMB, "Recommendations from the Interagency Committee," p. 36874.

154. Edmonston and others, *Spotlight on Heterogeneity*, p. 9.

155. Kenneth Prewitt, "Public Statistics and Democratic Politics," in William Alonso and Paul Starr, eds., *The Politics of Numbers* (New York: Russell Sage Foundation, 1987), p. 270.

156. Edmonston and others, *Spotlight on Heterogeneity*, p. 9.

157. See Peter Skerry, "Many American Dilemmas: The Statistical Politics of Counting by Race and Ethnicity," *Brookings Review*, vol. 14 (Summer, 1996), pp. 36–39.

158. OMB, "Recommendations from the Interagency Committee," p. 36923.

159. OMB, "Standards for the Classification of Federal Data on Race and Ethnicity," p. 44683. For data and commentary, see Edward W. Fernandez, "Comparisons of Selected Social and Economic Characteristics between Asians, Hawaiians, Pacific Islanders, and American Indians (Including Alaskan Natives)," U.S. Bureau of the Census, Population Division Working Paper 15 (June 1996); see also *Review of Federal Measurements of Race and Ethnicity*, Hearing, p. 199.

160. Separating Native Hawaiians from Pacific Islanders while at the same time separating Pacific Islanders from Asians would have so reduced the number of "Non-Hawaiian Pacific Islanders" (to as few as 154,000) that it would have been difficult for survey researchers to get adequate sample data for such a group at state or local levels without costly oversampling methods. See OMB, "Recommendations from the Interagency Committee," p. 36923.

161. OMB, "Recommendations from the Interagency Committee," p. 36926. On American

Indian opposition, see Edmonston and others, *Spotlight on Heterogeneity*, p. 31. See confirming evidence on incomes in Fernandez, "Comparisons of Selected Social and Economic Characteristics."

162. See GAO, *Federal Data Collection*, pp. 4, 8.

163. See Lieberson, "The Enumeration of Racial and Ethnic Groups in the Census," p. 32.

164. Omi and Winant, *Racial Formation in the United States*, p. 3.

165. Lowry, *The Science and Politics of Ethnic Enumeration*, p. 21.

166. Thernstrom, "American Ethnic Statistics," p. 102.

167. See Ford, "Administering Identity."

168. Lowry, *The Science and Politics of Ethnic Enumeration*, p. 21.

169. See Mary Waters's remarks in "Focus for the Future," in Statistics Canada and U.S. Bureau of the Census, *Challenges of Measuring an Ethnic World: Science, Politics, and Reality* (GPO, 1993), p. 149.

170. Omi and Winant, *Racial Formation in the United States*, p. 3.

171. See Theodore J. Lowi, *The End of Liberalism: The Second Republic of the United States* (New York: Norton, 1979).

172. Steven A. Holmes, "Panel Balks at Multiracial Census Category," *New York Times*, July 7, 1997, p. A12.

173. OMB, "Recommendations from the Interagency Committee," p. 36883.

174. Public Law 94-311.

175. Katherine K. Wallman, Roundtable discussion, "Measuring Race and Ethnicity in an Age of Diversity," Population Reference Bureau, Washington, D.C., November 15, 1995.

176. Sidney M. Milkis, "Remaking Government Institutions in the 1970s: Participatory Democracy and the Triumph of Administrative Politics," *Journal of Political History*, vol. 10, no. 1 (1998), p. 16.

Chapter Four

1. Jeff Passel, "Discussion," in U.S. Bureau of the Census, *1993 Research Conference on Undercounted Ethnic Populations* (GPO, October 1993), p. 348.

2. See also David A. Freedman and Kenneth W. Wachter, "Planning for the Census in the Year 2000," *Evaluation Review*, vol. 20 (August 1996), pp. 359–61.

3. For more on this, see Barry Edmonston and Charles Schultze, eds., *Modernizing the U.S. Census* (Washington, D.C.: National Academy Press, 1995), pp. 75–83.

4. See Howard Hogan and Gregg Robinson, "What the Census Bureau's Coverage Evaluation Programs Tell Us about Differential Undercount," in U.S. Bureau of the Census, *1993 Research Conference on Undercounted Ethnic Populations* (GPO, October 1993), p. 9.

5. Barbara Everitt Bryant and William Dunn, *Moving Power and Money: The Politics of Census Taking* (Ithaca, N.Y.: New Strategist Publications, 1995), p. 2.

6. See Edmonston and Schultze, *Modernizing the U.S. Census*, p. 33–34. See also William P. O'Hare, "The Overlooked Undercount: Children Missed in the Decennial Census," p. 1, Annie E. Case Foundation website, www.aecf.org/kidscount/census.pdf.

7. This conclusion is based, as table 4-2 indicates, on the revised results of the 1990 postenumeration survey. Yet as table 4-1 highlights, demographic analysis leads to a much higher estimate of the 1990 black-nonblack undercount differential (4.4 versus 3.25 percent), which then undermines this conclusion.

8. Hogan and Robinson, "What the Census Bureau's Coverage Evaluation Programs Tell Us about Differential Undercount," pp. 17–18; Howard Hogan, "The 1990 Post-Enumeration Survey: Operations and Results," *Journal of the American Statistical Association*, vol. 88 (September 1993), p. 1055.

9. Hogan and Robinson, "What the Census Bureau's Coverage Evaluation Programs Tell Us about Differential Undercount," pp. 14–15, 25.

10. Note that this net undercount figure is higher than those cited earlier because of errors that were subsequently discovered in the estimation methodology used to derive this number.

11. General Accounting Office (GAO), *1990 Census: Reported Net Undercount Obscured Magnitude of Error*, GAO/GGD-91-113 (August 1991), p. 1.

12. See Eugene P. Ericksen and Teresa K. Defonson, "Beyond the Net Undercount: How to Measure Census Error," *Chance*, vol. 6, no. 4 (1993), pp. 38–43.

13. Edmonston and Schultze, *Modernizing the U.S. Census*, p. 33.

14. Joseph Duncan, "Technology, Costs, and the New Economics of Statistics," in William Alonso and Paul Starr, eds., *The Politics of Numbers* (New York: Russell Sage Foundation, 1987), pp. 396–98.

15. See "C. Louis Kincannon: Oral History" (Washington, D.C.: Bureau of the Census, History Staff, n.d.), pp. 15, 17; James T. Bonnen, "Federal Statistical Coordination Today: A Disaster or a Disgrace?" *American Statistician*, vol. 37 (August 1983), pp. 179–84.

16. Despite its relatively low undercount, the 1980 census is regarded by most census professionals as a near disaster. In any event, this view of what happened in 1980 was also voiced publicly by former chief statistician at the bureau, Barbara Bailar, who resigned in protest in 1987 when the decision not to adjust the 1990 census was first announced. See her testimony before Mervyn Dymally's committee in *The Decennial Census Improvement Act*, Hearing before the Subcommittee on Census and Population of the House Committee on Post Office and Civil Service, 100 Cong. 2 sess. (GPO, 1988), p. 85.

17. On the difficulty of getting survey data on nonrespondents, see Eleanor Singer and others, "The Impact of Privacy Concerns on Survey Participation: The Case of the 1990 U.S. Census," *Public Opinion Quarterly*, vol. 57, no. 4 (1993), p. 465. Surveys on census participation have found that nontraditional households are much less likely to mail back census forms than traditional households. According to the 1990 Survey on Census Participation, 56 percent of nontraditional households mailed back their census forms, compared with 80 percent of traditional households. See Robert E. Fay and others, "Low-Mail Response Rate in the 1990 Census: A Preliminary Interpretation," paper presented at the 1991 Annual Research Conference of the U.S Census Bureau, Arlington, Va., March 17–20, 1991.

18. Mary Romero, "Ethnographic Evaluation of Behavioral Causes of Census Undercount of Undocumented Immigrants and Salvadorans in the Mission District of San Francisco, California," U.S. Bureau of the Census, Ethnographic Evaluation of the 1990 Decennial Census, Report 18 (July 1992), p. 4.

19. Alfredo Velasco, "Ethnographic Evaluation of Behavioral Causes of Undercount in the Community of Sherman Heights, California," U.S. Bureau of the Census, Ethnographic Evaluation of the 1990 Decennial Census, Report 22 (October 1992), pp. 9–12.

20. Velasco, "Ethnographic Evaluation of Behavioral Causes of Undercount in the Community of Sherman Heights," pp. 9–10.

21. Romero, "Ethnographic Evaluation of Behavioral Causes of Census Undercount of Undocumented Immigrants and Salvadorans in the Mission District of San Francisco," p. 7.

22. Sarah Mahler, "Alternative Enumeration of Undocumented Salvadorans on Long Island," U.S. Bureau of the Census, Ethnographic Evaluation of the 1990 Decennial Census, Report 20 (January 1993), p. 2.

23. Mahler, "Alternative Enumeration of Undocumented Salvadorans on Long Island," p. 9.

24. Ansley Hamid, "Ethnographic Follow-Up of a Predominantly African American Population in a Sample Area in Central Harlem, New York City: Behavioral Causes of the Undercount of the 1990 Census," U.S. Bureau of the Census, Ethnographic Evaluation of the 1990 Decennial Census, Report 11 (April 1992), p. 11.

25. Hamid, "Ethnographic Follow-Up of a Predominantly African American Population," p. 2.

26. Martin Dale Montoya, "Ethnographic Evaluation of the Behavioral Causes of Undercount: Woodburn, Oregon," U.S. Bureau of the Census, Ethnographic Evaluation of the 1990 Decennial Census, Report 25 (November 1992), p. 7.

27. Velasco, "Ethnographic Evaluation of Behavioral Causes of Undercount in the Community of Sherman Heights," p. 11.

28. See Douglas S. Massey and others, *Return to Aztlan: The Social Process of International Migration from Western Mexico* (University of California Press, 1987), pp. 174–78.

29. Romero, "Ethnographic Evaluation of Behavioral Causes of Census Undercount of Undocumented Immigrants and Salvadorans in the Mission District of San Francisco," pp. 6–7.

30. Nestor P. Rodriguez and Jacqueline S. Hagan, "Investigating Census Coverage and Content among the Undocumented: An Ethnographic Study of Latino Immigrant Tenants in Houston," U.S. Bureau of the Census, Ethnographic Evaluation of the 1990 Decennial Census, Report 3 (December 1991), pp. 1, 11.

31. Judith Wingerd, "Urban Haitians: Documented/Undocumented in a Mixed Neighborhood," U.S. Bureau of the Census, Ethnographic Evaluation of the 1990 Decennial Census, Report 7 (March 1992), pp. 5–6.

32. Alex Stepick and Carol Dutton Stepick, "Alternative Enumeration of Haitians in Miami, Florida," U.S. Bureau of the Census, Ethnographic Evaluation of the 1990 Decennial Census, Report 8 (March 1992), pp. 4–5.

33. Joyce Aschenbrenner, "Census Undercount in a Black Neighborhood in St. Louis, MO.," U.S. Bureau of the Census, Ethnographic Evaluation of the 1988 Dress Rehearsal Census, Report 6 (December 1990), pp. 5–8.

34. Hamid, "Ethnographic Follow-Up of a Predominantly African American Population," p. 15.

35. Hamid, "Ethnographic Follow-Up of a Predominantly African American Population," p. 15.

36. Hamid, "Ethnographic Follow-Up of a Predominantly African American Population," p. 15.

37. Manuel de la Puente, "Why Are People Missed or Erroneously Included by the Census: A Summary of Findings from Ethnographic Coverage Reports," in U.S. Bureau of the Census, *1993 Research Conference on Undercounted Ethnic Populations* (GPO, October 1993), pp. 41–42.

38. Pamela A. Bunte and Rebecca M. Joseph, "The Cambodian Community of Long Beach: An Ethnographic Analysis of Factors Leading to Census Undercount," U.S. Bureau of the Census, Ethnographic Evaluation of the 1990 Decennial Census, Report 9 (March 1992), p. 1.

39. De la Puente, "Why Are People Missed or Erroneously Included by the Census," p. 42.

40. Stepick and Stepick, "Alternative Enumeration of Haitians in Miami, Florida," p. 3.

41. Boanerges Dominguez and Sarah Mahler, "Alternative Enumeration of Undocumented Mexicans in the South Bronx," U.S. Bureau of the Census, Ethnographic Evaluation of the 1990 Decennial Census, Report 28 (January 1993), p. 8.

42. Dominguez and Mahler, "Alternative Enumeration of Undocumented Mexicans in the South Bronx," p. 8.

43. Mahler, "Alternative Enumeration of Undocumented Salvadorans on Long Island," p. 8.

44. Rodriguez and Hagan, "Investigating Census Coverage and Content among the Undocumented," pp. 12–13.

45. See Mercer L. Sullivan, "An Ethnograpic Study of the Number of Persons in Households in Selected New York City Neighborhoods," U.S. Bureau of the Census, Ethnographic Exploratory Research, Report 13 (September 1990).

46. Romero, "Ethnographic Evaluation of Behavioral Causes of Census Undercount of Undocumented Immigrants and Salvadorans in the Mission District of San Francisco," p. 10.

47. Rodriguez and Hagan, "Investigating Census Coverage and Content among the Undocumented," p. 8; Mahler, "Alternative Enumeration of Undocumented Salvadorans on Long Island," p. 12.

48. Rodriguez and Hagan, "Investigating Census Coverage and Content among the Undocumented," p. 8.

49. De la Puente, "Why Are People Missed or Erroneously Included by the Census," p. 49.

50. Rodriguez and Hagan, "Investigating Census Coverage and Content among the Undocumented," p. 11; De la Puente, "Why Are People Missed or Erroneously Included by the Census," p. 33.

51. Bunte and Joseph, "The Cambodian Community of Long Beach," p. 18.

52. De la Puente, "Why Are People Missed or Erroneously Included by the Census," p. 34.

53. Betty Lee Sung, "Behavioral Causes of Census Undercount in New York City's Chinatown," U.S. Bureau of the Census, Ethnographic Evaluation of the 1990 Census, Report 6 (August 1991), pp. 19–20.

54. Tom Shaw and Patricia Guthrie, "An Alternative Enumeration of a Heterogeneous Population in a San Francisco Housing Project," U.S. Bureau of the Census, Ethnographic Evaluation of the 1990 Decennial Census, Report 13 (May 1992), p. 9.

55. Joyce Aschenbrenner, "A Community-Based Study of the 1990 Census Undercount in a Racially Mixed Area," U.S. Bureau of the Census, Ethnographic Evaluation of the 1990 Decennial Census, Report 1 (November 1991), p. 13.

56. Sullivan, "An Ethnographic Study of the Number of Persons in Households in Selected New York City Neighborhoods," pp. 14–21; De la Puente, "Why Are People Missed or Erroneously Included by the Census," pp. 38–39.

57. At least according to Sullivan, "An Ethnographic Study of the Number of Persons in Households in Selected New York City Neighborhoods," p. 21.

58. Tai Kang, "Ethnography of Alternative Enumeration among Korean Immigrants in Queens, New York," U.S. Bureau of the Census, Ethnographic Evaluation of the 1990 Decennial Census, Report 15 (May 1992), pp. 19–20.

59. Dominguez and Mahler, "Alternative Enumeration of Undocumented Mexicans in the South Bronx," p. 7.

60. Dominguez and Mahler, "Alternative Enumeration of Undocumented Mexicans in the South Bronx," p. 1.

61. Census takers were shot at as they approached one building in Brooklyn during the 1990 count. See City of New York v. U.S. Department of Commerce, 739 F. Supp. 761, at 763 (1990).

62. Dominguez and Mahler, "Alternative Enumeration of Undocumented Mexicans in the South Bronx," p. 11.

63. Romero, "Ethnographic Evaluation of Behavioral Causes of Census Undercount of Undocumented Immigrants and Salvadorans in the Mission District of San Francisco," p. 3.

64. Stepick and Stepick, "Alternative Enumeration of Haitians in Miami," p. 13. Despite this specific example of duplicative counting, there was an overall undercount of Haitians in this study area. See pp. 15–16.

65. Romero, "Ethnographic Evaluation of Behavioral Causes of Census Undercount of Undocumented Immigrants and Salvadorans in the Mission District of San Francisco," p. 11.

66. Karen Bracken and Guillermo de Bango, "Hispanics in a Racially and Ethnically Mixed Neighborhood in the Greater Metropolitan New Orleans Area," U.S. Bureau of the Census, Ethnographic Evaluation of the 1990 Decennial Census, Report 16 (June 1992), pp. 5–7.

67. Michael J. Piore, *Birds of Passage: Migrant Labor and Industrial Societies* (Cambridge University Press, 1979), pp. 52–59.

68. Sullivan, "An Ethnographic Study of the Number of Persons in Households in Selected New York City Neighborhoods," pp. 23, 25.

69. Aschenbrenner, "A Community-Based Study of the 1990 Census Undercount in a Racially Mixed Area," p. 3.

70. Dominguez and Mahler, "Alternative Enumeration of Undocumented Mexicans in the South Bronx," pp. 4–5, 8; De la Puente, "Why Are People Missed or Erroneously Included by the Census," p. 32.

71. Kang, "Ethnography of Alternative Enumeration among Korean Immigrants in Queens," p. 19.

72. In census undercount ethnography by Kang, "Ethnography of Alternative Enumeration among Korean Immigrants in Queens," p. 18. See also Mahler, "Alternative Enumeration of Undocumented Salvadorans on Long Island," p. 7.

73. Mahler, "Alternative Enumeration of Undocumented Salvadorans on Long Island," p. 10.

74. Dominguez and Mahler, "Alternative Enumeration of Undocumented Mexicans in the South Bronx," pp. 8–9; Hamid, "Ethnographic Follow-up of a Predominantly African American Population," p. 7.

75. Sullivan, "An Ethnographic Study of the Number of Persons in Households in Selected New York City Neighborhoods," p. 26, also 21.

76. Shaw and Guthrie, "An Alternative Enumeration of a Heterogeneous Population in a San Francisco Housing Project," p. 6; Rodriguez and Hagan, "Investigating Census Coverage and Content among the Undocumented," pp. 7–8.

77. Kang, "Ethnography of Alternative Enumeration among Korean Immigrants in Queens," pp. 18–19.

78. Bunte and Joseph, "The Cambodian Community of Long Beach," p. 13.

79. Anthropologist Mahler reports that a Peruvian leaseholder whom she knew well simply lied to her about the five boarders who were sharing his dwelling with his family. Mahler, "Alternative Enumeration of Undocumented Salvadorans on Long Island," p. 11.

80. Romero, "Ethnographic Evaluation of Behavioral Causes of Census Undercount of Undocumented Immigrants and Salvadorans in the Mission District of San Francisco," p. 9 ; Mahler, "Alternative Enumeration of Undocumented Salvadorans on Long Island," p. 5.

81. Mahler, "Alternative Enumeration of Undocumented Salvadorans on Long Island," p. 7.

82. Dominguez and Mahler, "Alternative Enumeration of Undocumented Mexicans in the South Bronx," pp. 9–10.

83. For a revealing analysis of the degrees of free movement and choice available to illegal aliens, see Leo R. Chavez, *Shadowed Lives: Undocumented Immigrants in American Society* (Harcourt Brace College, 1992). For insight into the more restrictive environment for illegals in rural areas, see Montoya, "Ethnographic Evaluation of the Behavioral Causes of Undercount."

84. Shaw and Guthrie, "An Alternative Enumeration of a Heterogeneous Population in a San Francisco Housing Project," p. 7.

85. Shaw and Guthrie, "An Alternative Enumeration of a Heterogeneous Population in a San Francisco Housing Project," p. 8. This problem of the weakness of these ties is reminiscent of the point made by Jane Jacobs, in *The Death and Life of Great American Cities* (New York: Random House, 1961), pp. 59–63. See also Mark S. Granovetter, "The Strength of Weak Ties," *American Journal of Sociology*, vol. 78, no. 6 (1973), pp. 1360–80.

86. See Shaw and Guthrie, "An Alternative Enumeration of a Heterogeneous Population in a San Francisco Housing Project," p. 8: "When Shaw and Guthrie held conversations with

some individuals, we were never really sure if the person's responses were based on reality. We were expecting reason and logic from persons who may have been strung out on drugs or alcohol, who were living in fear of their neighbors, or any combination of these factors. During the course of the research Shaw was threatened with physical harm in a stairwell and Guthrie was locked in a room and verbally abused by a White male resident of the Projects who took his complaints about her all over the city, and then to the Census Bureau itself."

87. U.S. Bureau of the Census, *Report to Congress—The Plan for Census 2000* (July 1997), p. 5. See also De la Puente, "Why Are People Missed or Erroneously Included in the Census," p. 30.

88. See Shaw and Guthrie, "An Alternative Enumeration of a Heterogeneous Population in a San Francisco Housing Project," pp. 12–13.

89. Shaw and Guthrie, "An Alternative Enumeration of a Heterogeneous Population in a San Francisco Housing Project," pp. 6–8; and Dominguez and Mahler, "Alternative Enumeration of Undocumented Mexicans in the South Bronx," pp. 3–4, 8.

90. I base this on the singularly intense opposition of black leaders to greater reliance by the Census Bureau on administrative records, which they argue would have a negative impact on their group's participation in social welfare programs.

91. Barabba points to the unique challenge of counting illegals, though this conflicts with ethnographic evidence that illegal status per se is the problem. See "Vincent P. Barabba: Oral History" (Washington, D.C.: Bureau of the Census, History Staff, August 1997), p. 46.

92. Edward W. Fernandez, "Measurement of Hispanic Undercount by Demographic Analysis: Problems and Possible Solutions," paper prepared for presentation at the annual meeting of the Population Association of America, Washington, D.C., March 21–23, 1991, pp. 16–17.

93. See Shaw and Guthrie, "An Alternative Enumeration of a Heterogeneous Population in a San Franciso Housing Project," p. 13. Yet research indicates that privacy concerns are not generally an important factor in census nonresponse. See, for example, Robert E. Fay and others, "Low Mail Response Rate in the 1990 Census: A Preliminary Interpretation," paper presented at the 1991 Annual Research Conference of the U.S. Census Bureau, Arlington, Va., March 17–20, 1991; and Eleanor Singer and others, "The Impact of Privacy and Confidentiality Concerns on Survey Participation: The Case of the 1990 U.S. Census," *Public Opinion Quarterly*, vol. 57, no. 4 (1993), pp. 465–82.

94. See "For Political Justice, Adjust the Census," *New York Times,* June 15, 1991, p. A22; "Not the Best Census Ever," *New York Times,* April 25, 1991, p. A24.

95. For an exposition and critique of this methodology, see Lawrence D. Brown and others, "Statistical Controversies in Census 2000," University of California at Berkeley, Department of Statistics Technical Report 537 (April 30, 1999), pp. 15–16.

96. *Department of Commerce v. U.S. House of Representatives,* 525 U.S. 316 (1999).

97. See P. B. Stark, "Differences between the 1990 and 2000 Census Adjustment Plans, and Their Impact on Error," University of California at Berkeley, Department of Statistics Technical Report 550 (March 16, 1999), pp. 14–21.

98. Morris L. Eaton and others, "Planning for the Census in the Year 2000: An Update," University of California at Berkeley, Department of Statistics Technical Report 484 (June 19, 1997), pp. 2–3.

99. Stark, "Differences between the 1990 and 2000 Adjustment Plans," p. 6.

100. Eaton and others, "Planning for the Census in the Year 2000," p. 3.

101. Eaton and others, "Planning for the Census in the Year 2000," pp. 2–3.

102. For good specific examples on matching problems and the basic logic of matching, see Stark, "Differences between the 1990 and 2000 Census Adjustment Plans," pp. 12 and 6–7, respectively. See also David A. Freedman and others, "Adjusting the Census of 1990: The Smoothing Model," *Evaluation Review,* vol. 17 (August 1993), pp. 375–77.

103. Stark, "Differences between the 1990 and 2000 Census Adjustment Plans," p. 3.

104. Quoted in Rochelle Stanfield, "Sorting Our Nation's 2000 Headcount," *National Journal*, September 14, 1996, pp. 1956, 1958.

105. Freedman and Wachter, "Planning for the Census in the Year 2000," p. 362.

106. Committee on Adjustment of Postcensal Estimates, *Assessment of the Accuracy of Adjusted versus Unadjusted 1990 Census Base for Use in Intercensal Estimates* (Census Bureau, August 7, 1992), p. 8. (Hereafter cited as the Report of the Committee on Adjustment of Postcensal Estimates.)

107. Eaton and others, "Planning for the Census in the Year 2000," p. 3.

108. David A. Freedman, "Adjusting the Census of 1990," *Jurimetrics Journal*, vol. 34 (Fall 1993), pp. 102–03.

109. Freedman and others, "Adjusting the Census of 1990: The Smoothing Model," p. 379.

110. John E. Rolph, "The Census Adjustment Trial: Reflections of a Witness for the Plaintiffs," *Jurimetrics Journal*, vol. 34 (Fall 1993), p. 93.

111. Freedman and others, "Adjusting the Census of 1990: The Smoothing Model," pp. 379–80.

112. Report of the Committee on Adjustment of Postcensal Estimates, pp. 8, 17.

113. Freedman and others, "Adjusting the Census of 1990: The Smoothing Model," p. 380.

114. Freedman, "Adjusting the Census of 1990," pp. 103–06. For a contrary point of view, see Rolph, "The Census Adjustment Trial," pp. 86–96.

115. Department of Commerce (DOC), "Final Guidelines for Considering Whether or Not a Statistical Adjustment of the 1990 Decennial Census of Population and Housing Should Be Made for Coverage Deficiencies Resulting in an Overcount or Undercount of the Population; Notice," *Federal Register*, vol. 55 (March 15, 1990), p. 9841.

116. Rolph, "The Census Adjustment Trial," pp. 88–90.

117. Rolph, "The Census Adjustment Trial," pp. 95–96; Report of the Committee on Adjustment of Postcensal Estimates, pp. 17–18.

118. Brown and others, "Statistical Controversies in Census 2000," p. 6.

119. Brown and others, "Statistical Controversies in Census 2000," p. 7; Freedman and Wachter, "Planning for the Census in the Year 2000," p. 363.

120. Brown and others, "Statistical Controversies in Census 2000," pp. 2, 17; Nathan Keyfitz, "The Case for Census Tradition," *Society*, vol. 34 (March/April 1997), p. 46.

121. Freedman, "Adjusting the Census of 1990," p. 100–02.

122. See Brown and others, "Statistical Controversies in Census 2000," p. 10; Eaton and others, "Planning for the Census in the Year 2000," p. 9.

123. See Kenneth Darga, *Sampling and the Census: A Case against the Proposed Adjustments for Undercount* (Washington, D.C.: AEI Press, 1999), p. 56. See also Barbara Everrit Bryant, "Census-Taking for a Litigious, Data-Driven Society," *Chance*, vol. 6 (Summer 1993), p. 47.

124. Darga, *Sampling and the Census*, p. 52.

125. Report of the Committee on Adjustment of Postcensal Estimates, p. 15.

126. Freedman, "Adjusting the Census of 1990," p. 102. See also Brown and others, "Statistical Controversies in Census 2000," p. 2.

127. Stark, "Differences between the 1990 and 2000 Census Adjustment Plans," p. 5.

128. I am following closely here the exposition of this method in Stark, "Differences between the 1990 and 2000 Census Adjustment Plans," pp. 5–8.

129. As one statistician put it: "In terms of their undercount rates, young Hispanic men in Tombstone, Arizona, may not be the same as young Hispanic men in Napoopoo, Hawaii. They may not be the same in Tempe as in Boise. But the adjustment is calculated assuming

their undercount rates are the same." See Kenneth M. Wachter, "The Census Adjustment Trial: An Exchange," *Jurimetrics Journal,* vol. 34 (Fall 1993), p. 110.

130. Wachter, "The Census Adjustment Trial," pp. 113–14.

131. Report of the Committee on Adjustment of Postcensal Estimates, p. 25.

132. DOC, "Decision of the Director of the Bureau of the Census on Whether to Use Information from the 1990 Post-Enumeration Survey (PES) to Adjust the Base for the Intercensal Population Estimates Produced by the Bureau of the Census; Notice," *Federal Register,* vol. 58 (January 4, 1993), p. 76.

133. Wachter, "The Census Adjustment Trial," p. 109.

134. Report of the Committee on Adjustment of Postcensal Estimates, pp. 21–23.

135. Kenneth Wachter suggests there may have been millions. See Wachter, "The Census Adjustment Trial," p. 109. See also Brown and others, "Statistical Controversies in Census 2000," pp. 10–13.

136. Wachter, "The Census Adjustment Trial," pp. 112–13; Freedman and Wachter, "Planning for the Census in the Year 2000," p. 367.

137. Keyfitz, "The Case for Census Tradition," p. 46.

138. Bryant, "Census-Taking for a Litigious, Data-Driven Society," pp. 46–47.

139. See for example the remarks by Paul Voss, in *Using the Census: What It Tells Us about America's People, Workforce, and Small Communities* (Washington, D.C.: Consortium of Social Science Associations, May 2, 1997), p. 39. See also Bureau of the Census, *Report to Congress— The Plan for Census 2000,* p. 7; Riche quotation in Margo J. Anderson and Stephen E. Fienberg, "Who Counts? The Politics of Censustaking," *Society,* vol. 34 (March/April 1997), p. 23.

140. Thomas L. Brunell, "Using Statistical Sampling to Estimate the U.S. Population: The Methodological and Political Debate over Census 2000," Unpublished paper, Department of Political Science, SUNY-Binghamton, N.Y., May 17, 1999, p. 22.

141. Felicity Barringer, "Decision Today on Adjusting the Census," *New York Times,* July 15, 1991, p. A12.

142. Stephen E. Fienberg, "New York City Adjustment Trial: Witness for the Plaintiffs," *Jurimetrics Journal,* vol. 34 (Fall 1993), p. 72.

143. Brown and others, "Statistical Controversies in Census 2000," p. 13; see also Stark, "Differences between the 1990 and 2000 Census Adjustment Plans," p. 2.

144. Letter from Kirk M. Wolter, member of the Secretary's Special Advisory Committee, to Robert A. Mosbacher, secretary of commerce, June 21, 1991, p. 3.

145. See Thomas R. Belin and John E. Rolph, "Can We Reach Consensus on Census Adjustment?" *Statistical Science,* vol. 9, no. 4 (1994), p. 495.

146. Brown and others, "Statistical Controversies in Census 2000," p. 16. As statistician Morris Eaton concludes: "Sampling [sic] seems inherently more complex than a census." See Eaton and others, "Planning for the Census in the Year 2000," p. 4.

147. Belin and Rolph, "Can We Reach Consensus on Census Adjustment?" p. 486.

148. See the debate between the "Benthamites" and the "abolitionists" described in Paul Meier and others, "What Happened in Hazelwood: Statistics, Employment Discrimination, and the 80% Rule," in Morris H. DeGroot and others, eds., *Statistics and the Law* (John Wiley, 1986), pp. 24–26.

149. Steven A. Holmes, "Census Fight Is Put on Hold until a Count Is Completed," *New York Times,* October 31, 1999, sec. 1, p. 34.

150. *City of New York* v. *U.S. Department of Commerce,* 822 F. Supp. 906, at 929 (1993).

151. U.S. Bureau of the Census, *The 2000 Decennial Census Plan,* March 12, 1996, p. 3.

152. These NAS panels are the Panel on Census Requirements in the Year 2000 and Beyond, chaired by Charles Schultze; the Panel to Evaluate Alternative Census Methods, chaired by

Norman Bradburn; and the Panel to Evaluate Alternative Census Methodologies, chaired by Keith Rust.

153. U.S. Bureau of the Census, *Report to Congress—The Plan for Census 2000*, p. 7.

154. Marc K. Landy and Martin A. Levin, "The New Politics of Public Policy," in Marc K. Landy and Martin A. Levin, eds., *The New Politics of Public Policy* (Johns Hopkins University Press, 1995), p. 292.

155. Stark, "Differences between the 1990 and 2000 Census Adjustment Plans," p. 3.

156. To be sure, not all the error I have been addressing here is additive. Indeed, there is evidence that the correlation bias discussed above, at least at the national level, offsets some processing error. See Freedman and Wachter, "Planning for the 2000 Census," p. 367.

157. Fienberg, "The New York City Census Adjustment Trial," p. 80; see also Edmonston and Schultze, *Modernizing the U.S. Census*, pp. 248–49.

158. Darga, *Sampling and the Census*, pp. 35–41, 44–45.

159. "Barbara Everitt Bryant: Oral History" (Washington, D.C.: Bureau of the Census, History Staff, n.d.), pp. 28–29.

160. Undercount Steering Committee, *Technical Assessment of the Accuracy of the Unadjusted Versus Adjusted Census Counts* (Census Bureau, June 21, 1991), p. 6. (Hereafter cited as Report of the Undercount Steering Committee.)

161. Barbara Everitt Bryant, "Recommendation to Secretary of Commerce Robert A. Mosbacher on Whether or Not to Adjust the 1990 Census," June 18, 1991, p. 3.

162. Belin and Rolph, "Can We Reach Consensus on Census Adjustment?" p. 493.

163. Report of the Undercount Steering Committee, p. 6; see also Bryant, "Recommendation to Secretary of Commerce Robert A. Mosbacher," pp. 13–14. This is echoed in the testimony of statistician John Tukey in *Oversight Hearing to Review the Process of Coverage Evaluation Procedures*, Hearing before the Subcommittee on Census and Population of the House Committee on Post Office and Civil Service, 102 Cong. 1 sess. (GPO, 1991), pp. 55–56.

164. Fienberg, "The New York City Census Adjustment Trial," p. 76.

165. Rolph, "The Census Adjustment Trial," p. 97.

166. See *Oversight Hearing to Review the Process of Coverage Evaluation Procedures*, Hearing, p. 48.

167. A similar point is made in Keyfitz, "The Case for Census Tradition," p. 46.

168. Belin and Rolph, "Can We Reach Consensus on Census Adjustment?" p. 491.

169. Wachter, "The Census Adjustment Trial," p. 110.

170. Freedman, "Adjusting the Census of 1990," p. 100; Brown and others, "Statistical Controversies in Census 2000," p. 2.

171. DOC, "Adjustment of the 1990 Census for Overcounts and Undercounts of Population and Housing; Notice of Final Decision," *Federal Register*, vol. 56 (July 22, 1991), pp. 33592–93.

172. Belin and Rolph, "Can We Reach a Consensus on Census Adjustment?" pp. 491–92.

173. Morris Janowitz, *The Last Half-Century: Societal Change and Politics in America* (University of Chicago Press, 1978), pp. 300–05.

Chapter Five

1. Both examples are discussed in Michael P. Murray, "Census Adjustment and the Distribution of Federal Spending," *Demography*, vol. 29 (August 1992), pp. 330–31.

2. T. R. Reid, "Billion-Dollar Nosecount of '80 Fated to Be Wrong," *Washington Post*, June 10, 1979, p. A2. See also James K. Glassman, "A Virtual America?" *Washington Post*, May 13, 1997, p. A17.

3. When I address the risks of adjustment, I use "adjustment" in a generic sense, referring to all efforts to improve census data relying on sophisticated statistical sampling methodologies. This usage is consistent with the terms on which virtually all participants have conducted the ongoing public policy debate, and for this reason it is useful. But as I have already touched on in chapter 4 and will discuss later in this chapter, this usage is also misleading. In fact, adjustment is the goal of postcensus surveys such as the PES, ICM, and now ACE, while programs such as sampling for nonresponse follow-up (SNRFU) are designed not to adjust census numbers but to improve census coverage. Moreover, SNRFU poses different risks from a postcensus survey. Nevertheless, the two programs have been collapsed together by the Census Bureau, among others, as "sampling," and so too has discussion of "adjustment."

4. "Taking Leave of the Census," *New York Times*, January 17, 1998, p. A12.

5. On science, see John Patrick Diggins, *The Lost Soul of American Politics: Virtue, Self-Interest, and the Foundations of Liberalism* (New York: Basic Books, 1984), pp. 153–56.

6. General Accounting Office (GAO), *Formula Grants: Effects of Adjusted Population Counts on Federal Funding to States,* GAO/HEHS-99-69 (February 1999), pp. 4–5.

7. Journalists are particularly prone to cite these gross and misleading figures. One of the few exceptions is David Shribman, "Local Politicians Fear Harm Census Data Can Do to Funding, but Their Worry May Be Overdone," *Wall Street Journal,* January 2, 1991, p. A8.

8. See Barry Edmonston and Charles Schultze, eds., *Modernizing the U.S. Census* (Washington, D.C.: National Academy Press, 1995), pp. 40–41. The actual study cited by Edmonston and Schultze is Murray, "Census Adjustment and the Distribution of Federal Spending," pp. 319–32. Because Murray used undercount estimates that were subsequently reduced, the adjustment effects reported here might well be even lower.

9. Murray, "Census Adjustment and the Distribution of Federal Spending," p. 319.

10. GAO, *Formula Grants: Adjusted Census Data Would Redistribute Small Percentage of Funds to States,* GAO/GGD-92-12 (November 1991), p. 2.

11. For a review of these earlier studies, see Murray, "Census Adjustment and the Distribution of Federal Spending," pp. 319–20; and especially Constance F. Citro and Michael L. Cohen, eds., *The Bicentennial Census: New Directions for Methodology in 1990* (Washington, D.C.: National Academy Press, 1985), pp. 59–70, 76–77. The one study that departs from this research consensus is Barbara Steinberg and Howard Hogan, "Effects of Population Adjustment on the Allocations of Three Government Programs," in *Proceedings of the Social Statistics Section* (Washington, D.C.: American Statistical Association, 1985), pp. 256–60.

12. Quoted in Rochelle L. Stanfield, "Feel Shortchanged in Federal Aid? Don't Blame the Census Undercount," *National Journal,* March 29, 1980, p. 518.

13. GAO, *Formula Grants: Effects of Adjusted Population Counts,* p. 9.

14. See Murray, "Census Adjustment and the Distribution of Federal Spending," pp. 327–28.

15. GAO, *Formula Grants: Effects of Adjusted Population Counts,* p. 9.

16. GAO, *Formula Grants: Effects of Adjusted Population Counts,* pp. 4–6.

17. GAO, *Formula Grants: Effects of Adjusted Population Counts,* p. 26.

18. This figure excludes "nongovernmental cost funds," such as retirement funds. See the California Department of Finance website: www.dof.ca.gov/html/bud_docs/charts/chart-b.pdf.

19. GAO, *Formula Grants: Effects of Adjusted Population Counts,* p. 8.

20. GAO, *Formula Grants: Effects of Adjusted Population Counts,* p. 80.

21. Murray, "Census Adjustment and the Distribution of Federal Spending," p. 330. Again, it should be noted that this finding relies on undercount estimates that were subsequently reduced, which might further minimize the effects of any adjustment. See also Edmonston and Schultze, *Modernizing the U.S. Census,* pp. 40–43.

22. Murray, "Census Adjustment and the Distribution of Federal Spending," p. 328.

23. Peter Passell, "Economic Scene: Federal Gold, Census Rainbow," *New York Times*, August 7, 1991, p. D2.

24. Arthur J. Maurice and Richard P. Nathan, "The Census Undercount: Effects on Federal Aid to Cities," *Urban Affairs Quarterly*, vol. 17 (March 1982), p. 266.

25. Maurice and Nathan, "The Census Undercount," p. 251.

26. For a very brief discussion of this point, see Edmonston and Schultz, *Modernizing the U.S. Census*, p. 43.

27. Barbara Everitt Bryant and William Dunn, *Moving Power and Money: The Politics of Census Taking* (Ithaca, N.Y.: New Strategist Publications, 1995), pp. 160–61; "Barbara Everitt Bryant: Oral History" (Washington, D.C.: Bureau of the Census, History Staff, n.d.), p. 27.

28. On Gingrich, see "House Power Fuels Struggle over Census," *Atlanta Constitution*, June 5, 1997, p. A10. On Pete Wilson, see Herbert A. Sample, "Court Backs 1990 Census Results," *Orange County Register,* March 21, 1996, p. A1; John Jacobs, "GOP Counting on Census Undercount," *Fresno Bee*, October 5, 1997, p. B7.

29. For a slightly different take on this, see Harvey M. Choldin, *Looking for the Last Percent: The Controversy over Census Undercounts* (Rutgers University Press, 1994), p. 222.

30. The volatility and unpredictability of public policy statistics more generally are emphasized in Raymond Vernon, "The Politics of Comparative Economic Statistics: Three Cultures and Three Cases," in William Alonso and Paul Starr, eds., *The Politics of Numbers* (New York: Russell Sage Foundation, 1987), pp. 71–72.

31. Both items are recounted in "Barbara Everitt Bryant: Oral History," p. 28.

32. *Department of Commerce* v. *U.S. House of Representatives*, 525 U.S. 316 (1999).

33. For an exposition and analysis of this formula and of apportionment more generally, see Michel L. Balinski and H. Peyton Young, *Fair Representation: Meeting the Ideal of One Man, One Vote* (Yale University Press, 1982).

34. Of the twenty-one states that gained or lost at least one seat in 1990, the Census Bureau's 1988 projections were correct in twelve of the twenty-one states. For the 1988 projections, see Richard Cohen, "House Heading for a Big Reshuffling," *National Journal*, January 7, 1989, p. 25. For the results of the 1990 reapportionment, see "A Democratic Problem, Where's the Base?" *CQ Weekly*, March 23, 1991, p. 765.

35. David C. Huckabee, *House Apportionment Following the 2000 Census: Preliminary Projections* 97-94 GOV (Washington, D.C.: Congressional Research Service, January 10, 1997).

36. One projection was issued by Election Data Services on December 29, 1999 (see its website: www.electiondataservices.com). A second was done by Polidata, also released on December 29, 1999 (see www.polidata.org).

37. See David C. Huckabee, *House Apportionment Following the 2000 Census* 98-135 GOV (Washington, D.C.: Congressional Research Service, January 3, 2000), pp. 2–3.

38. Allen L. Schirm, "The Effects of Census Undercount Adjustment on Congressional Apportionment," *Journal of the American Statistical Association*, vol. 86 (June 1991), pp. 534–35.

39. Schirm, "The Effects of Census Undercount Adjustment on Congressional Apportionment," pp. 532–33. For a more conservative estimate, see Citro and Cohen, *The Bicentennial Census*, pp. 54–56.

40. Jeffrey S. Passel, "What Census Adjustment Would Mean," *Population Today*, vol. 19 (June 1991), p. 7.

41. Cited by Bryant and Dunn, *Moving Power and Money*, pp. 160–61.

42. David C. Huckabee, *Census Adjustment: Impact on Reapportionment and Redistricting* 94-649 GOV (Washington, D.C.: Congressional Research Service, October 12, 1995).

43. Passel, "What Census Adjustment Would Mean," p. 7.

44. Recommendations on 1990 Census Adjustment to the Honorable Robert A. Mosbacher from Kenneth W. Wachter, Special Advisory Panel (June 18, 1991), pp. 25-26.

45. Bryant and Dunn, *Moving Power and Money*, pp. 160–61. A similar point is made in Tim Noah, "Mosbacher, While Admitting Undercount of Minorities, Won't Adjust 1990 Census," *Wall Street Journal*, July 16, 1991, p. A9.

46. This projection was released by Polidata on May 29, 1997, and can be found at the Polidata website (www.polidata.org).

47. See Huckabee, *House Apportionment Following the 2000 Census.*

48. Passel, "What Census Adjustment Would Mean," p. 7.

49. One of the few studies available on the effects of adjustment at the state level suggests minimal changes. See Rachel J. Snow, "1990 Census Counts, Districting, and Representation: A Case Study of North Carolina," thesis presented to the Department of Political Science at Bates College; December 8, 1992.

50. David Butler and Bruce Cain, *Congressional Redistricting: Comparative and Theoretical Perspectives* (Macmillan, 1992), p. 15.

51. Butler and Cain, *Congressional Redistricting*, p. 8.

52. Butler and Cain, *Congressional Redistricting*, p. 9.

53. Butler and Cain, *Congressional Redistricting*, p. 109.

54. Butler and Cain, *Congressional Redistricting*, p. 9.

55. Butler and Cain, *Congressional Redistricting*, p. 107.

56. Butler and Cain, *Congressional Redistricting*, pp. 9–10.

57. Paul R. Abramson, John H. Aldrich, and David W. Rhode, *Change and Continuity in the 1992 Elections*, Revised Edition (Washington, D.C.: CQ Press, 1995), p. 332.

58. Butler and Cain, *Congressional Redistricting*, p. 15.

59. Bruce E. Cain, *The Reapportionment Puzzle* (University of California Press, 1984), pp. 168–71.

60. See Charles S. Bullock, "Winners and Losers in the Latest Round of Redistricting," *Emory Law Journal*, vol. 44 (Summer 1995), pp. 943–77; Kevin Hill, "Does the Creation of Majority Black Districts Aid Republicans?" *Journal of Politics*, vol. 57 (May 1995), pp. 384–401; for a slightly different perspective, see John R. Petrocik and Scott W. Desposato, "The Partisan Consequences of Majority-Minority Redistricting in the South, 1992 and 1994," *Journal of Politics*, vol. 60 (August 1998), pp. 613–33.

61. For the 1991 data, see Butler and Cain, *Congressional Redistricting*, pp. 96–99. For the 2000 data, see the National Conference of State Legislatures website, www.ncsl.org.

62. Careful readers will note that I do not include Utah in this analysis, even though table 5- 4 suggests it should be. The fact is that Utah just barely meets the criterion of a high undercount state. In any case, its domination by Republicans reinforces my argument.

63. These are of course *net* undercount figures. See GAO, *Formula Grants: Effects of Adjusted Population Counts*, p. 24.

64. Passel, "What Census Adjustment Would Mean," p. 7.

65. Recall that the only projection we have of apportionment outcomes with adjusted census data was done in 1997 and relied on 1996 Census Bureau projections of 2000 population counts. At that time these census figures projected much lower population growth for California than is now anticipated. See the Polidata study, released May 29, 1997, at www.polidata.org.

66. Passel, "What Census Adjustment Would Mean," p. 7.

67. Calculations based on data assembled in Mark Gersh and Ken Strasman, *1990 Census Undercount by Congressional District* (Washington, D.C.: National Committee for an Effective Congress, September 28, 1998).

68. The point about African American organizations is confirmed by the results of a recent survey. See Eleanor Singer and others, "The Impact of Privacy and Confidentiality Concerns

on Survey Participation: The Case of the 1990 U.S. Census," *Public Opinion Quarterly*, vol. 57, no. 4 (1993), pp. 478–79.

69. Kenneth W. Wachter, "The Census Adjustment Trial: An Exchange," *Jurimetrics Journal*, vol. 34 (Fall 1993), p. 112.

70. This term is from the title of the NAS's widely cited report on census reform, advocating statistical adjustment, sampling for nonresponse follow-up, and the one-number census. See Edmonston and Schultze, *Modernizing the U.S. Census*.

71. Hyman Alterman, *Counting People: The Census in History* (New York: Harcourt, Brace and World, 1969), p. 283.

72. Cited in Peter Skerry, "The Census Wars," *Public Interest*, no. 106 (Winter 1992), p. 28.

73. Ira S. Lowry, "Counting Ethnic Minorities in the 1990 Census," unpublished paper, Pacific Palisades, Calif. (September 1989), p. 22.

74. Lowry, "Counting Ethnic Minorities in the 1990 Census," pp. 22–23. Others, including professionals at the Census Bureau, have also expressed such concerns.

75. *Joint Meeting of the Census Advisory Committee on the African American, American Indian and Alaska Native, Asian, and Pacific Islander, and Hispanic Populations* (Washington, D.C., December 11–13, 1995), p. 53.

76. See H.R. 3558. See also Andrew A. White and Keith F. Rust, *Preparing for the 2000 Census: Interim Report II* (Washington, D.C.: National Academy Press, 1997), pp. 30–33. For an informative news account of this episode, see Steven A. Holmes, "Census Plan for 2000 Is Challenged on Two Fronts," *New York Times*, June 6, 1996, p. A21.

77. Memorandum, Democratic Staff to Democratic members of the Committee on Government Reform and Oversight, "Hearing on Plans for the 2000 Census," June 6, 1996, p. 6. (Hereafter cited as the Democratic Staff Memorandum.)

78. See, for example, the discussion of sampling in Edmonston and Schultze, *Modernizing the U.S. Census*, p. 241.

79. See, for example, Andrew A. White and Keith F. Rust, eds., *Sampling in the 2000 Census: Interim Report I* (Washington, D.C.: National Academy Press, 1996), pp. 2–3. Several of the NAS panel reports provided very little analytic detail about sampling. On this point, see Lawrence D. Brown and others, "Statistical Controversies in Census 2000," University of California at Berkeley, Department of Statistics Technical Report 537 (April 30, 1999), p. 17.

80. U.S. Bureau of the Census, *The 2000 Decennial Census Plan* (March 12, 1996), p. 3.

81. Edmonston and Schultze, *Modernizing the U.S. Census*, pp. 47–49.

82. As the minority staff report of the Committee on Government Reform put it: "The major argument for sampling to estimate the last 10 percent of the population is to save money." See Democratic Staff Memorandum, p. 5.

83. Edmonston and Schultze, *Modernizing the U.S. Census*, pp. 48–50.

84. See Edmonston and Schultze, *Modernizing the U.S. Census*, p. 87.

85. White and Rust, *Sampling in the 2000 Census: Interim Report I*, p. 8. For a different perspective on the relationship between SNRFU and ICM, see David A. Freedman and Kenneth W. Wachter, "Planning for the Census in the Year 2000," *Evaluation Review*, vol. 20 (August 1996), p. 358.

86. Meeting, 2000 Census Advisory Committee, Embassy Row Hotel, Washington, D.C., May 16–17, 1996.

87. Edmonston and Schultze, *Modernizing the U.S. Census*, pp. 107–10.

88. U.S. Bureau of the Census, *The 2000 Decennial Census Plan*, p. 3.

89. Memorandum, William F. Clinger, chairman, to members of the Committee on Government Reform and Oversight, "Consideration of Committee Report: 'Sampling and Statistical Adjustment in the Decennial Census: Fundamental Flaws'," June 14, 1996, pp. 12–13. (Hereafter cited as Clinger Memorandum.)

90. Democratic Staff Memorandum, p. 5. See also Clinger Memorandum, pp. 12–13.

91. Quoted in Clinger Memorandum, p. 13.

92. Edmonston and Schultze, *Modernizing the U.S. Census*, p. 141.

93. Such negative sentiments were certainly in evidence among minority leaders at the 2000 Census Advisory Committee meeting in Washington, D.C., on May 16–17, 1996, shortly after the bureau officially announced its plans for the 2000 census.

94. See the formal dissent of Representative Carrie Meek in *Sampling and Statistical Adjustment: Fundamental Flaws*, Fourteenth Report of the House Committee on Government Reform and Oversight, 104 Cong. 2 sess. (GPO, 1996), pp. 35–37.

95. See A. B. Stoddard and Marcia Gelbart, "Black Caucus Creates Defense Fund in Effort to Help Threatened Districts," *The Hill*, June 19, 1996.

96. See John Stone, *Racial Conflict in Contemporary Society* (Harvard University Press, 1985), pp. 41–43.

97. See my discussion of the concept of "minority" in Peter Skerry, *Mexican Americans: The Ambivalent Minority* (Harvard University Press, 1995), pp. 11–15.

98. William A. V. Clark and Peter A. Morrison, "Demographic Foundations of Political Empowerment in Multiminority Cities," *Demography*, vol. 32 (May 1995), p. 183.

99. This point is made in Judy Scales-Trent, "Add 'Multiracial' to the Next Census," *Los Angeles Times*, July 3, 1996, p. A11.

100. See William Petersen, "Politics and the Measurement of Ethnicity," in William Alonso and Paul Starr, eds., *The Politics of Numbers* (New York: Russell Sage Foundation, 1987), pp. 217–18; Office of Management and Budget (OMB), "Recommendations from the Interagency Committee for the Review of the Racial and Ethnic Standards to the Office of Management and Budget Concerning Changes to the Standards for the Classification of Federal Data on Race and Ethnicity," *Federal Register*, vol. 62 (July 9, 1997), p. 36922. See also OMB, "Standards for the Classification of Federal Data on Race and Ethnicity," *Federal Register*, vol. 60 (August 28, 1995), p. 44679.

101. Nathan Glazer and Daniel Patrick Moynihan, *Beyond the Melting Pot: The Negroes, Puerto Ricans, Jews, Italians, and Irish of New York City*, 2d ed. (MIT Press, 1970), p. 137.

102. Rabbi Gary Greenebaum of the Los Angeles office of the American Jewish Committee, quoted in Alan Abrahamson, "Area's Jewish Population Held Steady by Migration," *Los Angeles Times*, July 4, 1998, pp. B1, B3.

103. Alan Abrahamson, "Debate Rises over Jewish Census," *Los Angeles Times*, July 25, 1998, pp. B4, B5.

104. Quoted in William Safire, "News about Jews," *New York Times*, July 17, 1995, p. A13.

105. See Lewis M. Killian, "The Collection of Official Data on Ethnicity and Religion: The U.S. Experience," *New Community*, vol. 11 (Autumn/Winter 1983), pp. 79–80.

106. Edward O. Laumann and others, *The Social Organization of Sexuality: Sexual Practices in the United States* (University of Chicago Press, 1994), table 8.2.

107. David W. Dunlap, "Gay Survey Raises a New Question," *New York Times*, October 18, 1994, p. B8.

108. Dunlap, "Gay Survey Raises a New Question," p. B8.

109. Thomas Stoddard, quoted in Boyce Rensberger, "How Many Men in U.S. Are Gay?" *Washington Post*, April 17, 1993, pp. A1, A13.

110. Petersen, "Politics and the Measurement of Ethnicity," p. 217.

111. Kenneth Prewitt, "Public Statistics and Democratic Politics," in William Alonso and Paul Starr, eds., *The Politics of Numbers* (New York: Russell Sage Foundation, 1987), p. 270.

112. Daniel P. Moynihan, "Foreword," in David M. Heer, ed., *Social Statistics and the City* (Cambridge, Mass.: Joint Center for Urban Studies, 1968), p. iii.

113. Judith Eleanor Innes, *Knowledge and Public Policy: The Search for Meaningful Indicators*, 2d ed. exp. (New Brunswick, N.J.: Transaction Books, 1994), pp. 126–28.

114. Dennis Havesi, "Census Count of Homeless Is Disputed," *New York Times*, April 13, 1991, p. B2; Barbara Vobejda, "Holding up the Homeless Tally," *Washington Post*, April 11, 1991, p. A19.

115. Nampeo R. McKenney and others, "The Quality of the Race and Spanish Origin Information Reported in the 1980 Census," paper presented at the Annual Meeting of the American Statistical Association, Las Vegas, Nev., 1985.

116. Nampeo R. McKenney and others, "Evaluating Racial and Ethnic Reporting in the 1990 Census," in American Statistical Association, *Proceedings of the Section on Survey Research Methods* (Alexandria, Va.: ASA, 1993), p. 73.

117. WNET Educational Broadcasting Company, Transcript of Charlie Rose Show (July 14, 1994), pp. 8–9.

118. Here I paraphrase Paul Starr but disagree with him on the bureau's institutional conservatism. See Paul Starr, "The Sociology of Official Statistics," in William Alonso and Paul Starr, eds., *The Politics of Numbers* (New York: Russell Sage Foundation, 1987), p. 50.

119. Choldin, *Looking for the Last Percent*, pp. 147–52.

120. Choldin, *Looking for the Last Percent*, pp. 134–35.

121. Choldin, *Looking for the Last Percent*, p. 146.

122. See, for example, the remarks by Representative Robert Garcia in *The Decennial Census Improvement Act*, Hearing before the Subcommittee on Post Office and Civil Service, 100 Cong. 2 sess. (GPO, 1988), p. 50. See also President's Commission on Federal Statistics, *Federal Statistics: Report of the President's Commission*, vol. 1 (GPO, 1971), p. 47.

123. Choldin, *Looking for the Last Percent*, p. 151.

124. Choldin, *Looking for the Last Percent*, p. 149.

125. See Barbara Bailar's testimony on the negative effect of litigation on the conduct of the 1980 census, in *The Decennial Census Improvement Act*, Hearing, p. 85.

126. Janet L. Norwood, *Organizing to Count: Change in the Federal Statistical System* (Washington, D.C.: Urban Institute Press, 1995), pp. 26–29, 80–83.

127. See Choldin, *Looking for the Last Percent*, pp. 151–52, 154–55, 165–66.

128. "Barbara Everitt Bryant: Oral History," p. 29.

129. Bureau of the Census, *The Plan for Census 2000*, rev. (February 28, 1996), p. III-02.

130. Thomas R. Belin and John E. Rolph, "Can We Reach Consensus on Census Adjustment?" *Statistical Science*, vol. 9, no. 4 (1994), pp. 502–03.

131. Belin and Rolph, "Can We Reach Consensus on Census Adjustment?" p. 502.

132. U.S. Bureau of the Census, *The 2000 Decennial Census Plan*, p. 3.

133. For example, a redistricting specialist with the National Conference of State Legislators argued that a "one-number census" would be an estimate that would necessarily have upper and lower bounds. In effect, there would be three different numbers. Whether true or not, this was how many legislators reacted to the concept of a one-number census. See the remarks by Tim Storey, National Conference of State Legislatures, at the 2000 Census Advisory Committee meeting in Washington, D.C., May 16–17, 1996.

134. See statement of Dr. Martha Farnsworth Riche in *Oversight of the Census Bureau: Preparations for the 2000 Census*, Hearing before the Subcommittee on National Security, International Affairs, and Criminal Justice of the House Committee on Government Reform and Oversight, 104 Cong. 1 sess. (GPO, 1995), p. 85.

135. "Barbara Everitt Bryant: Oral History," p. 29.

136. See interview with Dr. Alan Heslop in Stephen Mansell, "The Virtual Census: The Political and Mathematical Consequences of Using Sampling in the 2000 Census," senior honors thesis, Claremont McKenna College, April 26, 1999, pp. 90–92.

137. Starr, "The Sociology of Official Statistics," pp. 50–51.

138. Bryant and Dunn, *Moving Power and Money*, pp. 47–48.

139. Moynihan, "Foreword," p. iii.

140. Interview with John J. Pitney, associate professor of government, Claremont McKenna College, September 8, 1998. I am indebted to Professor Pitney for generously sharing with me his insights about Republican responses to census adjustment.

141. Michael Doyle, "Former Democratic Lawmaker Tony Coelho Gets Census Post," *Sacramento Bee,* July 6, 1998.

142. This point is made by Butler and Cain, *Congressional Redistricting,* p. 4; also by Abigail Thernstrom, *Whose Votes Count?: Affirmative Action and Minority Voting Rights* (Harvard University Press, 1987), pp. 232–35.

143. Prewitt, "Public Statistics and Democratic Politics," p. 271.

144. Quoted in Rochelle Stanfield, "Sermons on the Count," *National Journal,* August 8, 1998, pp. 1854–55.

145. Clinger Memorandum, p. 35.

146. Affadavit of Jessica F. Heinz, assistant city attorney for Los Angeles, April 2, 1998, included among Affidavits in Support of Motion to Intervene as Defendants of Intervenors City of Los Angeles, in the case of *United States House of Representatives* v. *United States Department of Commerce,* United States District Court for the District of Columbia (Case No. 1: 98CV00456-RCL), p. 9.

147. In 1995, for example, total expenditures for the city of Los Angeles were $4.4 billion, according to Deirdre A. Gaquin and Mark S. Littman, eds., *1990 County and City Extra: Annual Metro, City, and County Data Book,* 8th ed. (Washington, D.C.: Bernan Press, 1999), p. 923. An increase of $18 million through an adjustment would represent only 0.4 percent of the city's annual expenditures, as of 1995.

148. Similar dynamics leading once again to exaggerated claims by local governments were evident in the Census Bureau's fiasco with Local Government Review of preliminary 1990 census results, retold by Bryant and Dunn, *Moving Power and Money,* pp. 132–37.

149. Maurice and Nathan, "The Census Undercount," pp. 252–53.

150. Quoted in Shrihman, "Local Politicians Fear Harm Census Data Can Do to Funding, but Their Worry May Be Overdone," p. A8.

151. White and Rust, *Preparing for the 2000 Census: Interim Report II,* p. 8.

152. *Census 2000: Putting Our Money Where It Counts,* Hearing before the House Committee on Government Reform and Oversight, 104 Cong. 2 sess. (GPO, 1996), p. 108.

153. Edmonston and Schultze, *Modernizing the U.S. Census,* pp. 87–88.

154. White and Rust, *Preparing for the 2000 Census: Interim Report II,* p. 10.

155. Clinger Memorandum, p. 11.

156. See the testimony of Francis D. DeGeorge, inspector general, U.S. Department of Commerce, in *Oversight of the Census Bureau: Preparations for the 2000 Census,* Hearing, pp. 11–12. See also the remarks by Associate Census Director John Thompson in David Kestenbaum, "Census 2000: Where Science and Politics Count Equally," *Science,* vol. 279 (February 6, 1998), p. 798.

157. Nathan Keyfitz, "The Case for Census Tradition," *Society,* vol. 34 (March/April 1997), p. 47.

158. U.S. Bureau of the Census, *Creating a Census for the 21st Century: The Plan for Census 2000* (February 1997), pp. 5–7.

159. U.S. Bureau of the Census, *Creating a Census for the 21st Century,* pp. 8–10.

160. White and Rust, *Sampling in the 2000 Census: Interim Report 1,* p. 1.

161. White and Rust, *Sampling in the 2000 Census: Interim Report 1,* pp. 6–7.

162. See *Census 2000: Putting Our Money Where It Counts,* Hearing, p. 55.

163. Kenneth Wachter testimony in *Census 2000: Putting Our Money Where It Counts,* Hearing, pp. 96–97.

164. Bryant and Dunn, *Moving Power and Money*, p. 137.

165. See Richard A. Kulka and others, *The Potential Impact of Adjusting or Not Adjusting the 1990 Census: Evidence from a Telephone Reinterview to the Survey of 1990 Census Participation* (National Opinion Research Center, University of Chicago, June 10, 1991), pp. 10–11.

166. See Kulka and others, *The Potential Impact of Adjusting or Not Adjusting the 1990 Census*, figs. 27 and 30.

167. Hugh Heclo, "Issue Networks and the Executive Establishment," in Anthony King, ed., *The New American Political System* (Washington, D.C.: AEI Press, 1978), pp. 118–19.

168. The phrase is from Mary Ann Glendon, *Rights Talk: The Impoverishment of Political Discourse* (New York: Free Press, 1991).

169. For example: "Unless the relief requested below is granted, the defendants will take a census that discriminates with respect to fundamental rights against individuals residing in legislative districts that are disproportionately undercounted, in violation of the equal protection guarantee of the Fifth Amendment to the Constitution." See Complaint, *City of New York v. U.S. Department of Commerce,* filed in U.S. District Court, Eastern District of New York, November 3, 1988, p. 14.

170. See *Proposed Guidelines for Statistical Adjustment of the 1990 Census,* Hearing before the Subcommittee on Census and Population of the House Committee on Post Office and Civil Service, 101 Cong. 2 sess. (GPO, 1990), p. 8.

171. Moynihan, "Foreword," pp. v–vi.

172. Quoted in Charles Pope, "Census: A Political Calculation," *CQ Weekly,* July 11, 1998.

173. Peter Zimroth quoted in Richard Levine, "Big Gain Predicted in New York City if Census is Adjusted," *New York Times,* April 20, 1991, sec. 1, p. 25.

174. Dick Kirschten, "Watching for Undercount in 1990 National Census," *National Journal,* March 31, 1990, p. 796.

175. Quoted in Louis Sahagun, "Local Leaders Urge U.S. to Adjust Census Undercount," *Los Angeles Times,* June 21, 1991, p. B3.

176. See, for example, the reasoning of the U.S. Court of Appeals for the Second Circuit in *City of New York v. State of Wisconsin,* 34 F. 3d 1114 (2d Cir. 1994), esp. pp. 1125–32.

177. Jessica Heinz, "2000 Census," *Los Angeles Times,* September 14, 1997, p. M4. The Republican leadership in Congress similarly invoked voting rights in *opposing* statistical adjustment: "Voters should not be disenfranchised through the use of statistical guessing." See letter from Speaker Newt Gingrich and others to Census Director Martha Farnsworth Riche, May 7, 1997, p. 1.

178. Miguel Perez, "The Right to Be Counted," *Hispanic Link Weekly Report,* May 5, 1997, p. 5.

179. Quoted by Carleton R. Bryant in "Too-Low Census Tally to Stand," *Washington Times,* July 16, 1991, pp. A1, A5.

180. See John E. Rolph, "The Census Adjustment Trial: Reflections of a Witness for the Plaintiffs," *Jurimetrics Journal,* vol. 34 (Fall 1993), p. 87: "If the rate of net undercount were about the same across the population, there would be little concern since the basic uses of the census—apportionment, redistricting, and fund allocation—largely depend on population *shares.*"

181. 13 U.S.C. 221.

182. Indeed, only two individuals have ever been brought to trial for failing to answer questions on the census form. See Dan Halacy, *Census: 190 Years of Counting America* (New York: Elsevier/Nelson Books, 1980), pp. 149–50.

183. Halacy, *Census*, p. 52.

184. Edmonston and Schultze, *Modernizing the U.S. Census*, p. 108. In fairness, it should be noted that in this volume the right to be counted is not emphasized.

185. This argument is alluded to in OMB, "Standards for the Classification of Federal Data on Race and Ethnicity," p. 44678.

186. David A. Freedman, "Adjusting the 1990 Census," *Science*, vol. 252 (May 31, 1991), p. 1235.

187. William P. O'Hare, "The Overlooked Undercount: Children Missed in the Decennial Census," www.aecf.org/kidscount/census.pdf.

188. R. Shep Melnick, "The Courts, Congress, and Programmatic Rights," in Richard A. Harris and Sidney M. Milkis, eds., *Remaking American Politics* (Boulder, Colo.: Westview Press, 1989), p. 195.

189. Barbara Vobejda, "Sampling for 2000 Census: Statistical Approach Still Dividing Lawmakers," *Washington Post*, June 11, 1997, p. A4. See also letter from Douglas S. Massey, president, Population Association of America, to Honorable William F. Clinger, chairman, Committee on Government Reform and Oversight, U.S. House of Representatives, June 28, 1996.

190. Dr. Paul Voss, Department of Rural Sociology, University of Wisconsin–Madison, at the 2000 Census Advisory Committee meeting, Washington, D.C., May 16–17, 1996.

191. See, for example, American Statistical Association, *Report of the Census Blue Ribbon Panel* (September 1996), www.amstat.org/outreach/execsummary.html.

192. Edmonston and Schultze, *Modernizing the U.S. Census*.

193. Citro and Cohen, *The Bicentennial Census*, p. 53.

194. For a contemporary assessment of Thomas Kuhn's work, see Steven Weinberg, "The Revolution That Didn't Happen," *New York Review of Books*, October 8, 1998, pp. 48–52.

195. Innes, *Knowledge and Public Policy*, p. 115.

196. Starr, "The Sociology of Official Statistics," p. 41.

197. White and Rust, *Preparing for the 2000 Census: Interim Report II*, pp. 30–33.

198. See White and Rust, *Preparing for the 2000 Census: Interim Report II*, p. 39.

199. Undercount Steering Committee, *Technical Assessment of the Accuracy of Unadjusted versus Adjusted 1990 Census Counts* (Census Bureau, June 21, 1991), p. 12. (Hereafter cited as Report of the Undercount Steering Committee.)

200. Report of the Undercount Steering Committee, p. 1.

201. Report of the Undercount Steering Committee, p. 6.

202. Report of the Undercount Steering Committee, p. 6.

203. See Department of Commerce, "Final Guidelines for Considering Whether or Not a Statistical Adjustment of the 1990 Decennial Census of Population and Housing Should Be Made for Coverage Deficiencies Resulting in an Overcount or Undercount of the Population; Notice," *Federal Register*, vol. 55 (March 15, 1990), Guideline 3, p. 9841.

204. Report of the Undercount Steering Committee, pp. 9–11.

205. David A. Freedman and others, "Adjusting the 1990 Census: the Smoothing Model," *Evaluation Review*, vol. 17 (August 1993), pp. 393–94.

206. See Rolph, "The Census Adjustment Trial," pp. 92–93.

207. Report of the Undercount Steering Committee, p. 9.

208. Rolph, "The Census Adjustment Trial," p. 97.

209. Belin and Rolph, "Can We Reach Consensus on Census Adjustment?" p. 503.

210. Statistician Bruce Hoadley quoted in James Gleick, "The Census: Why We Can't Count," *New York Times Magazine*, July 15, 1990, p. 54.

211. Committee on Adjustment of Postcensal Estimates, *Assessment of Accuracy of Adjusted versus Unadjusted 1990 Census Base for Use in Intercensal Estimates* (Census Bureau, August 7, 1991), p. 1.

212. Barbara Everitt Bryant, "Census-Taking for a Litigious, Data-Driven Society," *Chance,* vol. 6 (Summer 1993), p. 48.

213. Bryant and Dunn, *Moving Power and Money*, p. 167.

214. Bryant, "Census-Taking for a Litigious, Data-Driven Society," p. 48.

215. Bryant and Dunn, *Moving Power and Money,* p. 167.

216. John W. Kingdon, *Agendas, Alternatives, and Public Policies* (New York: Scott, Foresman, 1984), pp. 122–51.

217. Decennial Census Improvement Act of 1987, *Congressional Record,* October 20, 1987, p. E4053.

218. Bryant and Dunn, *Moving Power and Money*, p. 155.

219. See John W. Tukey, testimony in *Oversight Hearing to Review the Progress of Coverage Evaluation Procedures*, Hearing before the Subcommittee on Census and Population of the House Committee on Post Office and Civil Service, 102 Cong. 1 sess. (GPO, 1991), p. 46. Yet not every expert even grants this. See David A. Freedman, "Adjusting the Census of 1990," *Jurimetrics Journal,* vol. 34 (Fall 1993), pp. 99–106.

Chapter Six

1. Anthony King, ed., *The New American Political System*, 2d ed. (Washington, D.C.: AEI Press, 1990).

2. Kenneth Prewitt, "Public Statistics and Democratic Politics," in William Alonso and Paul Starr, eds., *The Politics of Numbers* (New York: Russell Sage Foundation, 1987), p. 270–73.

3. Peter Skerry, "E Pluribus Hispanic?" *Wilson Quarterly*, vol. 16 (Summer 1992), pp. 62–73.

4. A similar tendency to pursue representation at the expense of participation and mobilization is identified in the Depression era labor movement by James A. Morone, in *The Democratic Wish: Popular Participation and the Limits of American Government* (New York: Basic Books, 1990), pp. 162–68.

5. See William Petersen, "Politics and the Measurement of Ethnicity," in William Alonso and Paul Starr, eds., *The Politics of Numbers* (New York: Russell Sage Foundation, 1987), pp. 206–08, esp. fn. 33.

6. Barbara Everitt Bryant and William Dunn, *Moving Power and Money: The Politics of Census Taking* (Ithaca, N.Y.: New Strategist Publications, 1995), p. 149.

7. On the NAACP, see Steven A. Holmes, "From One Problem to Bigger One for N.A.A.C.P." *New York Times*, August 23, 1994, p. A18; and William Raspberry, "What Ails the NAACP?" *Washington Post*, November 7, 1994, p. A23. On MALDEF, see Karen O'Connor and Lee Epstein, "A Legal Voice for the Chicano Community: The Activities of the Mexican American Legal Defense and Educational Fund, 1968–1982," *Social Science Quarterly*, vol. 65, no. 2 (1984), pp. 245–64.

8. Jeffrey M. Berry, *The Interest Group Society*, 2d ed. (Glenview, Ill.: Scott, Foresman/Little, Brown, 1989), p. 55.

9. Robert D. Putnam, "Bowling Alone: America's Declining Social Capital," *Journal of Democracy*, vol. 6 (January 1995), p. 71.

10. Albert O. Hirschman, *Exit, Voice, and Loyalty: Responses to Decline in Firms, Organizations and States* (Harvard University Press, 1978).

11. Jack L. Walker, *Mobilizing Interest Groups in America: Patrons, Professions, and Social Movements* (University of Michigan Press, 1991), p. 61.

12. Neil K. Komesar and Burton A. Weisbrod, "The Public Interest Law Firm: A Behavioral Analysis," in Burton A. Weisbrod and others, eds., *Public Interest Law: An Economic and Institutional Analysis* (University of California Press, 1978), pp. 80–101.

13. Walker, *Mobilizing Interest Groups in America*, p. 107.

14. Walker, *Mobilizing Interest Groups in America*, p. 106.

15. Putnam, "Bowling Alone," p. 71.

16. To be sure, American Indians may also stand to benefit from maximized census totals in the ways other minorities do. My point is simply that there is a countervailing dynamic among Indians that is not present among other groups.

17. See, for example, the recently launched effort by the Mexican American Legal Defense and Educational Fund (MALDEF) urging Latinos, "Hagase Contar" (Make yourself count); Julia Ha, "Latino Group Launches Census Outreach Campaign," *Los Angeles Times*, March 31, 1999, pp. A3, A16.

18. I develop this analysis in Peter Skerry, "The Affirmative Action Paradox," *Society*, vol. 35 (September-October 1998), pp. 8–16.

19. James MacGregor Burns, *The Deadlock of Democracy: Four-Party Politics in America* (Englewood Cliffs, N.J.: Prentice-Hall, 1963); Daniel J. Boorstin, *The Genius of American Politics* (University of Chicago Press, 1953).

20. Sidney M. Milkis, *The President and the Parties: The Transformation of the American Party System since the New Deal* (Oxford University Press, 1993).

21. Theodore J. Lowi, *The End of Liberalism: The Second Republic of the United States*, 2d ed. (New York: W. W. Norton, 1979).

22. Robert A. Katzmann, *Institutional Disability: The Saga of Transportation Policy for the Disabled* (Brookings, 1986), pp. 15–18, 93–94, 152–54.

23. For a detailed examination of the growth of Congress's oversight function, see Joel D. Aberbach, *Keeping a Watchful Eye: The Politics of Congressional Oversight* (Brookings, 1990).

24. James Q. Wilson, "The Politics of Regulation," in James Q. Wilson, ed., *The Politics of Regulation* (New York: Basic Books, 1980), pp. 370–72.

25. R. Shep Melnick, "The Courts, Congress, and Programmatic Rights," in Richard Harris and Sidney M. Milkis, eds., *Remaking American Politics* (Boulder, Colo.: Westview Press, 1989), p. 188.

26. See for example Peter H. Schuck, "The Politics of Rapid Legal Change: Immigration Policy in the 1900s," in Marc K. Landy and Martin A. Levin, eds., *The New Politics of Public Policy* (Johns Hopkins University Press, 1995), pp. 47–87.

27. See James Q. Wilson, "New Politics, New Elites, Old Publics," in Marc K. Landy and Martin A. Levin, eds., *The New Politics of Public Policy* (Johns Hopkins University Press, 1995). See also Martin Shapiro, "Of Interests and Values: The New Politics and the New Political Science," in Marc K. Landy and Martin A. Levin, eds., *The New Politics of Public Policy* (Johns Hopkins University Press, 1995), pp. 3–19.

28. The distinction drawn by Steven Teles between advocates and representatives in the context of welfare policy parallels the point I make here. See Steven M. Teles, *Whose Welfare? AFDC and Elite Politics* (University of Kansas Press, 1998), p. 16.

29. Dan Schnur, "Everybody's Mad at Davis on Prop. 187," *Los Angeles Times*, April 29, 1999, p. B9.

30. Gregg Easterbrook, "Why the Sky Is Always Falling," in William Lasser, ed., *Perspectives on American Government: A Comprehensive Reader*, 2d ed. (Lexington, Mass.: D. C. Heath, 1996), pp. 304–05.

31. See Donald R. Brand, "Reformers of the 1960s and 1970s: Modern Anti-Federalists?" in Richard A. Harris and Sidney M. Milkis, eds., *Remaking American Politics* (Boulder, Colo.: Westview Press, 1989), p. 38.

32. Hugh Heclo, "The Sixties' False Dawn: Awakenings, Movements, and Post-Modern Policy-Making," *Journal of Political History*, vol. 8, no. 1 (1996), p. 57.

33. Hugh Heclo, "The Emerging Regime," in Richard A. Harris and Sidney M. Milkis, eds., *Remaking American Politics* (Boulder, Colo.: Westview Press, 1989), p. 304.

34. Heclo, "The Emerging Regime," pp. 312–13.

35. Sidney M. Milkis, "The Presidency, Policy Reform, and the Rise of the Administrative State," in Richard A. Harris and Sidney M. Milkis, eds., *Remaking American Politics* (Boulder, Colo.: Westview Press, 1989), p. 177.

36. See Wilson Carey McWilliams, "Two-Tier Politics and the Problem of Public Policy," in Marc K. Landy and Martin A. Levin, eds., *The New Politics of Public Policy* (Johns Hopkins University Press, 1995), pp. 268–76.

37. Heclo, "The Emerging Regime," p. 311.

38. For a similar point about the antibureaucratic ethos of Republicans and Democrats during the 1970s, see Melnick, "The Courts, Congress, and Programmatic Rights," p. 197.

39. Quoted in Sidney M. Milkis, "Remaking Government Institutions in the 1970s: Participatory Democracy and the Triumph of Administrative Politics," *Journal of Political History*, vol. 10, no. 1 (1998), p. 22.

40. Hugh Heclo, "Issue Networks and the Executive Establishment," in Anthony King, ed., *The New American Political System* (Washington, D.C.: AEI Press, 1978), p. 118.

41. Lowi, *The End of Liberalism*, pp. 37–39.

42. Heclo, "The Sixties' False Dawn," p. 52.

43. Heclo, "The Sixties' False Dawn," p. 56.

44. Heclo, "The Sixties' False Dawn," pp. 54–55.

45. U.S. Bureau of the Census, *Creating a Census for the 21st Century: The Plan for Census 2000* (February 1997), p. 4.

46. Prepared statement of Everett M. Ehrlich, Under Secretary of Commerce for Economic Affairs, before the Senate Committee on Governmental Affairs, March 11, 1997.

47. U.S. Bureau of the Census, "Census 2000: A New Plan for the Decennial Census," conference at the Herbert C. Hoover Building, U.S. Department of Commerce, February 28, 1996.

48. Again, Kenneth Prewitt, though not addressing adjustment, makes a related point forcefully when discussing the implications of our reliance on statistical formulas: "This of course does not eliminate politics; it simply pushes politics back one step." See Prewitt, "Public Statistics and Democratic Politics," p. 272.

49. These articles are brought together in Lani Guinier, *The Tyranny of the Majority: Fundamental Fairness in Representative Democracy* (New York: Free Press, 1995).

50. Paul Starr, "The Sociology of Official Statistics," in William Alonso and Paul Starr, eds., *The Politics of Numbers* (New York: Russell Sage Foundation, 1987), p. 57.

51. Here I paraphrase Paul Starr very slightly. See Starr, "The Sociology of Official Statistics," p. 57.

52. Apologies here to Hugh Heclo, who distinguishes between the powering and the puzzling functions of governments. See his *Modern Social Politics in Britain and Sweden: From Relief to Income Maintenance* (Yale University Press, 1974), pp. 304–26.

Chapter Seven

1. Daniel P. Moynihan, "Foreword," in Ian I. Mitroff and others, eds., *The 1980 Census: Policymaking amid Turbulence* (Lexington, Mass.: D. C. Heath, 1983), p. xxiv.

2. See Stephen Kinzer, "For One Day, Every Turk Hides in Plain Sight," *New York Times*, December 1, 1997, p. A1.

3. Richard A. Kulka and others, *The Potential Impact of Adjusting or Not Adjusting the 1990 Census: Evidence from a Telephone Reinterview of Respondents to the Survey of 1990 Census Participation* (National Opinion Research Center, University of Chicago, June 10, 1991), pp. 19–20.

4. For example, see the comments of Representative William Zeliff (Republican of New Hampshire) in *Census 2000: Putting Our Money Where It Counts,* Hearing before the House Committee on Government Reform and Oversight, 104 Cong. 2 sess. (GPO, 1996), pp. 69–70.

5. See, for example, Eugene P. Ericksen and Teresa K. Defonso, "Beyond the Net Undercount: How to Measure Census Error," *Chance,* vol. 6 (Spring 1993), pp. 42–43. An experimental study found that a shortened census questionnaire improved the response rate by about 5 percent in high-response areas, but substantially less in low-response (minority) areas. See Don A. Dillman and others, "Effects of Questionnaire Length, Respondent-Friendly Design, and a Difficult Question on Response Rates for Occupant-Addressed Census Mail Surveys," *Public Opinion Quarterly,* vol. 57, no. 3 (1993), pp. 298–99, 301–03.

6. P. B. Stark, "Differences between the 1990 and 2000 Census Adjustment Plans, and Their Impact on Error," University of California at Berkeley, Department of Statistics Technical Report 550 (March 16, 1999), pp. 14–15.

7. U.S. Bureau of the Census, *Report to Congress—The Plan for Census 2000* (August 1997), pp. 21–22.

8. U.S. Bureau of the Census, *Report to Congress,* pp. 10–11.

9. For an overview, see Andrew A. White and Keith Rust, eds., *Preparing for the 2000 Census: Interim Report II* (Washington, D.C.: National Academy Press, 1997), pp. 62–78. Reservations on this proposal are expressed in David A. Freedman and Kenneth W. Wachter, "Planning for the Census in the Year 2000," *Evaluation Review,* vol. 20 (August 1996), p. 358.

10. See 2000 Census Advisory Committee, *The American Community Survey* (September 26, 1996). See also Bryant, "Census Taking for a Litigious, Data-Driven Society," p. 49.

11. Freedman and Wachter, "Planning for the Census in the Year 2000," pp. 359–60, 364–65; Lawrence D. Brown and others, "Statistical Controversies in the Census 2000," University of California at Berkeley, Department of Statistics Technical Report 537 (April 30, 1999), pp. 17–18.

12. Margo J. Anderson, *The American Census: A Social History* (Yale University Press, 1988), pp. 26–28, 72–82, 154–58.

13. See Barry Edmonston and Charles Schultze, eds., *Modernizing the U.S. Census* (Washington, D.C.: National Academy Press, 1995), pp. 246–48. See also Bernard Grofman, "Statistics without Substance, A Critique of Freedman et al. and Clark and Morrison," *Evaluation Review,* vol. 15 (December 1991), p. 752.

14. This point was made some time ago in Constance F. Citro and Michael L. Cohen, eds., *The Bicentennial Census: New Directions for Methodology in 1990* (Washington, D.C.: National Academy Press, 1985), p. 65.

15. Nampeo R. McKenney and others, "Evaluating Racial and Ethnic Reporting in the 1990 Census," paper presented at the 1993 Joint Statistical Meeting of the American Statistical Association, San Francisco, Calif., August 1993, p. 56.

16. John Higham, *Send These to Me: Jews and Other Immigrants in Urban America* (New York: Atheneum, 1975), p. 243.

17. See Mary C. Waters, *Ethnic Options: Choosing Ethnic Identities in America* (University of California Press, 1990).

18. See John A. Hall and Charles Lindholm, *Is America Falling Apart?* (Princeton University Press, 1999).

19. See Newt Gingrich quotation in Barbara Vobejda, "Hill Reassured on Racial Checkoff Plan for Census," *Washington Post,* July 26, 1997, p. A4.

20. For another critique of the Census Bureau collecting racial and ethnic data, see John J. Miller, *The Unmaking of Americans: How Multiculturalism Has Undermined the Assimilation Ethic* (New York: Free Press, 1998), p. 24.

21. William Petersen, *Ethnicity Counts* (New Brunswick, N.J.: Transaction Books, 1997), pp. 276–78.

22. For a discussion of the tension between democracy and administration, see Bernard Crick, *In Defense of Politics,* 2d ed. (Penguin Books, 1982), pp. 106–10.

Index

DATE DUE